THE MAFIA

The MAFIA
A CULTURAL HISTORY

ROBERTO M. DAINOTTO

REAKTION BOOKS

Published by Reaktion Books Ltd
33 Great Sutton Street
London EC1V 0DX, UK
www.reaktionbooks.co.uk

First published 2015

Printed and bound by TJ International, Padstow, Cornwall

A catalogue record for this book is
available from the British Library

ISBN 978 1 78023 443 4

Contents

Preface

I know, there have been more depressing editions. But that of 21 October 2013 was certainly not an uplifting one: under the masthead – the *New York Times* – one after the other came stories of contaminated milk being sold for infant consumption, soaring anti-Semitism in the West, the rise of China's arms industry, the endemic corruption in our financial markets . . . It was only after the daily dose of gloom and doom that a title finally came, tucked inside the sombre reports on worldly catastrophes, to cast a glimmer of light: 'Mario Cuomo, Vocal Foe of Italian Stereotyping, Finally Sees *The Godfather*'!

Sure, Cuomo watching *The Godfather* may not reverse the crisis of the American arms industry or save us all from more credit default swaps – not to mention poor infants. It was still, in good conscience, epochal news:

> Mario M. Cuomo's hate–hate relationship with *The Godfather* has been well documented. For four decades, he refused even to see any of the movies or, presumably, to read Mario Puzo's book. He all but denied that the Mafia existed. And who could forget that unfortunate slip of the tongue during the 1992 presidential campaign, when Bill Clinton suggested that Mr Cuomo, then the governor of New York, acted like a Mafioso? But over the weekend, Mr Cuomo, 81, did the unthinkable: he finally watched *The Godfather*. And, somewhat grudgingly, he offered that 'maybe this thing was a masterpiece'.[1]

Born and raised in Sicily, I admit to being quite familiar with Mr Cuomo's grudge – a grudge, mind you, that has not fully dissipated as I write these pages. I still feel torn between pleasure and *ressentiment*. While utterly unconvinced by Cuomo's contention that the existence of the

Mafia is 'a lot of baloney', like him, I am prickly and sensitive about the whole affair of cultural stereotyping. Worse, I confess I understand well why someone might have 'refused even to see any of the [*Godfather*] movies or, presumably, to read Mario Puzo's book'. (But why 'presumably'? Is life without Mario Puzo, with all due respect, truly unconceivable?)

How anyone could enjoy and find entertainment or cultural nourishment in Mafia stories had, for a good part of my life, remained a mystery to me. All but entertaining or culturally satisfying, the Mafia was, for me, a sad and often depressing reality: endemic corruption, nepotistic management of the res publica, illiteracy never completely eradicated, half a million emigrants leaving their Sicilian homes and families year after year, entire cities engulfed in endless sprawls of cement, misery, violence, prevarication and abuse. Nor did the Mafia I knew have anything to do with spectacular ambushes and killings, or with customary wit – 'Leave the gun, take the cannoli' – despite how the cultural industry seemed determined to represent it. The Mafia was, rather, a prosaic, unheroic, dull, everyday affair.

If you asked me to single out the most realistic representation of the Mafia in any movie I have seen or book I have read, I would have to say that it is the moment in Marco Tullio Giordana's film *One Hundred Steps* (2000) when mafioso Tano Badalamenti drinks a cup of coffee with Peppino Impastato – just before having him murdered. In the movie, Impastato himself seems aware that the real Mafia is hidden precisely in those kinds of small, everyday gestures – gestures that, far away from the glossy adventures of Hollywood, always hide real power and submission in the dull rituals of daily routines:

IMPASTATO: You drink coffee at the same bar . . . 'Good Morning, Tano.' 'Good day to you, Peppino.' 'My regards to the family' . . . And they are the lords of the city!

The beating heart of the Mafia – its real power and lordship – was always hidden in the banality of these little gestures, not in the grand deed. The Mafia I knew, in short, had nothing to do with the spectacular dreams of grandeur of Howard Hawks's *Scarface* – 'The World is Yours' – or with the lavishness of gangsters' lives. That was Hollywood. In Sicily, as in a Dostoevsky novel, the Mafia looked like the devil that visited Karamazov: it always had a shabby, dull and vulgar look.

Take for instance the arrest of the feared Mafia boss Bernardo Provenzano in 2006, in the countryside near the town of Corleone made famous by the Godfather stories of Mario Puzo and Francis Ford Coppola. Provenzano had eluded the police since 1963. Through the years, he had ravaged Sicily by shooting, bludgeoning, strangling, knifing and drowning his enemies to death. In April 2006 Provenzano – 73 years old, in poor health, overweight, bespectacled and shabbily dressed – lived in what newspapers consistently described as a 'ramshackle farmhouse . . . an abandoned . . . run-down farmhouse with sheep corralled outside and a single bed within'.[2] It was there that the police found him, wearing shoddy jeans, his pockets stuffed not with dollars or small-calibre revolvers, but with pizzini (as he called them in Sicilian dialect) – little scraps of paper through which he communicated with his men. He did not resist arrest. Hardly a movie worth seeing could possibly come out of such a banal script. Indeed Provenzano's story was just one more 'lesson of the fearsome, word-and-thought-defying banality of evil'.[3]

Peppino Impastato was killed on 9 May 1978 by the Mafia, in the small town of Cinisi near Palermo. On the 'free radio' station that he ran, he had made explicit accusations that the city's boss, Badalamenti, could not tolerate. Impastato was beaten to death, his body then dismembered by a charge of TNT. On the same day Italy's ex-Prime Minister Aldo Moro was murdered by the terrorist group, the Red Brigades in Rome. At the movie theatre, in the meantime, Pasquale Squitieri's Corleone, an exploitation of the successful Godfather franchise, was selling tickets for one more Mafia show. Impastato's murder, in that context, was neither big news for the national press, nor filmic entertainment. It passed unnoticed. For me, working for a free radio station like Impastato's, 190 km (120 miles) from Cinisi, his death was a different story. The news of his murder had come between the broadcasting of Gloria Gaynor's 'I Will Survive' (those were the days) and the always-present (and given the occasion, gloomily allegorical) 'The End' by The Doors. The sour taste of real-life tragedy soon settled in over the music. Then loathing: how could anyone watch one more Corleone movie when this was the Mafia? Like Cuomo, my relationship with Mafia movies was growing to be hate–hate.

A few years after that, I cannot remember exactly when, but decidedly before Mr Cuomo, I grudgingly acquiesced to making peace with Mafia movies. You know how these things go: a friend intercedes, brings a DVD (though, in my case, it must have been a VHS) to your home, you put up a fight – 'Let's watch it', 'Let's not' – and before you understand what is happening, you are lying on the sofa watching *The Godfather* with fondness in your eyes. Maybe this thing *is* a masterpiece! After that *Scarface* was not bad either, although I preferred the original one to De Palma's over-the-top remake. And then came *The Sopranos*, which glued me like nothing ever before to the TV set for years on end. Slowly but surely, watching Mafia shows became an impassioned affair.

Was it real peace? Well, passion notwithstanding, I would say it was more like an armistice. My attitude towards the real thing was unchanged, but Mafia movies, and novels too, were a different story. Was it the adventure, the fast-paced action, the shootings? Not quite. *The Godfather* often moves with the slowness of an Antonioni movie, and *The Sopranos*, with its dream sequences and off-the-wall irony, seems more like David Lynch's *Twin Peaks* than a shooting match. What was it then? What made me love the Mafia in fiction, while loathing the one in real life?

The book that follows is an attempt to understand this apparent contradiction, which I suspect is not only my (or Mr Cuomo's) private idiosyncrasy. The tension between the *real* Mafia – with its brutal, often abusive connotations – and the *imaginary* Mafia surrounding it – a mythical potpourri of codes of honour, family values, and chivalric machoism – is the topic of the following pages. Rather than solving or explaining away such tension by dismissing the social imaginary around the Mafia as merely untrue, this book's ambition is to understand the social needs, the desires and fears, the kind of material and ideal fantasies that are satisfied by cultural representations of the Mafia. What makes Tony Soprano so likeable? Why, after the usual nine-to-five routine, would we rather leave the cannoli and take the gun? While the daily news continuously reports on a world where all dreams, even those of infants drinking tainted milk, are corrupted by dishonourable greed, what sort of dreams does the Mafia revive for us?

This book is organized chronologically and traces the development of the Mafia from its rural beginnings in western Sicily to its evolution into what could be aptly described as a global multinational of crime. To tell a coherent story, the focus is on the Sicilian and American Mafia and their tight interconnections. The other so-called 'mafias' – the Japanese Yakuza, the Chinese Triad, the Russian 'mafia', Latin American drug cartels – belong to a rather different narrative. So do other Italian criminal organizations such as the Camorra and the 'Ndrangheta, which developed autonomously and independently from the Sicilian Mafia and the Sicilian-American

Cosa Nostra. Only in the last chapter, at the conclusion of our story, will these mafias make a fleeting appearance.

While this book offers the coordinates to understand the Mafia as a historical, social, political and economic reality, it is not a history book. Excellent texts of this genre, such as Salvatore Lupo's *History of the Mafia* and John Dickie's *Cosa Nostra*, are recommended for this purpose. My concern here is to trace a history of the Mafia's growth into our cultural imaginary: what the Mafia meant in specific historical contexts of artistic production and reception.

The materials discussed include films, literary pieces, television shows, music, figurative arts and, last but not least, video games. *The Mafia: A Cultural History* does not attempt to compile an exhaustive list of cultural products on the Mafia; there are already books and encyclopaedias doing just that, which the reader can find in the list of works cited. Here the plan is to choose and discuss in some depth a few representative moments and works which, at least in my opinion, were milestones in the cultural history of the Mafia. To begin we will start with Sicily in the 1870s where fact and fiction, as in a *verismo* opera by Mascagni, became *trompe l'œil* of each other.

Of Rustic Knights and Godfathers: The Origin of the Mafia

MICHAEL: We're in Sicily – it's opera!
– *The Godfather Part III*, dir. Francis Ford Coppola

Truth be told, the third *Godfather* (1990) is hardly a masterpiece in the history of cinema. Not even Francis Ford Coppola, its enormously talented director, had much patience with it: was yet another sequel to the blockbuster of 1972 *really* necessary?

After years spent at UCLA's prestigious film school, Coppola entered Hollywood in the early 1960s with great artistic ambitions. Alas, they were to be short-lived: the movie industry, Coppola soon realized, did not need his art after all. 'You don't make films on anything but money', he scoffed in an interview.[1] Since, to make money, 'businessmen like predictability' rather than artistic experimentation, Coppola had, by 1972, all but lost hope: as the immense fortune of *The Godfather Part I* had established the predictable success of gangster film conventions, his artistic life was now 'ruined . . .'

> In some ways [that film] did ruin me. It just made my whole career go this way instead of the way I really wanted it to go . . . The great frustration of my career is that nobody really wants me to do my own work . . . *The Godfather* made me violate a lot of the hopes I had for myself.[2]

So, when approached by Paramount for a third time, Coppola resisted as much as he could. After all there was still enough money left from the first and second *Godfathers* for him to 'do [his] own work', and even to establish an alternative studio, Zoetrope Studios that could welcome new and unpredictable talents to the heart of Hollywood. It was only after the costly Vietnam War epic *Apocalypse Now* (1979), and following the financial demise of Zoetrope Studios, that Coppola's economic situation became so dire that Paramount's insistence became, so to speak, an offer he could no longer refuse. He was, yet again, at the mercy of 'businessmen'.

Full of misgivings Coppola and Mario Puzo, who had scripted the first two parts of the *Godfather* saga, negotiated a deal with Paramount: they requested six months to put together the semblance of a story – they had no more time to waste on a sequel! – and a hotel room in Reno, Nevada. There the boredom of weaving together yet another Mafia plot could at least be interrupted by the thrill of the casino. Paramount agreed to the room; but – and executive Frank Mancuso admitted no reply – Coppola and Puzo had no more than six *weeks* to come up with something, take it or leave it.[3] Coppola – less than willing, but in need of a contract – took it.

Necessity, as the saying goes, is the mother of invention: what Puzo and Coppola concocted in those six weeks, however, was hardly a feast of human inventiveness. The meandering plot involved a series of scandals that had occupied the international press throughout the 1980s: the mysterious death of Pope John Paul I (rumours were of an assassination, since the 'good Pope' was determined to put an end to the Vatican Bank's corruption); the allegations of money laundering involving Archbishop Paul Marcinkus, president of the Vatican Bank; the gruesome death of 'God's banker' Roberto Calvi, hanged from London's Blackfriars Bridge; and the financial speculations of Michele 'the Shark' Sindona, prince of Wall Street working for both the American and the Sicilian Cosa Nostra. The narrative was to lead to the improbable redemption, 'almost too ludicrous to believe', of the ruthless boss Michael Corleone (played by Al Pacino).[4] The final product was, alas, no better than such scripted questionable premises. An 'All Things Considered' report by Bob Mondello for National Public Radio, which ran on the vigil of the film's New York premiere on Christmas Day 1990, set the tone for what would become the customary take on the film: 'preposterous' bad acting (that of Sofia Coppola, the director's own daughter, did not help) and superficial editing had added to the successful *Godfather* franchise nothing more than a new 'flawed epic'.[5]

True enough. But what, then, to make of the final, masterful sequence of the movie? Bob Mondello himself – 'all things considered', indeed! – had to make concessions: the final hour of the movie was, in contrast to the disappointment of all the rest, a 'majestic feast of cross-cutting and sweeping camera movement'. Nor was Mondello the last critic to bestow unqualified praise onto the last hour or so of *The Godfather Part III*: for Naomi Greene, this was a 'most dramatic culmination' of the entire saga;

for Marcia Citron it was simply 'unforgettable'; while George de Stefano – who thought the movie overall 'sucked' – found the ending of the third *Godfather* 'riveting, and not even Sofia Coppola's amateurish performance [could] vitiate its power'.[6]

It is in these last moments of the film, in fact, that Francis Ford Coppola ultimately shows his artistic (if repressed) talents in spite of both businessmen and predictability. It is as if, approaching the end of the saga that had 'frustrated' him so much, Coppola finally feels entitled to give free rein to his true ambitions as an artist and a director. This is, no doubt, a masterpiece of cinematographic technique: in the manner of D. W. Griffith, Coppola executes a masterful parallel montage – 'actions taking place at a geographical distance by means of alternating shots of each'[7] – of no less than five different plot lines: in Palermo, a bloodthirsty assassin slaughters Michael's bodyguards; in Rome, Calò stabs to death the corrupt politician Don Lucchesi; in Vatican City, Neri fires his gun on the Archbishop (guilty of having poisoned the 'good Pope'); back in Palermo's opera house, Don Altobello slumps down in his seat, poisoned by Connie's cake; and finally, in Switzerland, the evil banker Keinszig is suffocated by Michael's men.

Not yet content with such magnificent interlacing of parallel plots, Coppola even measures himself here with the mastery of Sergei Eisenstein. Famously Eisenstein had maintained that 'montage is an idea that arises from the *collision* of independent shots – shots even opposite to one another: the "dramatic" principle.'[8] As he had with his experimentation in the first *Godfather* (the scene of the baptism juxtaposed with the killings of Michael's enemies), Coppola makes the brutality of the five assassinations – from Switzerland to Palermo (a hint to the globalization of the Mafia of the 1980s) – collide with the kindly, beautiful harmonies of an operatic bel canto – '*Oh Lola, ch'ai di latti la cammisa*' – sung by Michael's son, Anthony, who is making his debut as a tenor in a *mise en scène* of Pietro Mascagni's *Cavalleria rusticana* at the Teatro Massimo in Palermo.[9]

Coppola's weaving of an opera into a gangster movie to create an Eisenstein-like 'collision' redeems, in the end, if not Michael Corleone, an otherwise mediocre film: the heightened 'dramatic tension', along with an estranging effect of 'theatricality', qualify undoubtedly as high points in Coppola's artistic career.[10] Film criticism still wonders, though: 'Why did Coppola and Puzo choose Mascagni's *Cavalleria rusticana* to counterpoint the conclusion of *Godfather* III?'[11] Why not some Verdi, Wagner or Puccini? Why precisely that opera?

The hitman, Mosca, enters the Teatro Massimo, Palermo, while Anthony Corleone makes his debut in the opera *Cavalleria rusticana*. Francis Ford Coppola (dir.), *The Godfather III* (Paramount Pictures, 1990).

We know that Coppola 'had been familiar with *Cavalleria* since childhood, and its themes resonated with his ethnic upbringing'.[12] Since the demise of Michael Corleone was to be set in Sicily, Coppola was attracted by the Sicilian setting of *Cavalleria* and more precisely by a 'particular vision of violence [associated] with the deeply ceremonial, death-haunted, and religious culture of Sicily'.[13] In the introduction to the VHS release by Paramount, Coppola himself suggested that the 'rituality' of *Cavalleria* (the opera's climactic murder happens on Easter Sunday) was one reason for this choice:

> It is a style of the *Godfather* movies that a ritual is going on, and interwoven with the ritual are the resolutions, which are usually murders, and so for *Godfather III* I thought it was very appropriate that the opera *Cavalleria Rusticana* would be ritual.[14]

Drama, ethnic 'italianicity',[15] theatricality, a Sicilian setting, ritualistic killings: all these are good enough reasons for Coppola's selection of *Cavalleria rusticana*.

Yet some irony remains in the fact that Coppola stumbled on this precise opera to put an end to his trilogy. As he felt increasingly 'frustrated' and a victim of a cultural industry that had forced him into making one Mafia movie after another, it must have been a mocking fate that took him, perhaps unaware, to the very origin of the cultural industry's fashioning of the myth of the Mafia. He landed on *Cavalleria rusticana*, the very work that invented the Mafia: not the real Mafia, to be sure, but an imaginary one, grown out of the nostalgia for a lost world of mythical codes of honour, family values and rustic chivalry.

Giovanni Verga: In Search of Rustic Chivalries

The story of *Cavalleria rusticana* had originally been penned by Giovanni Verga. Born in 1840 into a wealthy landowning family of Catania, Verga had two, not unrelated, ambitions: to become a successful writer and to make lots of money out of writing. For these reasons he moved to Florence in 1865 and then to Milan in 1872. These were the years when the old dream of Italian liberation had finally been realized: Giuseppe Garibaldi's volunteer army of one thousand men had landed in Marsala, western Sicily, on 11 May 1860. Promising liberation from colonial Bourbon rule to the locals, republicanism to the middle classes tired of aristocratic privileges and redistribution of ecclesiastical and Bourbon estates to the peasantry, Garibaldi had managed to form (and arm) a powerful movement of rebellion against the Bourbons – a movement whose growth would soon intersect with the rise of the Sicilian Mafia. Sicily was liberated within a few days. By 14 May Garibaldi had assumed dictatorship over the island – in the name, however, of Vittorio Emanuele II, King of Savoy.

The Savoys, whose ambition was to rule the whole of Italy from their capital city of Turin, had cunningly financed Garibaldi's enterprise, thereby retaining control over the entire operation. Once Sicily and the whole South had been freed of the Bourbon presence, it did not take long for the king's government in Turin to oust Garibaldi from his dictatorship and eliminate the most radical demands that had stirred the enthusiasm of the local population: republicanism and the redistribution of land. On 18 February 1861 Vittorio Emanuele, after a successful northern offensive that had conquered the rest of northern Italy from Austrian colonial rule, became the first king of the united Italy. On 9 October 1870 the last symbolic city of Italian unification – Rome – was liberated from the Pope's armies and annexed to the new kingdom. The glorious resurrection, the Risorgimento of the Italian nation already fantasized by Dante, had come to fruition.

For an ambitious man like Verga, it was now easier than ever to move to the peninsula in search of fortune. Both Florence and Milan offered comparably more opportunities than Catania for an aspiring writer: closely knit intellectual communities, theatres, salons and, last but not least, the growing publishing industry. There Verga managed to publish his first books: *A Sinner* (1866), *Story of a Blackcap* (1871) and *Eve* (1873). They were fairly 'traditionalist novels': stories of unrequited love set invariably in middle- to upper-class urban environments, and written in a typical late Romantic, *larmoyant* style.[16] Some of them, such as *Story of a Blackcap*, achieved respectable sales.

Competition for this kind of narrative, however, was steep to say the least. The market was flooded by all-too-similar stories written on the wave of Francesco Mastriani's schmaltzy best-seller of 1852, *The Blind Woman of Sorrento*, a sorrowful tale of beautiful, blind Beatrice, restored to sight by Doctor Baldieri, who marries her in the last pages to live happily ever after. In late nineteenth-century Italy, 'everybody', as Benedetto Croce scornfully remarked, read this kind of narrative – 'with the exception of those who read literature'.[17] The problem for Verga was that everybody, even authors with literary ambitions such as himself, wrote that kind of narrative too. His hopes to make a fortune from writing soon cooled. In such a competitive market, he wrote bitterly to his friend Luigi Capuana, 'editors offer me 300 lire and pretend they are *paying me* with that!'[18] Undoubtedly new and unique products had to be invented, and quickly, to make the stocks of the Verga brand rise in the developing national market of literary exchange.

Verga met Capuana, like him a Sicilian émigré in search of fortune, in Florence. In their quest for something new, the two would-be best-selling authors began reading the new literary fashions coming from France: Gustave Flaubert first and foremost. Albeit plagued by a funda-mental inability to restitute in full the world of 'passions',[19] *Madame Bovary* (1856) did at least offer the opportunity to recast the usual love drama in a new light: as the almost-scientific analysis of a 'human document.'[20] Posing as a scientist in a laboratory, Verga started playing the Flaubertian role of the writer 'eclipsing . . . from the scene of story-telling', the one 'studying' reality, dispassionately, as it unfolds.[21] By 1873 he had begun work on two new novels, *Eros* and *Royal Tiger*, written in the detached style of *Madame Bovary*. *Royal Tiger* was turned down by the Treves's publishing house.

The problem was that, scientism notwithstanding, *Royal Tiger*, like *Madame Bovary* that had inspired it, remained essentially the same old story: an urban, bourgeois love drama. As Émile Zola had understood, 'Flaubert's love stories are still elegant and refined . . . they do not move in the mud.'[22] So, to escape elegance and refinement, Verga and Capuana started reading the *Rougon-Macquart* cycle: whether Zola described the city (*The Underbelly of Paris*, 1873) or the rural province (*The Fortune of the Rougons*, 1871), he certainly had a taste for 'mud' and the unusual. Differences of characters, dialects, customs, history and even landscapes enlivened Zola's narrative – set in the 'underbelly' of bourgeois society – in a way that could not be done in the propertied interiors of a *Madame Bovary*. So this was what was needed: a touch of local colour, a 'contrast with the unstable passions of the great cities, with their fictitious needs'![23]

This was the illumination that would take Verga's career on a radically new path. What if, instead of setting the love story in the usual urban middle-class milieu, he set it in the mud of Sicily? The island was as grimy and mysterious for the bourgeois urban public from the North as could ever be imagined; novelty was assured. The exotic distance of poor and illiterate Sicily from the refined readership in Florence or Milan would only give more prominence to the shockingly new effect of local colour:

> That is why I would like to take refuge in the countryside, or by the sea; among fishermen . . . at a distance from the hubbub of a city like Milan or Florence. Don't you think that certain things take more prominence when seen from a certain perspective?[24]

Italy had been unified, yes, but Sicily, growing poorer by the day, with its agricultural rhythms so unfamiliar to the public of an industrializing North, its peculiar rituals, its cults and superstitions and, last but not least, its passions often undistinguishable from sheer violence, remained a mystery indeed: 'Is this Italy? Is this Europe?', a military officer dispatched in the islands was reported to have exclaimed.[25] In sum Sicily offered, as Verga put it in a fantasized dialogue with his imagined typical reader – an elegantly dressed, well-read upper-class woman from the North – a new, estranging quality: 'a strange spectacle', indeed.[26] The attention bestowed by the public on the first novella of Sicilian Bovarysme, *Nedda* (1874), assured Verga he was on the path to success.

Sicily in those days excited Italian curiosity and imagination to the highest degree. Literature, to be sure, had not yet caught up with this public interest; readers had to satisfy their urges by turning to newspapers. In the dailies they could read with shock and awe of all the news coming from the faraway, mysterious island of Sicily.

Pasquale Villari's Southern Letters

Faced with the problem of having to cover the costs incurred in the wars of Italian independence, the central government of Vittorio Emanuele had imposed a number of new taxes on its new subjects – most pressingly on the southern provinces, who were bizarrely deemed, because of their optimal climate, to be potentially wealthier than all others. Taxes on newborns and on grain were particularly hard on agricultural economies like Sicily's, which relied heavily on bread for cheap nutrition and on large families to share the hard work in the fields. A new tax on inheritance was especially abhorred by the islanders; it prompted the sarcastic saying that 'in Sicily we are all relatives of the king', since His Majesty always took a share of the properties of the deceased. Another saying – It's better to be a pig than a soldier – reflected Sicilian distaste for a new law prescribing military conscription: the service, now compulsory for all Italians, took away much-needed youthful energy from the work in the fields.[27]

Rebellion against taxation and desertion from military duty quickly grew in the Italian South. The situation was particularly bad in the countryside: peasants, who had expected at least the redistribution of aristocratic and ecclesiastical estates, felt betrayed by the new nation. They had no intention of sacrificing the meagre revenues from their crops or the labour force of their youth to it. They preferred to evade taxes. They preferred to desert.

Already by 1861 – barely a few months into national unification – official announcements published in newspapers all over Italy and proclamations posted on the walls of southern villages initiated an open confrontation: the State would not compromise on taxation or conscription, and whoever evaded either was from now on to be considered an outlaw and a brigand.[28] Announcements and proclamations, unsurprisingly, had no effect. Paying heavy taxes and sending their sons to the army would, after all, have had devastating effects on the economies of many families. Breaking the law of a state perceived as distant, if not altogether inimical, quickly became the norm. The so-called Pica Law of 1863, named after its architect, Senator Giuseppe Pica of the party of the Right (Destra Storica), pushed things further by declaring a state of emergency in the southern provinces: 'between 1861 and 1865, almost two-thirds of the entire Italian army was deployed in trying to maintain order in southern Italy.'[29] The South was now under military siege and, in the new 'war' against brigandage, civil rights were suspended. The houses of alleged outlaws were burnt with no due process and their families imprisoned. Deserters were tortured and hanged and photos of their bodies were published in newspapers all over the nation to show the implacable might of the State.

The result of such criminalization of the South can easily be guessed: while the number of deserters – 26,000 in 1863 – did not decline one bit, the new laws de facto transformed draft-dodgers into wanted criminals and made just as many outlaws of their relatives, friends and parents.[30] The ranks of outlawry in Sicily had swelled out of proportion – and so had the enmity between the locals and the national government. In such a quick exacerbation of the conflict between the State and its South, official declarations defined Sicilians as 'barbarians' and 'outlaws'. Sicilians, in turn, became more convinced of having been wronged by a truly barbaric state – one that kept them, in the meantime, in unprecedented poverty. The conflict was spiralling out of control, with no solution in sight.

It was in this climate that public attention to the rebellious South began to grow. In this mysterious part of Italy that, like Africa, was still 'to be discovered' (as the *Gazzetta di Torino* put it in 1861), the locals – newspapers assured – were capable of ways of life and outbursts of violence that the mild, bourgeois northerners could not even begin to imagine. It may have been precisely because of their unimaginable nature, however, that the southern ways excited northern fantasies. The Turin daily *Gazzetta del popolo*, in part to justify the state of exception and in part to satisfy the morbid curiosity of its readership, went so far as to publish daily letters from northern soldiers fighting on the southern front. Some of them, appearing on the title page, talked quite explicitly of the 'barbarity of the southern man'.[31] It was in these fantasies of barbarism that the bases for the criminology of Giuseppe Sergi and for the anthropology of Cesare Lombroso, both proclaiming the existence of an essential racial difference between (normal) Italians and (criminally prone) southerners, were laid.[32]

In 1875 when the Florentine paper *L'opinione* asked Pasquale Villari, a professor of history at the University of Pisa, to start writing a series of 'Letters to the Editor' on the explosive southern question, it had a twofold objective: to capitalize on the public fascination for the exotic South, and to provide the political elites with strategies other than criminalization for the resolution of a problem that put into question the very unity of the State.[33] So successful that they were collected in a volume called *The*

Southern Letters in 1878, Villari's epistles warned that State repression was creating the preconditions that would allow popular rebellion to coalesce into forms of criminal organizations, if not altogether into revolutionary violence. The military occupation of the South only confirmed for southerners generally, and for Sicilians with their old tradition of autonomy more particularly, that what the king's government went on to call 'unification' was in fact the 'sacrificing' of the South as a colonial possession of the North.[34] Sicilians, in fact, still remembered the words of Prime Minister Camillo Benso, Count of Cavour, who conceived of unification as nothing more than the imposition of the North's will on its southern provinces: 'We must impose the unity on the most corrupt and weakest part of the country. We can have no doubts on the means to employ for such an end: moral force, and, if this is not enough, physical force as well.'[35]

To avoid a revolution, Villari maintained means other than militarization and physical force had to be found, and quickly. The State, in short, had to show a different, reformist face to the South, and start to tackle and eradicate the 'misery and hard conditions' which the South – Sicily first and foremost – was experiencing.[36]

A reformist liberal imbued with the positivist scientism of the late nineteenth century, Villari was a firm believer that material and economic conditions, rather than racial or cultural abstractions, determined social realities. According to such conviction, his goal was to convince his readers that a solution to the southern question, criminality included, could only be found in economic reforms: in short, 'the question of brigandage is an agrarian and social question', and not a criminal or anthropological one.[37] Still, in spite of the economic rigour he demanded of his readership, it was neither Villari's scientific analysis nor his proposals for agricultural reforms that the public of the Southern Letters was interested in. Instead they were fascinated by the appeal to the imagination that a single word in his texts had begun to stir: shrouded in mystery, eerie in sound, mysterious in origin, menacing in the images it evoked, the word 'mafia' entered the Italian cultural imaginary through a letter of March 1875.

'The Mafia' – Villari stated – 'is the logical, natural, necessary consequence of a particular social state, which must be modified in order to eradicate this evil.'[38] Surely in order to understand the consequences, one first needs to identify their causes; Villari described them: the feudal order of the Sicilian countryside, the class stratification of Sicily in aristocracy, landowning bourgeoisie, renters, wardens, and workers . . . But what was that Mafia, really? This seemed the only thing that truly interested Villari's readers.

To be precise, this was not the first time the word had appeared in writing. A record of the Inquisition of 1685 had referred to an episode of alleged witchcraft perpetrated by a 'Caterina of Licata, also known as Maffia'. While it is difficult to uncover the meaning of this nickname, it is unlikely that witchcraft had anything to do with the Mafia as a criminal organization.[39] A second written occurrence of the word, in a codex of eighteenth-century Sicilian poetry, is equally oblique: here the adjective *mafiusedda* appears with the meaning of 'finest looking'.[40] On the other hand a 'brotherhood' quite similar to what we might imagine the Mafia to be like today is described, in 1838, in a report sent by Pietro Ulloa, Attorney General of Trapani, western Sicily, to the Ministry of Justice in Palermo. The word 'mafia', however, is never used by Ulloa. Did the word not yet exist as the name for a criminal organization? Was Ulloa simply unaware of it? Or did he, perhaps, willingly refuse to name it as such?

Conjecture remains conjecture. What is certain is that a successful play of 1863, *The Mafiosi of the Vicaria* by Giuseppe Rizzotto and Gaspare Mosca, was single-handedly 'responsible' for allowing the word 'mafia' to enter into circulation with the precise meaning of a set of behavioural practices that were against the law.[41] Two years later the first police document to use the same word, describing Palermo's criminal organization, was signed by the prefect of Palermo, Filippo Gualterio. In 1866 the word was canonized in Antonino Traina's dictionary; the etymological fantasies regarding the mysterious origin of the word were soon to begin, with many suggested origins: *mahias*, an Arabic word meaning 'boasting', a leftover from the colonial domination of Sicily (827–1091); *marfud*, Arabic again, meaning 'swindler'; the French *mafler*, meaning 'gorging', inherited from the French Angevins who ruled Sicily between 1266 and 1282; *mafium*, meaning 'narrow minded' in the Piedmontese dialect; or even the Florentine *maffia*, meaning 'poverty'.[42]

It is around these dates, therefore, that a documentable codification of the term connoting a form of organized crime started to emerge. Lack of evidence for a Mafia that existed before the unified national state, to be sure, never pre-empted the possibility of imagining an older and almost mythical Mafia. Rather it simply divided the field of mafiologists into two opposing camps: on the one hand were those claiming that there was a prior, better time for Sicily when an honourable Mafia reigned rather than the abhorred Savoys; on the other were those determined to see the Mafia as a post-unification form of modern organization ready to exploit, 'deform and re-appropriate' a nostalgia for putatively better times in order 'to ensure the survival of the organization, its cohesiveness [and] its ability to create consensus.'[43]

There is no doubt that Pasquale Villari aligned with this second group. As 'the logical, natural, necessary consequence of a particular social state', the Mafia was, for Villari, the fruit of a particular social reality of post-unification Sicily. It exploited the weaknesses and advantages of the modern nation state. For Villari, in short, the Mafia was a *modern* institution, a response to the incomplete modernization of the South. His thesis was simple: with the French Revolution and the abolition of aristocratic privileges, a feudal system of vassalage and servitude had been replaced by the modern institution of private property. The land, which the king had once distributed to his own vassals in the form of counties and duke-doms – and which serfs had tilled to their masters' orders – was now redistributed among those same serfs who, as citizens, had become property owners. As Villari put it, 'Servitude was abolished, and the servant became not only a free man, but a property owner.'[44] In Italy, however, the national revolution, hijacked by a Savoy monarchy fearful of losing the favours of potentates in regions recently annexed to the State, had been reluctant to enforce new property laws, and even to establish clear ones. 'As we have conquered the governance of the country', noted Villari with despair, 'what have we done? Nothing. Absolutely nothing.'[45]

It was in the context of such passivity on the part of the State that the old aristocratic landlords, now reduced to mere citizens, decided to organize paramilitary groups to maintain possession over the feudal estates they had obtained from the now-deposed Bourbon king: such paramilitary groups were precisely 'the Mafia as an organization . . . [whose role was] to restrict the right to private property . . . It was precisely the defense of private property that served as the underlying motivation for most of the murders committed by the Mafia.'[46] Like the more recent Russian 'mafia' of today, grown from the demise of Soviet communism and the ensuing privatization of property, the original Sicilian Mafia was then, for Villari, a paralegal structure trying to capitalize on the new institution of private property in the absence of any clear norms.

Certainly this could not explain, by itself, why the Mafia grew in Sicily and not in other regions where a similar absence of clear laws had created the same preconditions. Villari, though, was certain that the context in which the Mafia had taken root was one in which the property of large

feudal estates was at stake. Tellingly the epicentre of the Mafia was neither in the poverty-ridden interior of the island nor in its economically
marginal eastern part. The Mafia, Villari noticed, existed where rich economic interests were at stake: 'The main centre, the very seat of the Mafia,
is in the surroundings of Palermo: from the surroundings, it extends its
web into the city. Here, the people are neither very poor nor oppressed.'[47]
It was essential, for Villari, to distinguish between mere brigandage, led
by 'poverty' and 'misery' and located in the inland and eastern part of the
island, and the true Mafia around Palermo, where 'the greatest estates
are to be found'.[48] From the estates of Villabate and Bagheria, the Mafia
wove its spiderweb to extend its control of substantial economic interests: orange and olive growth; wholesale; sulphur mines; and the nascent
industry of sweet wines.

Particularly attractive for the burgeoning Mafia observed by Villari were
the estates around Palermo's *Conca d'oro*, the 'golden valley' taking its name
from the citrus fruit industry. By 1870 the business was in the hands of
criminal organizations that controlled the growth, wholesale and price of
lemons, as well as the industry's labour and hiring practices. Weapons,
left over from Garibaldi's war of liberation, were readily taken up by those
willing to use them: those who were usually enlisted in the informal armies
of the big landowners seeking to defend themselves both from peasant
requests for 'lands for everybody' and from their competitors.

The economic elites thus surrounded themselves with an organization of landworkers, composed hierarchically; armed *campieri* (private
guards of farmland) supervising their work and quelling their attempts at
unionization; and *gabellotti* (renters and sub-lessors of parcels of farmland) at the head of them all. Recruited from the small-town elites, heavily
armed and controlling a militia of *campieri*, however, the *gabellotti* were
not exactly faithful vassals of their landlords. They soon started demon-
strating a lively entrepreneurial spirit of their own – Mafia style, to be
sure. Their objective was to take the lucrative citrus business away from
the feudal aristocracy that they serviced.

Dr Galati's Lemon Gardens

In 1872 a prominent Sicilian surgeon, Dr Gaspare Galati, inherited a ten-
acre lemon grove, Fondo Riella, on the outskirts of Palermo, from his
deceased brother-in-law. The farm was a jewel of modern agronomics.
Automated pumps provided the necessary irrigation, and the fruit was sold

far beyond Italy to the whole of Europe as well as the Americas. For such a modern farm, in such a lucrative business as lemons, it had never been a problem for Dr Galati's brother-in-law to get the necessary loans from the local bank, nor to obtain proper insurance for those rare cases of a poor harvest. By the time the doctor had inherited the farm, however, the warden of Fondo Riella, one Benedetto Carollo, had started to steal conspicuous quantities of the farm's fruit. His intention was not to sell, but to give Fondo Riella such a bad business reputation that it would run out of funding, so that he could acquire it for little money. As planned, by the time Galati had started managing Fondo Riella, the farm was in such disrepute that it was near bankruptcy – and Carollo was ready to buy it for a pittance.

As soon as Galati made sense of the situation, he fired Carollo. Not long after, Carollo's replacement was shot dead. After a very superficial and suspiciously short investigation, the police arrested two men, neither with a connection to the murder. Both men were soon released, and the murder went unpunished. Galati, unwilling to surrender, hired a new warden. It was at this time that threatening letters started being delivered to his door. The police were asked to intervene and did so with their customary lack of zeal: when asked if he had threatened anybody, Carollo had simply to deny it to be set free. The entire interrogation took only a few minutes.

At the end of his rope and convinced that the police were in cahoots with Carollo, Galati began his own investigation. He discovered a tight organization headed by Antonio Giammona, Sicilian don of the lemon business. It was Giammona, in partnership with Carollo, who wanted to bring Fondo Riella to bankruptcy in order to acquire it from Galati. Alas, this discovery too failed to ignite the zeal of the local police: such a pillar of the community as Signor Giammona, Galati was told, could not be inconvenienced for an interrogation. In the meantime, Galati's new warden was shot. More resilient than the first, he managed to survive, but refused to testify until, convinced he was about to die, he finally named Carollo as his attempted murderer.

Through the patient care of Galati's medical team, or perhaps graced by providence after his pious confession, the warden miraculously survived. Once in good health, it did not take him long before he visited Giammona, proposed a peaceful solution to the whole 'misunderstanding' and retracted his accusation. Vanquished, Galati abandoned Sicily and his lemon grove. He fled to Naples. There, in August 1875, when

Picking lemons in a grove on the *Conca d'Oro* (golden shell), outside Palermo, Sicily, *c.* 1906.

publication of the *Southern Letters* was underway, he sent a memorandum to the Minister of the Interior. In it he gave a detailed description of the Mafia family of Giammona, and even revealed the ritual of initiation to which all new adherents to the Giammona Mafia had to submit: the finger pricked with a needle by an officiating member; the drops of blood spilled on the image of St Anthony; the sacred image set on fire; the burning card passed from hand to hand; the oath . . . There it was: the whole pseudo-Masonic shebang.

Rituals and burning of saints notwithstanding, the episode of the Galati lemon grove suggests that Pasquale Villari had got it right: beneath the surface, the Mafia had little to do with feudal honour, ancient rituals or the banditry of the poor. It was, rather, a modern war 'opposing the landowners on the one hand and the guardian on the other, each against the other . . . It was part of the logic of competition.'[49] Monopoly of the lemon business was this war's trophy.

The three main characters in this story – Galati, the wealthy doctor, Giammona, the self-made man and Carollo the humble worker – confirmed Villari's most deep-seated fears. In the Mafia, as he understood it, 'we have three distinct classes: in Palermo the owners of great latifundia, . . . around Palermo, the wealthier peasants, [and] a third class of *gabellotti*.'[50] Among these classes, competition over land property and for the control of the lemon business had become open conflict. Reformist Villari had good reasons to be alarmed: a true class war, 'an antagonism of social classes' not altogether different from the one theorized by Marx and Engels in 1848, was brewing in Sicily.[51]

The Industry of Violence: Leopoldo Franchetti's Sicily in 1876

ANTHONY: Why is such a beautiful country so violent?
– *The Godfather Part II*, dir. Francis Ford Coppola

Just as alarmed as Villari was the Italian government, who now wanted to know more. The circulation of Galati's memorandum among the benches of the Italian parliament had turned the issue of the Mafia into a subject not only of public security, but of electoral politics. After the elections of 1874, Italian politics was divided into two major parties: a loose coalition of the Right, whose support came mostly from the industrialized provinces of the North; and an equally loose grouping of the Left, whose stronghold remained in the South. The despised war on brigandage, designed by Senator Giuseppe Pica and supported by his fellows on the Right, had turned Sicily into a hostile terrain for the conservative party. The evidence from the Galati memorandum, along with increasing rates of homicides in Sicily – one in every 3,194 inhabitants compared to one in 44,674 in Lombardy – became in this context an explosive political issue. Not only could the Right present itself as the party against the Mafia, but it could also portray its adversaries as being pro-Mafia. After Cesare Lombroso had theorized the genetic delinquency of the South, it was not a stretch for politicians from the Right to argue that the southern origin of many left-wing politicians genetically guaranteed their leaning towards crime. Southerners, put on the defensive, could only insist that the party in power was making instrumental use of the Mafia. The Mafia, they said, did not exist: it was a fantasy concocted by the Right to keep Sicily down and demonize the Left.

The confrontation reached its climax during a fiery parliamentary debate in June 1875, when a vote was requested by the Right on new special laws for Sicily. A senator on the Left, Diego Tajani, who had been chief prosecutor of the Palermo Court of Appeal from 1868 to 1872 and knew these matters well, attacked the members of his own party first, saying that denying the existence of the Mafia was like trying to 'deny the existence of the sun'. The Mafia, in Sicily, was something 'that you could see, you could feel, you could touch'. Tajani roared:

> There, crime is nothing more than an ongoing negotiation, an extortion note . . . that says: I could burn all your crops, your vineyards, I won't burn them, but give me something that corresponds to your wealth. There is a kidnapping, with the same mechanism: I won't kill you, but give me a certain amount and you will remain unharmed. You can see *capoccia* (chiefs) of the Mafia who take up a stance in the middle of an estate and tell you: I assure you that there will be no thefts, but give me a certain percentage of your harvests.[52]

With the members of his own party railing at him, Tajani turned his eyes – with a 'cold smile', as newspapers reported – to the other side of the aisle, flatly accusing the Right, always so willing to implement freedom-crushing measures in the South, to be just as willing in making use of criminals – the *gabellotti* protecting the large estates from the peasants' 'criminal' demands for land redistribution – as an instrument of 'local government' and electoral politics in Sicily:

> It has been stated by certain newspapers that we were opposed to the extraordinary law because we were friends to the Mafia, or, in other words, that we were abettors . . . Well, gentlemen of the Government, the center of the Mafia lies in the ranks of your law enforcement institutions, and, of course, without knowing it, you yourselves are the abettors.[53]

Vociferous protests ensued from both sides of the aisle. Tajani could not finish his speech until the next day, when he finally got to the point: 'The mafia in Sicily is not dangerous or invincible in itself. It is dangerous and invincible because it is an instrument of local government.'[54]

After the brouhaha, a parliamentary investigation was held in early 1876; the question became: who could be trusted with such an inquest? The senators from the Right were accusing those on the Left of protecting the peasants and brigands who threatened the order of private property in Sicily; those from the Left were sure that this was all a ploy to, once again, criminalize their party. As a result of such quarrels, two of Villari's students from the University of Pisa were dispatched to Sicily to conduct an independent private investigation that, it was hoped, could be trusted by all.

On 1 March 1876 Leopoldo Franchetti and Sidney Sonnino arrived in Palermo. The two Tuscans would publish their research in two separate reports. While Sonnino looked at the peasants' conditions on the island, Franchetti's *Sicily in 1876* was a sustained analysis of the Mafia, which focused on the specific ways in which this form of criminality differed from others. Written barely one year after Galati's memorandum had been circulated, the goal of Franchetti's report was to understand how the Mafia operated, why it had taken roots in Sicily and, above all, what it really was: 'the word "mafia" had been on everyone's lips . . . but there was great confusion about what it meant, if, indeed, it meant anything at all.'[55]

The Mafia, Franchetti began to explain, was a 'medieval sentiment' reflective of Sicily's still feudal culture:

A learned man who knows the island well has described [the Mafia] for us with these words: 'The Mafia is a medieval sentiment; a mafioso is a man who thinks he can provide for himself, for his safety and for the safety of his belongings, only through his own strength and valour and his personal influence, independently from authorities and the law'.[56]

This medieval idea would later find its supporters in those determined to legitimate and ennoble the Mafia as a form of honourable rebellion against 'authorities and the law'. From this perspective the popular yet fanciful idea of the Mafia having originated in the Sicilian Vespers was hypothesized. On Easter Sunday 1282, the Sicilians rebelled against French domination of the island and the slogan 'Death to the French, we want independence!' was written on the walls of Palermo. In Italian this reads as *Morte Ai Francesi Indipendenza Anela*, whose acronym produced the very word 'MAFIA'. This – rebellious but just – was the Mafia according to

American gangster Joe Bonanno, who called it, quite aptly, 'the Tradition'. And this was the Mafia according to Tommaso Buscetta, the 'boss of the two worlds' wanted by both the FBI and the Italian police: 'The Mafia was not born recently: it comes from the past. It fought for the poor against the rich . . . we still swear the same oath, we still have the same duties.'[57]

However, despite the fact that authoritative sources such as the *Encyclopædia Britannica Online* still put forward the idea that 'The Mafia arose in Sicily during the late Middle Ages, where it possibly began as a secret organization dedicated to overthrowing the rule of the various foreign conquerors of the island', the argument for a medieval origin – even a merely 'possible' one – has been amply disproved. Needless to say the illiterate people of Palermo in 1282 could hardly be imagined scribbling acronyms on the city's walls, and even the conceit of 'longing for independence' sounds more like an Enlightenment construct than the wisdom of trecento Sicily. As one historian writes, 'it is hard to imagine how anyone can believe such nonsense.'[58] Franchetti's intentions in claiming the medievalism of the Mafia, however, were quite separate from the nonsense concocted by its legitimators in search of an ancestral lineage. The Mafia, for him, was simply the paradox of the resilience of a medieval culture in a *modern* Italian state.

Like his teacher Villari, in fact, Franchetti was convinced not only that brigandage and Mafia were two very distinct phenomena, but that, while the former grew in the poverty and misery of the southern countryside and took the form of an archaic rebellion to state taxation and conscription, the Mafia was instead a *modern* form of delinquency.[59] In its sophisticated organization, its discipline, its division of labour, its dependence on economic prosperity and its urban texture, the Mafia was modern through and through:

> All so-called Mafia bosses are people of great economic means. It is easy for them to find enough workers, because the lower strata of the population in Palermo and its environs have a great familiarity with violence and are accustomed to blood . . . In this peculiar industry, the boss plays the roles of entrepreneur and manager. He determines the overall criminal plans, thus giving the Mafia its appearance of fatal and implacable power; he regulates the division of labour and of functions, and gives discipline to the workers of this industry.[60]

The Mafia, in sum, was the form of a perverted, 'abnormal' modernity. It grew parasitically, with the violence and modalities of a feudal 'medieval society', in the interstices of the modern Italian state, and protected a pre-modern feudal order of property at a moment when property, as Villari had taught Franchetti, was the privilege of the post-feudal modern citizen. It ordered labour in the manner of a modern industry, not for the production of social goods or services (the time of a 'social' Mafia providing prostitution or drugs to willing customers was still far away), but as an 'industry of crime', as Franchetti called it, or, mutatis mutandis, as an 'industry of violence'.[61]

Even worse was the fact that modern parliamentary democracy was being perverted by a latent Sicilian medievalism. What Franchetti meant by 'democratization of violence' was simple and yet terrifying: in the modern institution of the nation state, Franchetti explained, the right to use force, once the exclusive privilege of the king, had been legally transferred to the State.[62] Only the State, as the expression of the general will of its citizenry embodied in parliament, could use force, as in the case of war or police enforcement. In Sicily, however, the use of violence had been 'democratized', though in a perverted sense: while it was indeed no longer the privilege of the king, neither was it the prerogative of the State. It rather remained 'in the hands of private citizens, progressively involving new social groups and spreading beyond any rigid hierarchies of order or class'.[63]

It was exactly because the Italian state had failed to modernize Sicily and to eradicate its feudal system that the Mafia had now become a monstrous and parasitical version of modernity, 'a hellish parody of the capitalist economy' that Franchetti so enthusiastically supported.[64] The Mafia was an industry for no good; a democracy of abuse; the right of pure might. It was, in short, a paradox: a set of medieval orders, behaviours and cultural practices set in the heart of Italy's troubled modernity.

Turrisi Colonna and the Sect

MICHAEL: Italian politics have had these kind of men for centuries.
They're the true Mafia.
— *The Godfather Part III*, dir. Francis Ford Coppola

The paradoxes of the Mafia, however, went well beyond Franchetti's own expectations. The 'learned man who knows the island well' on whom Franchetti had relied as his main source of information was none other than Niccolò Turrisi Colonna, Baron of Buonvicino. 'A leading landowner of relatively recent status, forward-thinking and enlightened in the way he ran his businesses, a student of agricultural science, a patriot even before the unification, and thereafter a prominent member of the moderate left wing, as well as a senator, and the mayor of Palermo',[65] Turrisi Colonna had been the target of an assassination attempt in 1863.

One day in early summer he was returning home from his usual tour of his many estates around Palermo. As his cart approached the district of Olivuzza, five men began shooting, first at the horses, then at the carriage's occupants. Turrisi Colonna was quick to extract his revolver and return fire, hitting at least one of the assailants. At the noise, Turrisi Colonna's wardens rushed to the scene. There was nothing for the assassins to do but retreat, dragging their wounded accomplice away and leaving Turrisi Colonna alive and victorious. Soon after the incident, the baron wrote a study of organized crime titled *Public Security in Sicily*: 'it was the first of many books published after the unification of Italy that made the Sicilian mafia a subject of analysis, controversy, and confusion.'[66]

Confusion notwithstanding, what better source of information on the Mafia, Franchetti must have thought, than the courageous survivor of its violence? After all *Public Security in Sicily* was not only the first book ever published on 'the sect', but was also, as historian John Dickie describes it, a 'peculiarly well-informed and credible account' of the Mafia organization.[67] It described the hierarchical structure of the Mafia from the boss to the *gabellotto*, down to the simple 'soldiers'; it denounced the collusion of local police with Mafia families; it chastised the courts' unwillingness to touch the untouchables. In sum it gave a clear, if terrifying, picture of the Mafia's complete control of the Sicilian territory. That said, the problem with Turrisi Colonna's account was that it was so *peculiarly* well informed. How did he know so much about an organization whose very way of life was built on secrecy? Could it be that Turrisi Colonna was a mafioso in his own right, and that the assassination attempt was just a settling of accounts between Mafia families?

No clear answer has ever been given to these questions. Facts, however, accumulate to such an extent that Franchetti's naive trust should be fundamentally questioned. Turrisi Colonna's political ascent to the Italian parliament in the ranks of the Right, in fact, had been made possible by the endorsement of a man of honour whose name we have already encountered in the context of the Galati lemon grove affair: Don Antonio Giammona. Giammona manoeuvred and controlled a packet of 50 votes – votes that could make a substantial difference in Italy's regime of limited suffrage – in the countryside around Palermo. It was Giammona's electoral bloc that propelled Turrisi Colonna into national politics. Later, in 1875, when Giammona ran into legal trouble over the Galati affair, now-Senator Turrisi Colonna repaid the debt by giving moving speeches and writing 'recommendations' on his behalf. He also provided his own lawyers to prepare the defence.

Turrisi Colonna had always made consistent use of outlaws to defend his properties. At least three wardens of his farmlands were identified as mafiosi in police reports. When authorities on the track of mafiosi in 1874 were led by their investigations directly to his estates, Turrisi Colonna protested from the height of his senatorial seat. The prefect that had ordered the operation was immediately removed from Palermo and all investigations of the senator were closed. The chief of police, however, kept insisting that Mafia rituals of initiation were being celebrated on Turrisi Colonna's estates. It comes as no surprise that by 1876 members of the Italian parliament were already whispering the name of Turrisi Colonna as the Mafia's boss of bosses.

This was perhaps an exaggeration. More likely Turrisi Colonna was the first in a long series of politicians exchanging favours for votes with the Mafia: government contracts, land zoning or sales were cautiously leaked from Turrisi Colonna's office to Giammona; the latter then made sure that 'his' people would cast the right vote in the secrecy of the ballot box. As a result Franchetti's investigation into the Mafia was vitiated – to what extent we will never know – at its very source. Sicilians, perhaps, should not have been trusted. Those same Sicilians, in turn, hardly trusted the Tuscan author of *Sicily in 1876* who depicted the island in such gloomy tones that nothing good could come out of it for the islanders.

Don Raffaele and Giuseppe Pitrè

Precisely in this context, Giovanni Verga found the solution to all his marketing problems. It was not an easy feat: Verga had to balance, on the one hand, the public's eagerness to read more and more about the Mafia and, on the other, his own Sicilian pride that had been wounded by those, like Franchetti, who associated Sicily with unredeemable violence.

There was only one solution to such a balancing act: to transform the Mafia, or at least the violence that agitated Sicily, into something nobler, more antique, more genuine and more authentic than Franchetti's prosaic 'industry of violence'. Verga was not alone in this operation. The entire Sicilian intelligentsia, in one way or another, was determined to return lost honour to Sicily. Some, like Congressman Napoleone Colajanni, would remain critical of the Mafia while insisting that its origins were neither cultural nor ethnic but rather historical: centuries of colonial domination continued by the Savoys. By and large, however, the Sicilian intellectual class was on a more radical path. To rehabilitate Sicilian honour, the Mafia had to be either denied as the defaming invention of northerners like Franchetti or – better yet – reframed as a more romantic and beautiful thing: a rustic chivalry of sorts. At the heart of this movement was Don Raffaele Palizzolo, boss of Ciminna.

A true self-made man, Mafia style, Palizzolo came out of the Risorgimento wars as the owner of some lands near Palermo. These were not big or particularly profitable properties, especially when compared to the estates of those who really mattered in western Sicily like Baron Turrisi Colonna. Giuseppe Marchesano, the lawyer who would successfully prosecute Palizzolo in 1902, argued during his trial that he 'maintained these lands for no other reason than to give work to convicts'.[68] Convicts and outlaws, well armed since the times of Garibaldi, were indeed instrumental to Palizzolo's true ambitions, which went well beyond the narrow horizons of his lands. Not only could these convicts intimidate Palizzolo's farmers and curb their requests for just salaries and proper working conditions, they could also – and Palizzolo was a genius at this – convince or coerce the people in his district to vote him into public office for the Sicilian Autonomist Party, which at the time 'included some of Sicily's richest and most powerful aristocrats'.[69]

Voter intimidation and the clientelism of favours; as an attentive historian of the Mafia has observed, the Mafia operates by 'processes, however distorted and perverted, of democratization'.[70] In Sicily as in the New

World, careerism within the rank and file of the Mafia – petty criminal becoming man of honour, and later even the commander of a firing squad – had always reflected a larger context in which the immobility of societies based on birthright had made way for new processes of social mobility. It was in politics in particular, however, that the Mafia engendered a true, if perverted, process of democratization. Consider: how could a man of humble birth such as Palizzolo ever compete against Sicily's richest and most powerful aristocrats – say, in an electoral campaign in which money, yesterday as today, buys votes and media attention? Voter intimidation, clientelism and sheer corruption corrected the imbalance for Palizzolo so that, in a bitter triumph of representative democracy, even he – the humble man, the *umile* – could conquer his seat in parliament. It may not be mere chance, then, if the key word of biblical justice and political emancipation – humility – coincides with one of the Mafia's most emblematic terms: *umili*, of humble birth, is one likely etymological root for *umirtà* or *omertà*, the deadly code of silence.

Palizzolo was elected councillor for the province of Palermo in the late 1860s. The picture of Palizzolo in public office is starkly reminiscent of the opening sequence of the first *Godfather* film. In the morning, in what I like to imagine as a dim-lit office in Coppola's fashion, he would receive his postulants in the luxurious Palazzo Villarosa in Palermo, a stone's throw away from the royal palace that the Norman count Roger II of Hauteville had used as the administrative centre for his 'Southern Empire' of 1144. At Palazzo Villarosa the new king in town would dispense favours – a job, a pay rise, a licence, a better grade in school – in exchange for 'signs of respect' that could range from a purely symbolic kiss of the hand to the more pragmatic monetary 'gift'. Once in office Palizzolo also made a practice of embezzling public funds. Neither the police nor the magistrate, however, seemed capable of finding enough evidence against him. Perhaps they were not hoping to get a transfer, a promotion, a pay rise . . .

Palizzolo's luck started to change in 1873 when Marquis Emanuele Notarbartolo (from whose family, incidentally, Palizzolo had bought Palazzo Villarosa) was elected mayor of Palermo. The encounter between the two was nothing short of epochal for the history of the Mafia. It began with a profound reciprocal dislike and with Notarbartolo's mounting suspicions of Palizzolo's financial misdeeds. In 1876, when Notarbartolo was nominated manager of the Sicilian Bank and had complete access to bank records, the suspicions started to solidify into a heap of evidence.

By 1878 – one year after the publication of Franchetti's report – Notarbartolo had not only built a solid case against Palizzolo, but had forced the central government to intervene. The Bank of Sicily was a matter of national interest, and the government soon opened a parliamentary investigation for the impeachment of Palizzolo from the provincial government. On the wave of Franchetti's report, his looked like a case of Mafia infiltration into politics.

Palizzolo's reaction was to mount a campaign in defence of his honour, and the honour of *all* Sicilians. In those years, as historian Paolo Pezzino recounts, the political elites of Sicily were already at work creating a peculiar rhetorical 'paradigm': if they were accused of having Mafia connections, they would simply retort that the accusations were slanderous – not only for them, humble servants of the general will, but for the Sicilian people as a whole. The Mafia did not exist: northern politicians had invented it for their political gain. And if the Mafia existed, it was simply a respectable Sicilian tradition, which every senator was proud, democratically, to represent. As Senator Antonio Starrabba di Rudinì claimed unabashedly during a parliamentary interrogation on 10 March 1876:

> What is this Mafia? . . . I mean, there is a benign Mafia. This benign Mafia is a spirit of courage, a disposition not to accept abuses . . . So, in a sense, I could even be a benign mafioso. I mean, I am not, but could be, like any man who respects himself . . . and who does not tolerate abuses.[71]

Using this paradigm, Palizzolo built his own defence. All that was needed was to turn Franchetti's argument from negative to positive. Yes, Franchetti may have been correct, there may be a Mafia in Sicily and politics may even be linked to it. But are we sure that this is such a bad thing?

These arguments became the basis for Palizzolo's new regionalist party of the Right, unsurprisingly called Pro-Sicilia (Pro-Sicily). We find the coordinates of the party's campaign in the pages of one of the most ardent supporters of Don Raffaele Palizzolo, the Sicilian ethnographer Giuseppe Pitrè:

> The word Mafia . . . is most certainly not recent: if no dictionary before Traina's registers it . . . This does not mean that it did not exist before 1860, as many presume. Our dictionaries . . .

only represent a minimal amount of popular language . . . in the popular quarters of Palermo, in the Borgo . . . the word Mafia and its derivatives always meant, and still mean, beauty, grace, perfection, excellence. A pretty girl conscious of her beauty, well dressed and with a countenance of superiority, shows some Mafia, and is *mafiusa*, *mafiusedda* . . . In addition to the meaning of 'beauty', the word Mafia also signifies superiority and ability in the best sense of the word . . . but never self-importance in a bad sense, never arrogance, never haughtiness. The Mafia man or mafioso, in this proper sense, would not intimidate anybody, because no one is more courteous and respectful than him. Unfortunately, after 1860, things have changed, and the word *mafioso* no longer has, for many, its original and authentic meaning.[72]

Thus defined as neither a sect nor an association, the Mafia has then nothing to do with crime. Its original meaning is, instead, 'beauty'. In this true re-evaluation of all values, Pitrè was codifying the sort of respectable and honourable Mafia concocted by the fantasies of Palizzolo and his regionalist friends for their own political needs.

The terms of this re-evaluation should not pass unnoticed: first, the Mafia is said to be a very old tradition – it 'always meant' – and not a modern 'industry' as Franchetti had argued. Second, the fact that dictionaries did not include the word until recently only proves that the Mafia was not the instrument of the elites (Villari's thesis before Franchetti's) but a concept of the 'popular quarters of Palermo'. Third, there is nothing intimidating or abusive in the Mafia – 'never self-importance in a bad sense, never arrogance' – but only a sense of 'beauty, grace, perfection [and] excellence' symbolized by a most unthreatening 'pretty girl'. Fourth, and most importantly, it is essential to distinguish between the proper sense of the word – 'its original and authentic meaning' that has 'always' existed in 'popular' Sicily as a veritable ancestral tradition – and the 'unfortunate' new meaning attributed to this word after 1860. Who hides behind this unfortunate misinterpretation and corruption of origins? The *infami* – 'the habitual mafia insult for a traitor, "dishonoured scum"' – like Franchetti the northerner (or Sicilian Notarbartolo himself) who dishonour Sicily and the most beautiful of its traditions![73]

Palizzolo's autonomist right-wing party clung to the work of the ethnologist Giuseppe Pitrè just as German nationalists of the same period embraced the folklore of the Grimm brothers. Pitrè's ethnology claimed an original and untouchable *Volkgeist*, a spirit of the Sicilian people, in which the Mafia played a similar role to some German Cinderella, a racially pure heroine that Palizzolo – a true Prince Charming with an unspoiled instinct, able to distinguish true from false – could see in all her beauty and chose time and again over stepmother Italy.[74]

Palizzolo's pro-Sicily party was not alone in finding inspiration in such folklore. As soon as Giovanni Verga resolved to set his literary stories in Sicily, he turned to the works of Pitrè for inspiration: the ethnographer's collection of Sicilian folk tales, songs and popular sayings was exactly what he needed to add a touch of local colour to his writings.[75] By the time he started working on his *Cavalleria rusticana* in 1880, it seems that the whole paradigm of Palizzolo and Pitrè's beautiful, authentic and popular Mafia had begun to frame his regionalist fantasies. No longer the mere 'social conditions' of Villari's cold scientific analysis, nor the gloomy 'abnormal modernity' of Franchetti's disdainful report, the Mafia had acquired the status of a most powerful literary theme. It was all that Verga needed: the legend, the antiquity of traditions lost in a modernizing world, beauty misunderstood, the expression of a popular spirit and, above all, the affirmation of a passionate life.

Ten years after the glorious conclusion of the Risorgimento, after the ideal had been (somewhat) realized and the age of heroism was over, it was exactly life and passion that the new nation needed. The petty bourgeois existence of the Italian Madames Bovarys (and of their male counterparts too) needed new thrills, new passions and new life. No lesser authority than Francesco De Sanctis, Minister of Public Instruction, had said so. In a famous inaugural lecture at the beginning of the academic year 1872–3, De Sanctis warned the new Italy:

> Life today suffers an unknown disease, whose symptoms are apathy, boredom and emptiness . . . To create new blood, to rebuild the fibres, to raise new vital energies: this is the task not only of medicine, but of pedagogy as well; of historiography, but also of the arts. We must regenerate our vital energies, toughen our character once again; with a sentiment of strength we must regenerate our moral character, sincerity, initiative, discipline. We must regenerate the virile man, and therefore the free man.[76]

Like De Sanctis, Verga was convinced that modern existence 'has smoothed the corners, flattened, given uniformity to the way in which feelings and passions are manifested'.[77] What better theme than the Mafia, a pre-modern chivalric tradition, to combat the apathy, boredom and emptiness of modern life, the daily routine of work, family, hot soup and bed! The Mafia – Palizzolo's and Pitrè's 'beautiful' Mafia, to be sure – represented, after all, those very virtues that had characterized the Risorgimento: heroism, self-determination, resistance against authority and independence. As the heroic life of the Risorgimento could hardly be routinized in the instituted State and its bureaucracy, the Mafia, the new rustic cavalry, was to come to the rescue.

What better theme than the Mafia, indeed, to get a glimpse of that 'virile man' whose vital energies and unbridled passions are above and beyond any social order! Lola is married to Alfio? But social contracts and a marriage licence mean nothing compared to Turiddu's passion for Lola! Passions are passions, and life is life; neither can be contained in the social formulas of 'man and wife'! If 'new blood' is to be created – healthier and livelier – a good place to start is the Sicily of this romanticized Mafia. In this Sicily, rivers of blood are spilled for the sake of nothing more (or less) than sincere passion – for the sake of an authentic life still uncontaminated by the 'unknown disease' called modern bourgeois social norms.

In 1880 Verga began to exploit the theme of the Mafia popularized by Villari and Franchetti and rendered 'beautiful' and 'authentic' by the regionalism of Palizzolo and his followers.[78] *Cavalleria rusticana* narrates the story of Turiddu (Sicilian for Salvatore, 'the Saviour'), a soldier who is returning to his Sicilian village at the end of his military service on the continent. The tension between old and new – village life and the conscription of the modern state, Sicily and the new nation – is at the forefront. Back home, Turiddu finds that his beloved, Lola, has married Alfio, a wealthy carter from a nearby town. Jealousy and rage are his immediate reactions. After the initial furore, and with Lola quite willing, Turiddu begins an adulterous affair with her. When Alfio hears of the affair, he challenges the man who has dishonoured him to a duel – set, quite symbolically, on Easter Sunday.

Alfio's behaviour, like that of Pitrè's mafioso, is, by definition, legitimated by the invocation of honour – what Pitrè had called, precisely, 'chivalric honour'.[79] Honour, in turn, is defined by blood, the only symbol that can wash away dishonour and shame; 'only blood', Pitrè had written, 'can wash blood offences away.'[80] This is because, in the last analysis, honour is about 'the purity of flesh and blood . . . For this reason dishonour is caused by the shame of a relative no less than by an offence against one's own person.'[81] In other words, in the grand tragic drama of *Cavalleria*, Lola's adulterous relation with Turiddu threatens to give Alfio a child whose blood is impure – a bastard. In the pre-modern society described by Verga, 'property is given, transmitted by inheritance, not acquired through processes of social mobility.'[82] Lola is, then, the one who ought to preserve, with her honour, the effective purity of the bloodline – hence the transmission of property. An eye for an eye: once the bloodline has been compromised, only blood can repair the offence.

For Turiddu too, it is a matter of honour to accept the challenge. Once Turiddu has lost social prestige because Lola has chosen a wealthier man, spilling Alfio's blood is his only option to regain honour:

> Honour is a particular ability consisting in strength and cunning or in some other individual gift which inspires admiration and respect and helps one make one's way in life. For example, the man of honour, even if his origins are humble, has become wealthy and respected by bullying. Or he has killed . . . In this case, honour is conceived of as an extraordinary individual ability reinforced by the accumulation of a capital of successful violence. The more effectively a man is able to use violence the higher he rises on the scale of honour. The struggle for honour is therefore a competition . . . One fights to acquire honour and so to alter the pre-existing . . . distribution of honour.[83]

For both Alfio and Turiddu, honour is, moreover, about meeting social expectations. As the anthropologist Michael Herzfeld puts it, honour is – with its rituals of death and sacrifice appealing to allegedly timeless traditions – some kind of an operatic theatre, a 'strategy that leads social actors to capitalize on "tradition" . . . for what we call honor is a calculating claim to lineage, to a past, to history'.[84]

Turiddu senses that the duel will be his end, but honourable men have no choice. On the day of the duel, amidst the exotic prickly pears of the Sicilian countryside, the destiny of Turiddu is sealed:

> 'Ah!' screamed Turiddu, blinded. 'I'm done!' He tried to save himself by jumping desperately backwards, but Alfio caught him up with another stab in the stomach, and a third in the throat. '– and three! That's for the house which you adorned for me! And now

your mother can mind her fowls –'. Turiddu reeled about for a moment or two here and there among the cactuses, then fell like a stone. The blood gurgled frothing from his throat, he couldn't even gasp: Oh, Mother![85]

The duel fought for the sake of honour is not the only commonplace Verga draws from Pitrè's Mafia. Albeit 'elusively'[86] – the actual term never appeared explicitly in his writings – *Cavalleria rusticana* (along with the unfinished 'Golden Key') was cunningly packed with allusions to the Mafia. Turiddu's very entrance into the scene, 'swaggering about the village square ... showing himself off in his [military] uniform', is reminiscent of Pitrè's 'well dressed ... countenance of superiority' that makes someone 'mafioso'.[87] Lola's 'temper' – *sangue rissoso* or 'quarrelsome blood' in Verga's original Italian – certainly qualifies her as a *mafiusedda*.[88] Master Alfio too, 'one of those carters who go swaggering beside their horse with their cap over their ear', seems a model in a hypothetical fashion show of the Mafia.[89]

There is one further moment when the allusion to the Mafia becomes as explicit as possible without naming it. It is the scene that prepares the duel (repeated twice in *The Godfather Part III*), when 'Turiddu nipped the carter's ear between his teeth.'[90] Pitrè describes the gesture as typical of the honour code of the Mafia:

> Tom has called Dick 'low life'. Dick, who disagrees with the characterization, and feels he has been bloodily offended, calls Tom outside and asks him if he has anything to say. Tom embraces him and bites his ear (the mafioso embraces and kisses *for life and for death*. Biting the ear means: 'let's duel – one of us must die'). Dick reciprocates the kiss as a man of honor, thus accepting the challenge.[91]

In 1880, as Verga's short story was being published in the Roman paper *Fanfulla della domenica*, the Galati affair and Palizzolo's judicial troubles had already shown the less rustic face of the Mafia. In the same year, public prosecutor Ferdinando Lestingi had started an investigation of Sicilian 'Brotherhoods' devoted not so much to passion, but rather to extortion, robbery, cattle theft, murder and political intimidation on behalf of, once again, Raffaele Palizzolo.[92] In 1880 the rate of homicides in Sicily, which included the relatively peaceful eastern provinces, had risen to 119 murders per 100,000 inhabitants; in Palermo, this surely did not feel like chivalrous times. However, neither Giovanni Verga nor his readers were touched by all this: *Cavalleria rusticana* was a smashing success.

The prestigious Milan publishing house Treves immediately issued Verga a contract to allow them to publish the story, along with others in the same genre, in a collection entitled *Life in the Fields (Vita dei Campi)*. With *Cavalleria* being reprinted – in infringement of copyright – in other papers, Verga was thrilled by the offer from Treves. The collection was rushed through to press in a few months and was yet another success. Readers, critics and the publishing industry were in awe of Verga's Sicily. To meet public demand, *Life in the Fields* was reprinted in 1881. Even from France, publishers and translators were at Verga's door.

The Godfather Syndrome

Of all the stories collected in *Life in the Fields*, it was certainly *Cavalleria rusticana* that remained the most popular: the blood, the passion, the ritualistic murder of Turiddu in an exotic Sicily, was all the public wanted. Verga was happy to comply. On 14 January 1884 the theatrical adaptation of *Cavalleria* was ready to premiere at the Teatro Carignano in Turin. Turiddu's nipping of the ear was a hit. In 1887 a translation of Verga's short stories circulated in France with a preface by Guy de Maupassant, arguably the most influential writer of short stories at the time. The success was unprecedented. In 1899 Pietro Mascagni made *Cavalleria* into an opera and in 1907 another composer, Domenico Monleone, invited by Verga himself, wrote a second opera on the same story. While Verga and Monleone were brought to court by Mascagni for infringement of copyright, Mascagni's opera was applauded in Budapest and Vienna. In 1908 a French version of the play premiered in Paris to great acclaim. In the midst of legal action, Verga was already thinking about using the new media everybody had started talking about – cinema – to squeeze even more out of *Cavalleria*. No fewer than three movies based on the story were made between 1907 and 1916. The Mafia had become a cultural good, and quite profitable for business too.

On the wave of Verga's success, an outpouring of stories alluding to the Mafia (but, like Verga's, rarely mentioning it explicitly) populated Italian bookshelves. In 1885 Carolina Invernizio, one of the most successful writers of popular fiction at the time, released *An Episode of Brigandage*. In 1896 a collection of sonnets in dialect on the '*maffia*' was published by Nino Martoglio as *O' scuru o' scuru (In the Dark)*. In 1901 Capuana's *Marquis of Roccaverdina* presented a character 'whose behaviour is typical of a Mafia understood as [the] exercise of private violence'.[93] And in 1910 Luigi Natoli's *Blessed Paulists* became a national best-seller.

What was the public fascination with the Mafia? It was the same fascination, no doubt, which stands behind the success of the *Godfather* saga. In one word: nostalgia. The Mafia, here, is nothing less than the longing for a world we have lost, where honour and passions are pristine – or where, as D. H. Lawrence wrote after watching Mascagni's opera in 1911, 'life [is] more natural, naive, inartistic & refreshing.'[94] It is longing and nostalgia, to use the words that Lawrence penned for the preface to his translation of Verga's, for 'every manifestation of pure, spontaneous, passionate life, life kindled to vividness'.[95]

Nostalgia begins with the foreboding that passions and individuality are being sacrificed at the altar of social reason. Max Weber called this sacrifice – a true 'disenchantment' of the world – 'the practical rationalization of life from the viewpoint of utility'.[96] From such a viewpoint, a social contract or a law would prevent Alfio from killing Turiddu. A rational calculus of utility and convenience would intervene to prevent his revenge. Lawrence commented:

> We think of ourselves, ah, how stupid of Alfio . . . to have to go killing a man and getting [himself] shut up in prison for life, merely because the man had committed adultery with [his wife]. Was it worth it? . . . We ask the question with our reason, and with our reason we answer No! . . . We have got beyond all that. We are so much more reasonable. All our life is so much more reasoned and reasonable.[97]

Yet, 'the more the populations of the world become only rational in their consciousness, the swifter they bring about their destruction pure and simple.'[98] Fear – or sheer boredom – of such rationalization rekindles a nostalgia for passion.

Just as readers of *Cavalleria* are nostalgic for lost passions, so does nostalgia animate the whole of *The Godfather Part III*. True, since the first movie of 1972, Coppola's entire trilogy was 'imbued with mourning for a lost America', caught in the yearning desire 'to return to past forms that are either in the process of fading away or have already done so'.[99] Yet it is in *The Godfather Part III*, on the notes precisely of *Cavalleria rusticana*, that 'the sense of nostalgia does not end.'[100]

The faded sepia family photos; the house 'in disrepair, abandoned . . . on a cold, gray day'; the aged face of Michael . . . [101] From the very opening – on the notes of Nino Rota's melancholic waltz – nostalgia crawls over the screen. Far is the community from Michael's lonely, deteriorating villa on Lake Tahoe; far is his family; and lost is the harmony about which he cannot but reminisce in the most nostalgic, longing letter written to Anthony and Mary:

> My dear children. It is now better than several years since I moved to New York, and I haven't seen you as much as I would like to. I hope you will come to this ceremony of Papal Honors, given for my charitable work. The only wealth in this world is children, more than all the money and power on earth. You are my treasure. Anthony and Mary, although I entrusted your education to your mother for your own best interests, you know how I look forward to seeing you, and to a new period of harmony in our lives.

Michael Corleone has become an enviably successful, respectable businessman, about to receive the Papal medal of the insignia of St Sebastian. Yet the more reason tells him he has made it big, the swifter, to paraphrase Lawrence, his sense of what he has lost brings about his destruction. The wealth he has accumulated – 'money and power on earth' – has deprived him of the 'only wealth' that matters: his children and his family, his only

Faded photos on his desk remind Michael of the family harmony he has lost,
The Godfather III (1990).

true passions, are gone. As he will tell Vincent, his nephew: 'That's the price you pay.'

The price for Michael has been steep. He has lost not only his family but, as the film cuts on the pomp and circumstance of Michael receiving the papal honours, 'every manifestation of pure, spontaneous, passionate life'. 'All my life', Michael will later confess, 'I kept trying to go up in society . . . But the higher I go, the crookeder it becomes. How in the hell does it end?' How does it end, or what is that end: this is the less-than-Hamletish question.

Going 'up in society', to put it differently, no longer guarantees that life can retain meaning, and it is this meaning – pure, spontaneous, passionate life – Michael pays as his price for success. The crescendo of brutality, the hyperbolic bloodiness of one event after another, the senseless violence in search of at least *some* thrill of emotion, only end up highlighting and exasperating this ultimate loss of meaning for human life, up to the speechless last cry of Michael, and his death witnessed only by a sniffing dog. If the violence in *The Godfather Part III* is grotesque and absurd, it is so because it reflects, in the end, the grotesquery and absurdity of a life that has lost all passion and all meaning.[102] It is life itself that, being now meaningless, becomes dispensable: murders are the emblem of that dispensability.

Such a sense of loss pervades *The Godfather Part III* throughout: 'You were all that I loved, valued, most in the world', says Michael to Kay. 'And I'm losing you, I lost you, anyway. You're gone, and it was all for nothing'. And again: 'You know, every night here in Sicily, I dream, about my wife and my children. And how I lost them.' 'He's lost', says Don Altobello of Michael . . .

In truth, it is not only Michael who is, or has, lost. 'I lost all the venom, all the juice of youth', echoes Altobello. The young ones are not immune either. Mary has established a Vito Corleone Foundation 'dedicated to the resurrection of Sicily'. To the mourning of this dead, lost Sicily, she devotes her earnest existence. Michael's nephew, Vincent – young, hotblooded Vincent, reminiscent of Verga's Turiddu – has also made nostalgia his way of life. He takes Mary, whom he likes, to the old neighbourhood:

VINCENT: That's where our Grandfather got his start. Started as a delivery boy, made three bucks a week. Three years later, he owned the company.
MARY: Only in America!
VINCENT: That's it!

That's it: *only* in America! The problem, however, is that America in 1990, exactly like Michael, seems to live its success (the Berlin Wall having just crumbled) with a sense of aching nostalgia for the old days when delivery boys, making three bucks a week, were debonair and happy. As for now, Coppola mourns, 'the only priority . . . that's become uppermost in America today: to make a profit.'[103]

This is not an idiosyncratic claim of Coppola's. It is rather an epochal drama. The editorial boom of self-help manuals begun in the 1980s was already a symptom. Behind titles like *Miss Piggy's Guide to Life* or *The Be (Happy) Attitudes*, which consistently occupied the top ten lists of the decade, lurked a sense of something lost. In the same years, Dire Straits's 'Money for Nothing' and Bruce Springsteen's dystopic anthem 'Born in the USA', which sang of having 'Nowhere to run, ain't got nowhere to go'– were compulsively asking whether life in America had turned out worse than expected. Hollywood itself had not shied away from showing the deep malaise corroding American society at its core. Ridley Scott's *Blade Runner* (1982) opened the way by asking whether humans were becoming automata after all. Sergio Leone's nostalgic *Once Upon a Time in America* (1984) continued the trend by implying that perhaps America was no more. Wes Craven's *A Nightmare on Elm Street* (1984), mourning the loss of innocence of its teenage protagonists, filmed nothing less than the horror of dreams as they turned into reality.

In 1984 Leo Buscaglia's best-selling book *Loving Each Other* diagnosed the first symptoms and pointed its finger against a modern, rational and prosperous society that 'has perpetuated isolation and devalued basic human values'.[104] Both from the political Right (Allan Bloom's *The Closing of the American Mind*, 1987), and from the Left (Ravi Batra's *The Great Depression*, 1987), a sense of loss and nostalgia pervaded the American imaginary of the 1980s. Throughout the decade, 'Coppola's interest in nostalgia is most apparent in films like *Tucker: The Man and His Dream* (1988), *Peggy Sue Got Married* (1986), and *The Outsiders* [1983].'[105] In this context, *The Godfather Part III* handles the Mafia: as is America, so is Mafia boss Michael Corleone. With no sense of a purpose – 'How in the hell does it end?' – with no ultimate goal or meaning, Michael, like America, *has* become nostalgic for something he has lost.

'Michael, you must lead another life', Don Altobello warns him. 'Your life could be redeemed', insists Cardinal Lamberto. Yet what other life is possible? All, in this America, seems to be the same: all is business. Religion and banking? 'They're the same problem', asserts Michael. Politics and crime? 'They're the same thing', he continues. Finance and politics? 'Finance is a gun; politics, is knowing when to pull the trigger', concludes Don Lucchesi. And the Mafia? Could the Mafia, at least, be something else?

Even the Mafia, in *The Godfather Part III*, has been 'rationalized': it has become business. If the Mafia in the first and second *Godfather* still possessed a 'rose-coloured' quality that separated it from the drabness of everyday life, here 'the family' has been reduced to an indistinct, homogenized part of the same everyday: 'It's no different than any large corporation', states B. J. Harrison in the movie.[106] In short nostalgia remains the only escape.

Like the reader meeting Verga's Turiddu before him, Michael seems convinced that such escape into nostalgia can in fact lead to a different life: 'Let me show you Sicily. The real Sicily', he says.

The solar, saturated colours of the Sicilian second half of *The Godfather Part III* are captured by Emilio Lari, Coppola's photographic consultant for the Sicilian scenes. Idyllic shepherds move around the ruins of Greek temples with their flocks as a Romantic memento to a lost harmony. Sicily – imagined precisely in the colours of Verga – contrasts dramatically with the drab, grey atmospheres of the New York scenes, captured by consultant John Seakwood, master of *noir* photography for films such as *Family Business* and *Presumed Innocent*. In Sicily Michael finds the colour of something he has lost and yet fancies he can regain. Here he finds a different Mafia: Don Tommasino's.

The Don is old, frail and in a wheelchair; but how much wiser, alive and honourable is he, living in a rustic country house and dressed accordingly, than all those bankers, cardinals, politicians and businessmen! This, to Michael, is the real Mafia. Like that of Verga, it is as beautiful and passionate as an aria. Anthony sings folk songs. Michael reminisces about his past love. He cries. Vincent strokes Mary's hair . . . It's all as beautiful as the day of creation.

Moved to generosity, Michael invites us all to celebrate:

MICHAEL: I have invited you all here to celebrate my son's first appearance in an opera house. He will be appearing, in about three weeks, in the Teatro Massimo, in the opera *Cavalaria rusticani* [mispronounced by Michael].

ANTHONY: It's *Cavalleria rusticana* dad [correcting Michael's pronunciation].

MICHAEL: *Cavalleria* . . . (*Laughing*). I think I've got tickets to the wrong opera.

No doubt all of us, like Michael, got the wrong ticket if we believed for a moment that such regained harmony was within reach. As Tommasino is killed and Sicily too precipitates in a spiral of senseless violence, there comes the reckoning: there was no Utopia and there was no elsewhere. All was business as usual, like the unhappy business of Coppola unwillingly entertaining us with yet another Mafia movie – one produced, so he said, with money that the Mafia laundered through banker Roberto Calvi (on whose persona the character of Frederick Keinszig is based), money then moved through the Vatican-held real estate and construction company Immobiliare (which in the movie is supervised by the evil Archbishop Gilday) and finally invested in Paramount Pictures' Mafia movies.[107] If a tragedy climaxes in *The Godfather Part III*, it is that of the inescapability of money – or of the Mafia, which, given the circumstances, is all the same. A different Mafia? Well, that was another opera.

Like Coppola, Verga had grown suspicious that he had bought a ticket to the wrong show. He developed increasing doubt regarding his success, especially for the much-applauded Parisian performance in which 'The Grasso Company . . . gives an exaggerated interpretation . . . to represent a grotesque aspect of the Sicilian character.'[108] This unexpected sense of displeasure in the face of a much-desired success was perhaps just a symptom of something more serious than a mere dislike for Grasso's

Pastoral Sicily welcomes the Corleones in *The Godfather III*.

interpretation, which 'aroused racist prejudice with his stage adoption of the jargon and the knife of the Mafioso'.[109] As we began this chapter with Coppola's resistance to the idea of a third instalment of his Mafia original of 1972, we could frame this 'symptom' by now calling it 'the Godfather syndrome'. Verga had made his fortune by opening his narrative to the allusive *mafiosità* of Sicily. Like Coppola he soon found out he had become completely enmeshed in it: the cultural industry, with its new mass public in search of cheap thrills, its logic of art on demand and its publishers or producers in business suits, offered no way out. The successful formula had to be repeated time and again.

An early diagnosis of Verga's syndrome came in 1892 when his friend Capuana, in the pages of *Sicily and Brigandage*, began his protest against the unjust criminalization of Sicily that was being made through 'the cliché of the Mafia'.[110] Capuana's prognosis was dire: Sicilian intellectuals had developed a bad case of 'remorse for not having defended . . . Sicily when it was being judged and defamed, which is unfortunately not a rare thing today'.[111]

It was on the wings of his own remorse that Capuana's thought went immediately to his friend Verga:

> Do you too . . . Giovanni Verga, feel the same sharp blade of remorse when you think of your *Life in the Fields* and your *Rustic Novellas* where the most humble of the Sicilian people lives happily ever after with their suffering, their Oriental resignation, their lively passions, their rebellious temper and their easy excesses? We were naive! . . . We believed we were producing art . . . and we never suspected that our sincere works, misunderstood and misinterpreted, could be used to reinforce prejudices, to strengthen wrong and malicious opinions, to prove, in the end, exactly the opposite of our true intention.[112]

The sad fact was that there was no cure in sight: continuing to write on the Mafia had become by then a terminal condition for Sicilian writers. All the public wanted and all the cultural industry was ready to concede was, as Capuana pointed a finger against Verga once more, 'the rustic duel between your Master Alfio and Turiddu Macca . . . that you have popularized, more than anybody else, with *Cavalleria rusticana*'.[113]

The Murder of Emanuele Notarbartolo

Not long after the publication of Capuana's words, the media sensation around the Notarbartolo murder severely worsened Verga's pathology. The assassination of the distinguished Sicilian – 'the mafia's first eminent corpse, its first victim among Sicily's social elite' – could not pass unnoticed. It had the potential to demolish, like a house of cards, all romantic fantasies of a rustic chivalry.[114] The rhetoric of naive passions and sense of honour could work no longer, in large part because the murder had implicated one of the very inventors of that rhetoric: Don Raffaele Palizzolo, whom we now find at the apex of his political career as candidate to the national parliament.

On 1 February 1893 on a train running between Altavilla Milicia and Trabia, two little towns in the province of Palermo, Emanuele Notarbartolo was stabbed to death. Following the trial and impeachment of Palizzolo in 1878, which were precipitated by Notarbartolo's accusations, the latter had been (suspiciously) removed from the directorship of the Sicilian Bank by Prime Minister Francesco Crispi. While Crispi was politically to the left of the pro-Sicily party, he had very cordial relations with its leader, Palizzolo. Italians have a name for this kind of realpolitik: *trasformismo*, a propensity to 'transform' one's position according to convenience. With the fall of the Crispi government in February 1891, however, the new minister Antonio Marchese di Rudinì, had thought it best to reinstate Notarbartolo. This made quite difficult, if not impossible, the illicit transfer of funds from the bank for the financing of Palizzolo's electoral campaign for the senate.

In short if there was one man in Sicily who might have had plenty of reasons to have Notarbartolo murdered, it was Palizzolo. His name was already whispered by many in Palermo on the day following the murder. It appeared soon in a secret report signed by Ermanno Sangiorgi, chief of police of Palermo.[115] Given the involvement of a candidate to the senate, a major bank and even an ex-prime minister, the Notarbartolo murder had all elements necessary to create the greatest media sensation on the Mafia ever.

The gruesome details of his demise added more; the killing seemed to come out of the pages of a thriller. In 1899 the writer Paolo Valera, a member of *Scapigliatura* (as Milan's bohemian scene at the time was known), decided to write his own pamphlet-novel about it. He began by paying a debt to the literary imagination of its perpetrators. They had stabbed Notarbartolo 27 times when the train had entered a tunnel. Drenched in blood, they had tried to dump the body over a bridge, but they had left it lying on the tracks. Valera wrote:

> The idea to assassinate a man on a train could not have been born but in the heads of people who had read Zola. The more I read [the reports on the investigation], the more I am convinced they have committed one of the most blatant cases of plagiarism in history. Change the names of the towns and the itinerary of the train, and you realize that the coach of [Zola's] *The Human Beast* represents exactly the same scene that happened in the first-class compartment of our Sicilian train. Monsieur Grandmorin and Signor Notarbartolo have been slaughtered in an identical manner.[116]

The investigations, which would last a record of eleven years, soon started unearthing one scandal after another: the financial, political and even judiciary elites not only of Sicily, but of the whole of Italy, were implicated.

On 16 November 1899 Notarbartolo's son, Leopoldo, rendered the following testimony to the court:

> I believe that the murder was a vendetta and that the only man who hated my father is Commendatore Raffaele Palizzolo, the member of parliament. I accuse him of being the instigator of the crime, of commissioning these and other killers.[117]

Palizzolo's parliamentary immunity was removed. He was jailed along with one of the two assassins – Giuseppe Fontana from the Villabate family, investigated for twenty other homicides – and the appeal trial of 1902 confirmed the sentence. The usual protests headed by Pitrè, expressing indignation at Palizzolo's conviction and lamenting the offence taken by Sicily as a whole, predictably ensued. This was an old tactic, which Palizzolo had engineered already, we remember, at the time of his creation of the pro-Sicily party.

The strategy, this time, worked better than in the past. Something had changed from 1878: with the ongoing peasant revolts known as the Sicilian Fasci (Workers' Leagues), begun in 1891, the Crispi government needed the support of the Right in order to curb the insurrection. The Right, especially Palizzolo's pro-Sicily party, was only too happy to comply.

Those peasants, with their calls for 'free land for all', were a direct threat to the very interests of landed property that those parties represented, interests which coincided with the those of the Mafia. In this sense the Fasci were the first movement of revolt against the Mafia,[118] as clarified in the bylaws of the Fascio of Santo Stefano Quisquina: 'Article 4. It is forbidden to accept as members of the Fasci: (a) those who have betrayed the goals of the Fascio . . . or who are known as vagrants, *mafiosi* and criminals in general.'[119] Similar measures were codified in the bylaws of the Fasci of Santa Caterina Villarmosa and Paternò.

The result of the alliance between Left and Right against the Fasci was a new military siege of Sicily, which eventually brought the Workers' Leagues to extinction in 1894. A supplementary result, however, was the weakening of the Sicilian Left, which in the eyes of its main constituency – the peasants – was guilty of outright betrayal in the wake of the repression. When, in 1901, one year before Palizzolo's appeal trial would begin, a weakened coalition of the Left (Giuseppe Zanardelli's) regained control of the national parliament, an alliance with the pro-Sicily party was absolutely essential for the stability of the government. The pro-Sicily party, in short, had become a strong pressure group of right-wing Sicilian landowners and *mafiosi* with whom the government had to negotiate. As John Dickie writes, 'The quashing of the . . . trial may well have been a peace offering to the powers organized around "Pro Sicilia".'[120] In 1902 the Court of Cassation (Italy's Supreme Court) annulled the sentence on a technicality. Palizzolo and Fontana were freed, and one more trial held in 1904 confirmed the innocence (by way of reasonable doubt) of the duo.

Despite the unlikely acquittal, the polemics around the Notarbartolo case had profoundly changed the terms of the debate in Sicily. For Verga, the Mafia could no longer be the pristine passion he had imagined only a few years before. Palizzolo's intrigues, corruption elevated to national politics, financial traffickings and the sheer brutality of the murder had shown a face of the Mafia that was hardly chivalric or rustic. 'The Golden Key', a new short story that Verga was writing on the Mafia, was taken out of circulation by its author; Verga could not associate his name with the Mafia again.[121] At the climax of his success, and perhaps remorseful like his friend Capuana, he was done with the Mafia. After one last serial novel – *From Yours to Mine* – he was done with literature, too.

Palizzolo, like Verga, disappeared from the public spotlight as well; he was too compromised by now for politics. Giuseppe Fontana too, the alleged material killer of Notarbartolo, disappeared from Sicily. He left the island to try his fortunes in the New World. Returning immigrants told of a land of plenty and opportunities on the other side of the Atlantic. There must have been room, amongst those huddled masses yearning to be free, for good hands well practised in theft, kidnapping, extortion and murder.

America, here comes the Mafia . . .

From Corleone to Hollywood

'Screw the Hays Office!' With these words, Howard Hughes, the flamboyant producer of *Scarface* (1932), began a quarrel with the powerful
Motion Picture Producers and Distributors of America (MPPDA) that
would last two years, make *Scarface* the most controversial film ever produced and change the history of Hollywood for years to come.[1]

Throughout the 1920s William Harrison Hays, the mousy-looking
president of MPPDA, had seen it as his most pious calling to monitor 'the
suitability for screening of current novels and stage plays'.[2] In 1927 he
had taken pen and paper to draft *The Don'ts and Be Carefuls*: 'Resolved –
That those things which are included in the following list shall not appear
in pictures produced by the members of this Association, irrespective of
the manner in which they are treated.'[3] Among the 'don'ts' on Hays's list
were 'illegal traffic' and 'any inference of sex perversion'. Producers
were also asked to exercise 'special care' in the treatment of subjects such
as 'international relations (avoiding picturizing in an unfavorable light
another country's . . . citizenry)', 'the use of firearms', 'theft', 'brutality
and possible gruesomeness', 'techniques of committing murder by whatever method' and – last but not least in the era of Prohibition – 'smuggling'.

The Don'ts and Be Carefuls formed the backbone of the Motion Picture
Production Code, prepared by Catholic editor Martin Quigley and Jesuit
priest Father Daniel Lord under the auspices of the Hays Office, and published with much fanfare in the weekly entertainment-trade magazine
Variety on 19 February 1930. The code stressed the moral duty for producers to educate the masses by avoiding unethical subjects such as crime.

Shoot! Cinema Discovers the Mafia

The life of their bodies, there, on the screen
of the cinematograph, is no more.
– Luigi Pirandello, *Shoot!*

Not many producers, in truth, were eager to abide by the code; faced with failing box office receipts brought about by the onset of the Depression, they knew that sex, violence and growing public fascination with the lives of gangsters could be their financial salvation. The marriage of gangsterism and cinema seemed a match made in heaven. After all, cinema had begun in 1882, thirteen years before the Lumière brothers' first private screening at the Salon Indien du Grand Café in Paris, with nothing less than a chronophotographic gun.

With this peculiar contraption capable of taking twelve consecutive frames a second, and looking eerily like a real gun, Étienne-Jules Marey had gone around France to shoot – yes, that term too! – slices of real life: birds flying, waves moving, men running, soldiers *en marche* . . . The camera is like a gun of sorts: you point, you shoot, and life is frozen, done with, arrested in an eternal present. As Luigi Pirandello put it, in what is arguably the first novel on cinema, the camera 'devours' life.[4]

It cannot be mere chance that the gun reigned as king of cinema since its origin: in *The Great Train Robbery* (Edwin S. Porter, 1903); in *The Birth of a Nation* (D. W. Griffith, 1915); in *Battleship Potemkin* (Sergei Eisenstein, 1925) . . . And then there is that famous scene of Griffith's *The Fatal Hour* (1908): the heroine is tied to a chair. Pointing at her is a gun. The trigger is attached with a rope to the hands of a clock. The villain has rigged the

Étienne-Jules Marey's chronophotographic gun.

gun to go off when the clock strikes twelve. As the life of the film goes on, the life of the heroine approaches its end. Cinema always happens at *High Noon*.

It is not only the camera that suggests this almost-natural, elective affinity of cinema, death and violence.[5] The framing of a scene? 'If . . . in a well-defined characterization the figure's headgear happens to be irrelevant, then it can simply be guillotined by the edge of the frame.'[6] Close ups? When Griffith showed one in Hollywood, panic ensued in the theatre at the vision of the 'severed head'. Montage? Listen to Eisenstein's description of it in 'The Montage of Film Attractions' of 1924: 'a throat is gripped, eyes bulge, a knife is brandished, the victim closes his eyes, blood is spattered on a wall, the victim falls to the floor, a hand wipes off the knife: each fragment is chosen to "provoke" associations.'[7]

Eliminating violence from movies – American producers must have thought in 1930 – was not simply a betrayal of the public's most insatiable appetite. The truth is that it was a betrayal of cinema *tout court!* To be sure, cinema should not encourage violence; on the contrary cinema, as a mass art, had a most pious and solemn social mission to accomplish. But how to deprive cinema of those guns that were so integral to its survival? The problem, in short, was to invent ways to have the cake of Hays's moralism and eat it too – crammed with ingredients pleasing to the public's palate.

Warner Brothers, for instance, widely publicized the fact that its blockbuster *Little Caesar* of 1931, while admittedly a Mafia movie, was in fact a moral crusade against those very bootleggers who had killed a close friend of producer Darryl Zanuck: 'the more ghastly, the more ruthless the criminal acts,' Warner Brothers argued, 'the stronger will be the audience reaction against men of this kind, and organized crime in general.'[8] The other blockbuster of that golden age of gangster cinema – *The Public Enemy* of 1931 – similarly rode the convenient white horse of the moral crusader. After 80 minutes of spectacular gangster violence, the end titles of the movie could, with self-congratulation and righteous moral rectitude, declare: 'The Public Enemy is not a man, nor is it a character – it is a problem that sooner or later WE, the public, must solve.'

While certainly not disinclined to follow suit and play the morality game like the rest of the entertainment industry, Howard Hughes was pushier than most in Hollywood. The movie he was preparing would have some high moral pedestals on which to stand, as was dramatized in the script: 'Murder, gang wars, killings . . . You are glorifying the gangsters by giving them all this publicity', a concerned citizen accuses the newspaper editor, writing about organized crime. The editor's retort to what might have well been Hays's own accusation against *Scarface* reframes the issue of morality in a more convenient light: 'You are trying to tell me you are going to get rid of the gangster by ignoring him? . . . That's ridiculous!', exclaims the editor, looking straight into the camera. 'You are the government, all of you! Instead of hiding the facts, get busy and see that laws are passed that'll do some good . . . Put teeth in the Deportation Act! These gangsters don't belong in this country! Half of them are not even citizens!' In agreement, another concerned citizen with a thick Italian accent exclaims: 'That's true! They don't bring anything but disgrace to my people!'

In other words Hughes was implying that cinema's moral mission did not consist of 'hiding the facts', but rather in exposing them – albeit in the most spectacular way possible. The fact that spectacle was also good for business remained, morally speaking, irrelevant. After all, if yet another Mafia movie had to be produced in America – and it *had* to be produced since the First World War was not selling as it once had done – such a movie, Hughes declared, had to be made 'as realistic, as exciting, as grisly as possible': no easy moralizing was to hinder its effects.[9]

Ironically, it was Hays's *Don'ts and Be Carefuls* that provided a ready-made list of all the ingredients needed to create the most spectacular gangster movie ever seen – one that, as the *New York Times* put it, made 'all the other gangster pictures appear almost effeminate' in comparison.[10] Illegal trafficking and the smuggling of liquor was the Prohibitionist background for the actions of mobster Tony Camonte, a barely disguised Alphonse 'Scarface' Capone. The use of firearms, theft and murders (no less than 43) were all but hidden in the movie. Brutality and gruesomeness were brought to levels of violence never before seen on the silver screen. The citizenry of another country – Italy – were 'picturized' in such an unfavourable light, starting with the monkey-like features of the protagonist Tony Camonte (played by the Austrian-born American actor Paul Muni), that protests from the Order of the Sons of Italy were to be expected. And if Hays's code prohibited 'any inference of sex perversion', Hughes began with a scandalous out-of-wedlock relationship between Camonte and his boss's wife, full of the eroticism of sex-symbol actress Karen Morley (Poppy in the movie). Still not content, Hughes added a few scenes alluding to the greatest sexual taboo of all – the incest between Tony and his sister Cesca:

Tony Camonte, enraged by his sister Cesca. Howard Hawks and
Richard Rosson (dir.), *Scarface* (The Caddo Company, 1932).

TONY: What do you think you're doing? I'm your brother.
CESCA: You don't act it. You act more like . . . I don't know . . .

Not everybody, in the end, agreed with Hughes that the morality of
cinema was in its ability to show it all. The weekly *Harrison's Reports* called
Scarface 'the most vicious and demoralizing gangster picture ever produced'.[11] Screw the Hays Office and *Harrison's Reports*, then! Hughes, after
all, had always seemed to thrive amid controversy. He had been the talk
of Hollywood since he had settled there in 1925, breaking the hearts of his
family, oil tycoons from Texas who had other plans for him. Howard, alas,
had no intention of continuing his father's business and was ready to put
every penny of his considerable fortune into the new American industry
of entertainment.

Hollywood had welcomed the young millionaire (he was nineteen years
old in 1925) with a mixture of opportunism and contempt: let's dry up
his money quickly and send the fool packing! But Hughes was no fool. By
the time *Two Arabian Nights* – a First World War movie starring William Boyd,
idol of the silent era – became a smashing success in 1927, Hollywood was

obliged to take note of the parvenu. When, the following year, Hughes started producing *Hell's Angels* – another war movie combining his interest in film-making with a growing passion for aeroplanes – not only Hollywood, but the entire American press started asking a single question: how much money can be invested in the making of a single film? For Hughes, the wannabe flyboy immortalized in Martin Scorsese's *The Aviator* (with Leonardo DiCaprio playing Hughes), the sky was the limit. *Hell's Angels* became the costliest movie ever produced to that date, but also, surprising the critics of conspicuous spending, a success at the box office.

So, even after the United States had entered the shadow of the Great Depression in 1929, and when parsimony had become a national virtue, no one dared question Howard Hughes as he embarked on yet another colossal enterprise: a Mafia movie like no other before, in which the thrill of gangster life – the speedy car chases, the shooting of machine guns, the escapes from the police, the living on the edge – had to come alive on the screen, no matter the cost. Hughes informed the press that this would be 'the last word' on the gangster genre, beginning production on *Scarface* in haste in June 1931 at three different locations: the Metropolitan Studios, Harold Lloyd Studios and the Mayan Theater in Los Angeles.

The Body in the Barrel

'It's not the Mafia, it's the Black Hand!'
'Same thing.'
'See! You know nothing!'
– Laurie Fabiano, *Elizabeth Street*

The timing for a Mafia movie, *pace* the Hays Office, was perfect: public awareness of organized crime was on the rise in the United States. What the New York dailies had titled 'The Body in the Barrel Mystery' had been the first incident to bring organized crime to the fore of public anxieties.

Early on an April morning in 1903 an Irish scrubwoman was heading to work when she noticed a coat draped over a barrel in a courtyard near the corner of 11th Street and Avenue D on the Lower East Side. Picking up the coat and peering into the barrel she saw the mutilated body of a murdered man. The body, still warm, was that of a husky 35-year-old with his ears pierced, a common practice among Sicilians. He bore several stiletto wounds sufficient to kill him, and his body had also been repeatedly slashed with a razor. Some accounts added a grisly final touch that marked him as a squealer, claiming his genitals had been removed and stuffed in his mouth.[12]

Giuseppe 'Joe' Petrosino, an immigrant from the southern Italian village of Padula who was raised from the age of fourteen in New York's Little Italy, was the detective put in charge of the case. Only a day after the murder, the police had arrested nine members of a gang suspected of having organized an import of forged U.S. currency, printed in Sicily and then circulated throughout the East Coast in the false bottoms of olive oil cans. It was Petrosino who connected the counterfeiters to the case of the barrel and to the Mafia 'family' of Giuseppe 'Piddu' Morello. An immigrant from Corleone, Morello had imported more than olive oil and fake currency from his native town: along with those counterfeit bills and olive oil cans came the Mafia.

To be sure, this was a different Mafia from the Sicilian one. The Sicilian system of territorial dominance in the areas surrounding Palermo had little effectiveness in the more mobile, modern and diverse American society. 'The population of Elizabeth Street, as in the other immigrant quarters', writes John Dickie, 'was in constant flux. People came and went from the Old World. Many new arrivals moved on to other parts of the U.S. Others, as they improved their living standards, moved up and out to more salubrious areas in Harlem, Brooklyn and beyond.'[13] No remnants of a feudal system or of Franchetti's 'medievalism' were to be found in the Americas. The structure of political power in the United States was also quite different from Sicily, where the government was perceived as a far-away, inimical, semi-colonial dominance. As far as private property was concerned, once the land-grab in the far West was over, a formal system of laws securely defined the terms of ownership. More significant still, contrary to what had happened in Sicily – where the Mafia, as we have seen, initially comprised informal militias at the disposal of the dominant classes – the American Mafia of the early twentieth century was the product of subaltern classes. As the historian Giuseppe Carlo Marino wrote, the early Mafia in the United States was 'a violent and cynical reaction expressed by a particular ethnic community of marginalized peoples'.[14] Given such radical differences, noted the sociologist Robert Anderson in his now famous 'From Mafia to Cosa Nostra', could the Sicilian Mafia ever 'survive . . . in an urban, industrial milieu?'[15]

Petrosino's investigation of the barrel case revealed that, despite such contextual and historical differences, the Mafia could survive and even flourish. Years ahead of Hobsbawm's understanding of the Mafia as a form of 'primitivism', the Mafia demonstrated an enviable capacity for adaptability and modernization: it readjusted quickly to the conditions of modern America.[16] It transformed itself from a *territorial* system of clientelism and corruption to a *transnational* venture mimicking the modus operandi of an import–export business. So what was a fundamentally land-based phenomenon in Sicily (a competition, as Lupo reminded us, for the control of land) transformed in the United States into a quite diverse operation. A new division of labour was one consequence of such diversification. No longer in the exclusive business of protecting or grabbing land, the Mafia, once in the New World, soon felt the need to create its own specialized groups and sub-groups, each particularly skilled in one specific business: narcotics, gambling, prostitution – and, needless to say, murder.[17] In this new situation Petrosino had not only solved a murder case, but shown the entire nation the arrival of a new Mafia in the new continent.

Immortalized in the silent movie *The Adventures of Lieutenant Petrosino* of 1912, the courageous officer then revealed how the 'feudal' Mafia Franchetti had gleaned in Sicily could truly ripen into a modern 'industry of violence' once settled in a properly modern environment. What Franchetti could only intuit in Sicily, Petrosino was able to see taking place in America, witnessing it with his own eyes. The lieutenant was eventually murdered in Palermo, Sicily, in 1909. He had grossly underestimated the real power of the Sicilian Mafia, still better organized and more lethal than its American counterpart (this was the point argued in another film on his life, *Pay or Die!*, in 1960). His investigations into the barrel case, however, had revealed once and for all to a frightened American public that the Mafia had crossed the ocean for good. In so doing, the zealous Italian-American officer had opened a Pandora's box that would have unexpected consequences for his own community.

The last meal of spaghetti found in the corpse in the barrel by the forensic team (the body belonging to Benedetto Madonia, another Sicilian immigrant who had crossed Morello); the pierced ears; the onion skins and Italian stogies that the police had found at the bottom of the barrel; and, above all, the long list of Italian names brought to trial – all this was evidence pointing to a rather picturesque, if terrifying, picture of Italian immigration. After the first wave of migration in the 1870s, which had been unrecorded because no national census had yet been instituted, between 1901 and 1913 alone an impressive 800,000 Sicilians emigrated to the United States. They were, to put it mildly, not well liked. Often dirt poor,

Detective Lt Joseph Petrosino (left) escorts Mafia hitman Petto the Ox (Tomasso Petto, second from left) to court.

illiterate and unaccustomed to modern metropolitan life, they were resilient to any attempt at acculturation. Some were mafiosi, connecting Palermo's lemon trade with New York (in fact, according to Palermo's commissioner Baldassare Ceola, Petrosino's killer was none other than Giuseppe Fontana, who we saw taking the boat to the United States in the previous chapter). All were undesirable. The Italians themselves, after Italy's unification in 1870, held them in contempt: they were, as the patriot Luigi Settembrini once put it, 'barbarians and beasts'.[18] Another patriot, Francesco Trinchera, considered them 'profoundly degraded'.[19]

It was the positivistic anthropology of Giuseppe Sergi that gave scientific status to the theory of southern Italian genetic inferiority and propensity for crime. In his research Sergi had determined that two races inhabited the European continent: one 'European' and one 'Mediterranean'. Whereas the former was sociable, industrious, intelligent and respectful of the law, the latter was anti-social, lazy, backward and irremediably violent.[20] Such a southern Mediterranean race was an example, in anthropologist Cesare Lombroso's words, of an 'atavistic primitiveness . . . the effect of a hindered development, in the collective moral sense, resulting in the permanence of a barbaric stage'.[21] When a book on southern barbarism by geographer Alfredo Niceforo was reviewed in the Italian daily paper Il Secolo in 1898, the reviewer exclaimed: 'Isn't it like living a nightmare!? Isn't it shocking to read that habits typical of Arab tribes before Mohammed are still alive today in some regions of Italy? Isn't it shocking to find that such behaviour is enacted not by Tuaregs and Bedouins, but by Italian citizens?'[22]

Having fled a country that seemed to have no place for them, these southerners, hunted at home by the 'war on brigandage' chronicled in the preceding chapter, had packed their hopes for the land of liberty: 'Give me your tired, your poor, Your huddled masses yearning to breathe free' was the augural inscription – if only they could read! – welcoming them near Ellis Island. The arrival, however, was not met by a welcome party.

The massive migration from southern Italy soon created a xenophobic reaction in the United States. Hostility towards these new immigrants was already on the rise when, on 16 October 1890, the homicide of New Orleans Chief of Police David Hennessy unleashed the rage against them. After six Italian men were found guilty, a mob formed outside the prison, broke the doors and lynched the eleven Italians found there, many of whom were not connected to the murder. The grand jury quickly cleared those involved in the lynching of all wrongdoing, and newspapers stumbled onto a hitherto unknown Italian word – 'Mafia' – to frame the incidents, and thus justify the killing of the Italians.[23]

While the u.s. government was still hard at work trying to restore broken diplomatic relations with Italy – including the payment of a $25,000 (about $600,000 today) indemnity to Italy for the incident – the case of the body in the barrel of 1903 further complicated an already tense situation. After the involvement of Morello and other Italians in the murder came to light, the New York Herald proclaimed in alarm: 'The boot [i.e. Italy] unloads its criminals upon the United States. Statistics prove that the scum of southern Europe is dumped at the nation's door in rapacious, conscienceless, lawbreaking hordes.'[24] As the trial was repeatedly hindered by the refusal of Italian witnesses to testify, the Herald deployed, as a last weapon, the word that would terrify all New Yorkers into action: 'New York Italians Kept Silent by Terror of the Far Reaching Arm of the Mafia.'[25]

Such Mafia rhetoric only exacerbated already strong xenophobic attitudes and engendered an open diffidence on the part of Italian immigrants towards America and its institutions. This could only benefit the Mafia, who seemed to be left alone to offer aid, protection and opportunities to a migrant group under siege.

That said, there certainly was abundant evidence of close relations between criminality in America and the Sicilian Mafia. One associate of the Morello gang was Don Vito Cascio-Ferro, from Bisacquino near Palermo, who had fled Sicily under suspicion of being involved in Mafia activities. In New York he worked – officially, that is – as a lemon importer. He barely escaped an arrest ordered by Petrosino in connection with the barrel case, moved to New Orleans and, from there, returned to Palermo. He was finally arrested and jailed in Sicily by the Fascist police in the 1920s. Another Sicilian mafioso, the seemingly ubiquitous Giuseppe Fontana from Villabate, was also a member of Morello's gang. The Morello gang hired its men from immigrant communities coming from different Sicilian towns and Mafia organizations. Unknown to – possibly even at war with – each other while in Sicily, these communities found a common identity in Morello's organization. It was here that the Mafia evolved from a series of small, unrelated, local organizations into one more ambitious body sharing a commonality of interests across the Atlantic. For Morello's New York gang, 'American business was becoming a matter of interest to the whole Sicilian mafia.'[26]

In the States, however, the sole concern was that the Mafia had crossed the ocean to threaten the land of liberty. With anti-Italian attitudes on the rise, an Immigration Commission headed by Senator William Paul Dillingham threw more wood on the fire. The Commission had been put in charge of drafting a report aimed at restricting immigration from 'undesirable' countries. Known as the Dictionary of Races of Peoples, the document was released in 1911. It singled out southern Italians as one of the most undesirable groups of all (only Africans fared worse). Backed by the 'scientific' findings of Italian anthropologists such as Sergi and

Lombroso, the report introduced the word 'Mafia' to immigration policies for the first time:

> The secret organizations of the Mafia (see *Sicilian*) and Comorra [*sic*], institutions of great influence among the people, which take the law into their own hands and which are responsible for much of the crime, flourish throughout Southern Italy. The chief difficulty in dealing with the crimes of Italians seems to be their determination not to testify in court against an enemy, but on settling their wrongs after the manner of vendetta.[27]

'Mafia (see *Sicilian*)': the slippage of one term into the other in a document concerning immigration is telling.

It is as if, by 1911, the word 'Mafia' had become the catalyst for all American fears of an albeit necessary immigration: it is the fear of contagion, of miscegenation, which threatens to degenerate the blood of the young and progressive nation with that of the racially inferior and backward southern Italian horde. The blood spilled by the Mafia on the streets of New York or New Orleans becomes *symbolic* blood: 'Blood as a symbolic device', the anthropologist Anton Blok claims, 'dominates the discourse and practices of mafiosi', creating ties of kinship (family consanguinity), ritualistic blood-relation (godfathering) and ritual belonging (the sharing of the blood of a new member with that of an old one in the Mafia initiation ceremonies described by Sangiorgi and later by Joe Valachi).[28] As in Pitrè's and Verga's 'chivalric' Mafia, symbolic blood also creates a specific juridical system, a code of honour prescribing that the vendetta be consummated in blood. The blood that started to preoccupy America in the years when eugenics was the leading demographic science was, however, of a different symbolic kind than the one described by Blok, or evoked by Verga: it was the blood of inferior races threatening to mix with that of the healthy Anglo-Saxon marrow of the nation.[29] A Mafia murder made visible that blood, but its threat transcended mere killings. A sadly influential book of 1916 written by the nativist Madison Grant summarized in its title the pervasive fear of Sicilian blood: *The Passing of the Great Race* argued with the tones of a Cassandra that the blood of the Nordic, Anglo-Saxon stock was being diluted and corrupted by the presence of southern Europeans on American soil.

Cinema was ready to capitalize on this fear. In 1906 Wallace McCutcheon directed *Black Hand: True Story of a Recent Occurrence in the Italian*

Quarter of New York for the American Mutoscope & Biograph Company. Depicting a good, Anglo-Saxon America besieged by the 'other', the film marked the passage, as Sergio Bertellini has argued, from the 'negro-phobic' attitudes of Griffith's *The Birth of a Nation* and the 'Indianophobia' of the early western to the Italophobia of the nascent Mafia film.[30]

McCutcheon's was the story of a Black Hand kidnapping of a child (the innocence of the nation corrupted in the Italian quarters of New York) for a $1,000 ransom. The Black Hand had entered the imaginary of America on 3 August 1903, only a few days after the case of the body in the barrel. Nicola Cappiello, an Italian-American working as a building contractor in Brooklyn, had received the following note written in semi-literate Italian:

> Meet us at 72nd Street and 13th Avenue, Brooklyn, tomorrow afternoon, or your house will be bombed and you and your family killed. The same fate awaits you in the event of your betraying our purposes to the police.

Similar letters would be delivered in the following months and years.

The Black Hand, which took its name from the hand printed in black ink in extortion letters, was not the Mafia. In fact it was not one specific organization. Historian John Dickie calls it a 'logo' that disparate criminal enterprises felt at liberty to use.[31] Another historian, Salvatore Lupo, similarly describes the Black Hand as 'not an actual organization but a criminal phenomenology, a form of crime practiced by groups operating independently'.[32] Independent as they might have been, however, all of these groups and gangs had one common denominator: they were generally Italian. It is unsurprising, then, that all American fears expressed through crime cinema targeted specifically the Italian migrant. As the film historian Kevin Brownlow has suggested, other ethnic groups as well – Jews, Chinese, Irish and African-Americans – were the target of cinema's representation of American anxieties about the melting pot.[33] However, it was specifically 'generally Italian' crime that was capturing the public's imagination. The Italian villain was becoming 'the paradigmatic urban criminal'.[34]

Following *Black Hand*, D. W. Griffith himself directed several shorts – *In Little Italy*, *The Cord of Life* and *At the Altar* in 1909 alone – to 'connect Sicilian ethnicity with murderous violence'.[35] By 1912 Griffith had moved from generic violence to organized crime; his *Musketeers of Pig*

Alley is arguably the prototypical gangster film, soon imitated by a quick succession of shorts on the Sicilian Mafia: *The Criminals* (1913), *The Padrone's Ward* (1914), *The Last of the Mafia* (1915) and *Poor Little Peppina* (1916). From these early works, interest in the ethnic Mafia of the Sicilian immigrants was soon to escalate.

For this to happen, however, a number of historical, social, cultural and aesthetic developments were first necessary. To begin with, the end of the First World War had returned home a number of veterans who found it difficult to find a job after having served their country. In the trenches they had developed skills that were not useful for civilian life: while they could form a firing squad and use machine guns and dynamite with ease, they remained conspicuously under-qualified for any clerical job. The situation was particularly dire for a community discriminated against such as the Italian – to a large extent illiterate and with poor verbal skills in English. The Volstead Act of 1919, which ordered that 'no person shall manufacture, sell, barter, transport, import, export, deliver, or furnish any intoxicating liquor', offered a perfect business opportunity for veterans to provide a service to those Americans – and there were many – who still wanted to consume alcohol against the law. Those unemployed veterans (many of them of Italian heritage) could now use, in confrontations with the law's enforcers (and with other gangs, too), those very skills they had learnt on the front. In this way they transformed the Mafia into a fully fledged business enterprise, working in the chain of supply and demand for much requested services: alcohol first and then, later, gambling and prostitution.

This was an epochal moment in the history of the Mafia: from a criminal organization limited to extortion, counterfeiting, murder and kidnapping (the 'violence industry' of Franchetti), the American Mafia of the 1920s morphed into a complex nationwide industry controlling all phases – from manufacture to delivery – of *socially desirable goods*. The Mafia, so to speak, was turning into an entertainment industry. For the Italians, the sudden increase of the price of alcohol following the Volstead Act also allowed for the possibility of finally realizing the promised American Dream of financial success in a very – very! – short time. Controlling all phases of production and distribution of alcohol – 'From the field to the consumer!', an apt advertising campaign might have read – Italian-American criminal organizations raked in immense (and tax-free) profits from the illegal sale of booze: according to one estimate, no less than $2 billion from 1919 to 1933.[36] And what was good for Italian-American business was also good for Hollywood. Between 1927 and 1928 many classics of what later would be called 'classic gangster cinema' were produced in short succession: Underworld, The Racket, Chicago After Midnight, The Heart of Broadway and Dressed to Kill.[37] Their background was the Prohibition act. Their protagonist, almost invariably, was the Sicilian immigrant dreaming, in the way of the Mafia, the American Dream.

Al Capone: Mafia, or the American Dream

He fulfilled his American Dream.
– Luciano Iorizzo, Al Capone: A Biography

No other figure became as emblematic of the Prohibition Mafia as the Italian-American Alphonse Capone, nicknamed 'Scarface'. Born in Brooklyn to Neapolitan parents on 17 January 1899, he moved to Chicago soon after the war. As one of the best gunmen of the Chicago syndicate, he soon rose to the top of Chicago's South Side gang. Spectacular ruthlessness and cunning were his trademark: on St Valentine's Day of 1929, his firing squad, disguised in police uniforms, killed seven associates of the North Side Irish gang led by 'Bugs' Moran.

Beyond his propensity for spectacular forms of violence, what made Capone the media sensation of the 1920s was his meticulous care in crafting his own persona. By the second half of the decade, the media were 'saturated' with stories of Mafia and racketeering, but no one was able to fill the dailies like Al Capone.[38] He loved the press and relished giving interviews. Always sumptuously (if gaudily) 'dressed in pinstripe suits, fedoras, and fancy neckties', he liked to pose for photographers.[39] He preferred never to show the left side of his face, however, where he had been slashed three times by Frank Galluccio, whose sister he had offended. But even scars could be turned by Capone into self-aggrandizing legends: he boasted he had got them on the Western Front, where he had also learnt to handle a machine gun.[40] When he heard that Howard Hughes was making a movie titled Scarface, Capone took a personal interest in the film. His men were offered as consultants, and Al himself purchased a copy of the film.[41]

Capone's greed for publicity – simply unthinkable for any Sicilian mafioso then or now – was largely reciprocated. Capone, like his contemporary Rudolph Valentino, was a figure of simultaneous attraction and repulsion for the American public. 'Racially positioned between

Louis 'Lepke' Buchalter handcuffed to J. Edgar Hoover, on the left
at the entrance to the courthouse.

alterity and familiarity', Capone, Italian and mobster, was certainly a figure
of repugnant alterity for Anglo-Saxon American norms.[42] He was also
an all-too-familiar and attractive emblem for that same culture – a culture
that had fashioned its own aspirations on the characters of Horatio Alger's
novels. Newspapers – such as the *Chicago Daily Tribune* – presented the
'True Story of Capone's Rise' from 'humble buyer of beer trucks' to the
king of organized crime, and consistently 'portrayed Capone as an Alger
character, a man from modest beginnings who made something of

himself'.[43] And when Fred Pasley, a reporter for the same *Tribune*, wrote the life story of Capone, he tellingly subtitled it – again with a nod to Alger – *The Biography of a Self-made Man*.

Compared to the landowning Mafia of Sicily, or even to the senatorial one of Raffaele Palizzolo, the American Mafia of the 1920s told a rather different story. In a seminal essay published in the *Partisan Review* in 1948, Robert Warshow argued that the figure of the gangster embodied everything that 'the American psyche' deeply desired: 'In ways that we do not easily or willingly define, the gangster speaks for us . . . Thrown into the crowd without background or advantages . . . the gangster is required to make his way, to make his life.'[44] The gangster, in short, was the ideal of the American self-made man who, albeit with ambiguous skills, made his life one of riches and success.

He was also, however, the prototype of yet another, if not unrelated story: that of the price to be paid for individual success, which in 1990, as we have seen, *The Godfather Part III* was still rehearsing. Success always comes at a price: the isolation of the self-made man *as* individual. As the lives of gangsters, tragic American heroes, invariably come to an end, 'the gangster heroes remain single and die alone.'[45]

> The gangster's whole life is an effort to assert himself as an individual, to draw himself out of the crowd . . . At bottom, the gangster is doomed because he is under the obligation to succeed, not because the means he employs are unlawful. In the deeper layers of modern consciousness, *all* means are unlawful, *every* attempt to succeed is an act of aggression, leaving one alone and guilty and defenseless among enemies: one is punished for success.[46]

As such, the gangster embodied both an attraction to the ideal of American individualism, and the fear that all sense of community and belonging could be fatally lost at the very altar of a much-desired individual success.

The typical story of Mafia novels and films of the 1920s and early '30s entailed a simple paradigmatic plot – the hero rises to the top, remains isolated, and dies alone in the end – which resonated with the desires and fears of society at large. It unfolded a true social dialectic: a desire, on the one hand, to make it big – nearly a social 'obligation to succeed' – and, on the other, the fear of submitting to such an obligation. Almost conscious of being a character in such a social script, Capone himself saw well how profoundly he was made to incarnate, for both good and bad, this very ideal of American individualism – the business-man: 'Everybody calls me a racketeer. I call myself a businessman. When I sell liquor, it's bootlegging. When my patron serves it on a silver tray on Lake Shore Drive, it's hospitality.'[47] Capone was right: he *was* America's own Everyman. He made manifest, in his excess, the very contradictions that words like 'racketeer' and 'bootlegging' barely hid; beyond nomi-nalistic distinctions, it was all business, as Coppola would later reiterate, and business was nothing else than raising one's own self above all others; above – which also meant out of – a community.

This was, in the end, the scandal of Al Capone, and this was the ambiguous complex of attraction and repulsion that his persona dispensed on the American public. As an ideal, he was the model of conspicuous and stylish consumption – of all that individual success can buy.[48] As an apotropaic mask, his was the scarred face of individual success, the fear, that is to say, of a waning sense of community in urban America.[49] The Italian ethnic origin of the prototypical American gangster allowed this dialectic of desire (identification) and fear (rejection) to work flawlessly.

The living room at 'the hideout'. The Northwood retreat of Al Capone during Prohibition, Couderay, Wisconsin.

White like a WASP and yet 'embodying the Italian community's racial difference in the figure of the Latin criminal', the mafioso was the perfect scapegoat for a social ritual that attempted to reconstitute a sense of community in the midst of a dream of unfettered individualism: he was punished for what ordinary America wanted.[50] On his white skin, desires were purified through his final sacrifice.

Can the Mafioso Speak?

Omertà. n. A Mafia code of honour which demands absolute loyalty to the organization and silence about its activities, esp. refusal to give evidence of criminal activity to the police.

– *Oxford English Dictionary*

It was a technical innovation – the advent of sound cinema in 1927 – that allowed the film industry to capitalize fully on all the fears and desires, anxieties and dreams that a subject such as the Mafia could offer. *Little Caesar*, released at a moment when 25 other gangster silent films were being made in Hollywood, rose above the competition and became an unprecedented success of the Mafia genre precisely because of its deft use of audio.[51] Certainly the fact that *Little Caesar* was a barely disguised biopic of Al Capone helped, but it was in the opening scene that sound operated its true magic: after Rico/Capone commits a robbery and enters a diner to eat a meal of spaghetti, we suddenly *hear*, clear and dreadful, 'a strong accent, and a poor command of the English language'.[52]

If in the years of the Great Depression studios intended to use the gangster film 'to reflect the discontent and alienation, the deep anxiety and hostility of many Americans facing the Depression'; if in those years Hollywood was determined to 'represent the gangster as scapegoat for the Depression' – it was then that the technical innovation of synchronized audio allowed the American film industry to turn fear of the Depression towards a specific organization (the Mafia) and a specific ethnic group (Italian-Americans) that sounded, with a strong accent and poor command of English, like corrupting pathogens of the American Dream.[53] To paraphrase Robert Warshow, the use of accent in *Little Caesar* allowed the (Anglo-Saxon) American public to see the self-made man from a distance, as an 'other' American of sorts. As an American, the gangster – with his dream of success – was the object of sympathy and identification; as an Other, however, he was the scapegoat punished for having wanted to rise above the community, thus corrupting the common Dream. The public could thus resolve its anxieties – the fear of not being able to realize the American Dream in the years of the Depression – on his person: 'The dilemma is resolved because of his death, not ours. We are safe; for the moment, we can acquiesce in our failure, we can choose to fail.'[54] In this sense the Mafia, silent in its code of omertà in Sicily, had started speaking loudly and clearly in Hollywood, voicing the desires and repulsions, attractions and fears, of the American Dream – in all their unresolved ambiguity.

When Howard Hughes entered the fray of the Mafia movie, he was determined not to let any opportunity go to waste. The movie had to be a compendium of all that America wanted and all that America feared. On the one hand, *Scarface* was to prove that the American Dream was still alive after the Depression. Tony Camonte, accordingly, climbs the ladder of success. Thirty minutes into the movie, he sits at the top of the syndicate, has conquered the blonde and sexy Poppy, bought a new 'purty hot' home – 'Expensive, eh?' – and a bunch of shirts with matching ties: 'See, what I'm gonna do is wear a shirt only once. Then I give it right away to the laundry. A new shirt every day.'

As Marilyn Roberts notices, the shirt scene was lifted from another popular story of the American Dream of the 1920s – F. Scott Fitzgerald's *The Great Gatsby* (1925):

> He took out a pile of shirts and began throwing them one by one before us, shirts of sheer linen and thick silk and fine flannel, which lost their folds as they fell and covered the table in many-colored disarray. While we admired he brought more and the soft rich heap mounted higher – shirts with stripes and scrolls and plaids in coral and apple green and lavender and faint orange with monograms of Indian blue. Suddenly with a strained sound, Daisy bent her head into the shirts and began to cry stormily. 'They're such beautiful shirts', she sobbed, her voice muffled in the thick folds. 'It makes me sad because I've never seen such – such beautiful shirts before.'[55]

The message conveyed through the allusion to Gatsby's shirts as symbol of that 'surrealism of dreams that money can buy' is paralleled in another scene, again quoting Fitzgerald: out of Camonte's window, a glittering

Tony Camonte tries to impress Polly with his new riches, *Scarface*.

sign from Thomas Cook's travel agency – 'The World is Yours' – parodies a similar one from *Gatsby*: 'God knows what you've been doing.'[56]

Like Fitzgerald before them, the scriptwriters of *Scarface* seem to hint at the fact that their heroes, much as allegories of a nation, have placed 'their faith in a highly material version of the American Dream'; such faith can only lead to their final demise.[57] The Depression, in other words, is not a structural economic crisis, but one of ideals: Americans, like Camonte, have put too much weight on material possessions and forgotten that the American Dream is more than that. It is time now to return to more ideal values.

Scarface harbours the doubts concerning the American Dream that are typical of the 'Depression-era audience, disenchanted with the success ethic of the 1920s': the suspicion that the climb for success is a Darwinian struggle; that money does not buy class; that the end is near.[58] Yet, at the same time, through the figure of the Italian-American mafioso, *Scarface* wants to salvage that very Dream: it is the Italians, with their Mafia, who are corrupting the Dream by making it into a gaudy quest for material success. The Italians are stealing the Dream from us. As the newspaper-man screams in *Scarface*: 'Put teeth in the deportation act! These gangsters don't belong in this country! Half of them are not even citizens!'

Script-writing on *Scarface*, based on Armitage Trail's pulp novel of the same name, was assigned to Chicago crime reporter Ben Hecht, aided by W. R. Burnett and Robert Lee (co-writers of *Little Caesar*), as well as Fred Pasley, author of *Al Capone: The Biography of a Self-made Man*. It had to chronicle the rise and fall, from humble origins to riches and final death, of the sacrificial Tony Camonte, a hoodlum in the liquor business. Ethnic themes had to play a big part: Camonte's Italian-American family; his accent (an over-the-top performance by Paul Muni, an actor discovered by Hughes in a Yiddish theatre in New York); the ever-present spaghetti; and even a Jewish lawyer named Epstein. Fast action and violence were to spice up the movie, along with spectacular car chases in quick montage. Not only were such scenes of brutality to *look* real, but they also had to refer to real and much publicized events that the public could easily recognize: the 1920 murder of gang leader James 'Big Jim' Colosimo under Capone's orders; Capone's murder of crime boss Dion O'Banion in 1924; the St Valentine's Day Massacre; and the 'Siege of West 90th Street' in 1931 in which the police killed Francis 'Two Gun' Crowley in his New York apartment. Finally a good dose of titillating sex scenes and innuendo had to be provided, from Poppy's breathtaking negligees to the incestuous overtones of the Camonte siblings' relationship.

In a move calculated to excite the press, Hughes assigned the direction of the movie to Howard Hawks, whom he had just brought to trial with the accusation of stealing the plot of his *Hell's Angels*. In exchange for the dropped lawsuit, and with no limits on expenses, Hawks was happy to assume direction of *Scarface*; he also quite liked the script. The problems for the two, however, were just beginning: 'inasmuch as they have everything in the story', read a memo delivered to Hays's desk on 11 July 1931, 'including the inferences of incest, the picture is beginning to look worse and worse to us, from a censorship point of view.'[59] The office of the censor was, to say the least, not happy.

Several modifications to the script were negotiated in haste between the Hays Office (which hired a psychologist, Carleton Simon, as consultant), Hughes's crew and MGM. The most notable was the addition of a 'foreword' aimed at reinforcing the moral frame of the film:

> This picture is an indictment of gang rule in America and of the callous indifference of the government to this constantly increasing menace to our safety and liberty. Every incident in this picture is the reproduction of an actual occurrence, and the purpose of

this picture is to demand of the government: What are you going to do about it? The government is your government. What are YOU going to do about it?

New York Police Commissioner Mulrooney was asked to declaim the forward. He declined; the film, as he saw it, remained such a raw glorification of gangster life that he'd rather not be mixed up with it at all.

Scarface went into production notwithstanding. Shooting took three months, with the cast and crew working seven days a week. Hughes and Hawkes were utterly pleased with the final product. The movie, however, was loaded with such unprecedented doses of violence and gore – 'not to mention overtones of incest between Scarface and his beautiful sister'! – that the Motion Pictures Producers and Distributors of America (MPPDA) refused to release the film unless substantial changes were made.[60] Among such changes, the MPPDA demanded with particular insistence a different ending: while in the original Scarface was unceremoniously gunned down by the police, the MPPDA's new finale required that Scarface be tried and executed with due process – a didactic, if anti-climactic, triumph of law and order. To please the censor, Hughes agreed to all revisions, and even subtitled the movie *Shame of the Nation*. When, after going through the MPPDA, the New York's State Board of Censors still refused to let *Scarface* be shown, Hughes decided to go on the offensive, mounting a press campaign in the name of nothing less than free speech and artistic freedom of expression. American liberties, he hinted, were at stake.

Hughes's counterattack began with a statement released to the press in late April 1932:

It has become a serious threat to freedom of honest expression in America when self-styled guardians of the public welfare, as personified by our film censor boards, lend their aid and their influence to the abortive efforts of selfish and vicious interests to suppress a motion picture simply because it depicts the truth about the conditions in the United States which have been front page news since the advent of Prohibition. I am convinced that the determined opposition to *Scarface* is actuated by political motives. The picture, as originally filmed eight months ago, has been enthusiastically praised by foremost authorities on crime and law enforcement and by leading screen reviewers. It seems to be the unanimous opinion of these reviewers that *Scarface* is an honest and powerful indictment of gang rule in America and, as such, will be a tremendous force in compelling our state and Federal governments to take more drastic action to rid the country of gangsterism.[61]

As Hughes instructed his lawyers to file suit against the MPPDA, and while public opinion was turning, as Hughes had planned, against the 'un-American' censors, *Scarface* was reassembled almost in its original version. On 31 March 1932 the film premiered in New Orleans. The subtitle *Shame of a Nation*, the foreword and the alternate ending with Camonte's execution by hanging were the only visible traces of a two-year-long controversy with the Hays office.

Peace did not last long. When the film was shown in New York on 25 June 1932, all hell broke loose. *Scarface* opened with a masterful travelling shot: after a location shot identifying 22nd Street and Wabash in Chicago – Capone's territory – as the setting for the action, the camera pans right-wards to a nightclub, enters the premises and looks around. There it finds nothing more than the leftovers of a bachelor party: balloons, confetti and a bra. It is at this point that we hear the first words. Barely audible at first, the voices soon acquire a distinct, if hyperbolic, Italian accent. The camera keeps travelling rightward until it finds two men sitting at a table with 'Big Louie', his name reminiscent of Big Jim Colosimo: the three men are wearing tuxedos. Their elegant dress, however, soon contrasts with the crassness and gaudiness of the dialogue:

> Look at me. A man-a always gotta know what he's got-a enough. I've gotta plenty. I gotta house, I gotta automobile, I gotta nice-a girl, (burp), I gotta stomach trouble, too.

It is not only the accent, the burps and the bad grammar that ruin the picture of gentlemanly restraint. The peasant-like gesticulating, the ethnic dark complexion of each member of the trio, the immigrant faces and Big Louie's moustachioed braggadocio quickly reveal the wannabes for what they truly are: three Italians, *nouveaux riches*, sitting uninvited at the banquet of the American Dream. Only God knows how they climbed the ladder to their garish success!

Well, in truth, viewers know, too. The secret of their success will be unveiled in just a moment: as Big Louie's companions leave, a doorway opens and the shadow of a fourth man appears in the back room of the nightclub. We see the silhouette (that of Tony Camonte, we soon learn) behind stained glass. The effect is reminiscent of early German expressionist cinema. Different to the nightmarish creatures from The Cabinet of Dr Caligari, however, this ghastly presence has more than a shadow to terrify the viewer. Born after the age of silent cinema, he has a voice, too. We hear him now. He whistles an operatic aria. The Italianate plot thickens: it is – we figure – the famous sextet (Chi mi frena in tal momento?, 'Who Dares to Stop Me Now?') from Gaetano Donizetti's Luciadi Lammermoor. From a melodrama of clan wars, family feuds and ghosts set amid the gothic castles and lakes of Scotland, this sextet was particularly well known in America: Enrico Caruso (who sang the part of murderous Edgar) had brought the aria to the top of the charts for Victor Records in 1908. The shadow, whistling Edgar's song of wrath, draws a gun. 'Hello, Louie' (that Italian accent again). Three shots, then whistling again. The body of Big Louie lies on the floor. That is the Italian way to success: the way of the Mafia.

The Grand Council of the Order of the Sons of Italy in America did not have to see more: from that first sequence, Scarface threw nothing but discredit on their race! The Italian-American Women's Club requested – at the very least – that all Italian names and references to Italy be deleted from the film. One sympathizes, but then again, would Joe Shmoe ever be as picturesquely terrifying as Tony Camonte? In Italy, in the meantime, while the Roman daily Giornale d'Italia urged the u.s. authorities to ban the film altogether, Duce Benito Mussolini had to see it with his own eyes. Evidently not amused, he forbade the showing of Scarface in his country. Fascism, his government claimed, had defeated the Mafia in Sicily. The American Mafia, which the movie now presented as a foreign threat from Italy, was in fact an all-American phenomenon, and America had no one else – certainly not Italy – to blame.

In the following chapter we will see how much of that Fascist claim was true. In the United States, however, Scarface had stirred up so much trouble that the controversy Howard Hughes had so purposefully engineered got completely out of hand. As planned, the movie had become the most talked-about picture in America, was voted among the top ten pictures of 1932 by the Film Daily Nation Wide Poll and was nominated best film by the National Board of Review. However, the Hays Office – screw it! – had the last word. No other film offered Hays a better example than Scarface to point out the dangers that a movie industry out of control could create for the whole nation. Scarface proved, by its very existence, that a stringent production code was needed. With the establishment of a nationwide Production Code Administration on 13 June 1934, the showing of guns (let alone mafiosi) in American cinema became virtually impossible.

Hughes had to withdraw the film from circulation. By the time MGM's *Manhattan Melodrama* came out later that year, the great era of Hollywood's gangster cinema had ended. *Scarface*, arguably the masterpiece of the genre, had been the last nail in its coffin. So, while the Mafia continued to operate and prosper on the streets of the United States, hardly any mention of it was made on the silver screen – not until the code was suspended in the late 1960s, and *The Godfather* could revitalize that tradition.

THREE

The Far West is Here

The wide angle reveals a landscape of monumental proportions: a desert still unmarked by human trails spreads open majestically. The framing 'emphasizes horizontal planes stretching into the distance . . . and horizontals slicing the image in two'.[1] The intersecting lines form a valley.

The overexposed photography makes the viewer sweat, imagining the toil of voyage across the uncultivated, godforsaken stretch of land; oppressed by dust and sun, barren and not yet dominated by human will, the land is a frontier. As a coach enters the screen from the distance, proceeding westward, the soundtrack, 'a mixture of American hymn, settler folk music, and cavalry fanfare', reaches symphonic proportions.[2] Hiding behind a boulder stands a man with a gun in his hand and a 'bandana covering the lower half of his face'.[3] He is ready to ambush the lone traveller riding the coach.

The landscape has become the theatrical stage, hosting an epic 'occasion for risk, adventure, and struggle'; the story is ready to unfold as a 'foundational narrative, the struggle to create a civilization in the wilderness'.[4]

This – you might have guessed – is John Ford's *Stagecoach*, a masterpiece of the western genre set in the mythical American frontier. Or is it? I have appropriated a number of excerpts from books and essays on Ford to describe a movie that, while not precisely a western, borrows quite generously from Ford in order to tell a story about a different myth and a different frontier. 'Borrow' is not even the proper term here. The viewer who, in 1949, would have started watching the movie I am referring to, must have been tricked quite intentionally by the film's director. The opening sequence *wants* to leave no doubt that what we are watching is a John Ford western set in some deserted corner of California. The voice-over then comes as a surprise:

Landscape in the Italian 'Western', Pietro Germi (dir.),
In the Name of the Law (Lux Film, 1949).

This land, this vast solitude oppressed by the sun, is Sicily. A Sicily
which is not only the teasing gardens, the oranges, the flowers,
the olive trees which you know, or think you know; but it is also
a bare and burned wilderness, oxidized walls of a blinding white,
hermetic men sealed by the ancient customs that the foreigner
does not understand; a world mysterious and beautiful, where a
tragic and bitter beauty reigns.

The film we are watching is, in fact, Pietro Germi's *In the Name of the Law*
(*In Nome della legge*), 'one of the most popular Italian films of 1949, and
probably the first film made in Italy to represent the Sicilian Mafia'.[5]

Germi, a northerner from Genoa whose *Seduced and Abandoned* and
Divorce Italian Style became blockbusters of 'Sicilian' cinema, shared a
passion for Sicily with the entire generation of post-Fascist film-makers.
Italian cinema had discovered Sicily as early as 1898 when, in response
to the Lumière Brothers' *Arrival of the Train in the Station of Ciotat*, a short
film titled *Passengers Landing from the Ferry* was filmed in Messina. It was
only during the Fascist period, however, and in response to a Fascist
cinema imprisoned in the bourgeois interiors of the Italian urban middle

classes, that a generation of young anti-Fascist intellectuals had started to imagine the liberating cinematic potentialities of the Sicilian landscape.

For a young generation educated in the myth of American cultural democracy – with Elio Vittorini's *Americana* (1941), an anthology of American literature from Washington Irving to John Fante, as their bible – anti-fascism meant, above all, the ability to translate into both cultural and cinematic terms the great democratic lesson of the United States of America. In an essay published on 25 April 1941 in the journal *Cinema* (edited by the Duce's own son, Vittorio Mussolini), Giuseppe De Santis, who would later join the Italian Communist Party, had penned an influential plea for Italian cinema to discover 'The Italian Landscape'. The model to follow, wrote De Santis, was 'early American western cinema': 'Do we Italians have less beautiful landscapes' than American western directors do? 'Is not ours the land that everybody envies for its beauties?'[6] On 10 October of the same year De Santis and Mario Alicata insisted on the necessity of Italian cinema to learn the lesson of the American western. And if Italy had never had its James Fenimore Cooper nor its 7th Cavalry Regiment, no doubt it could still boast one Giovanni Verga and his unforgotten *Cavalleria rusticana*: 'Not only has Giovanni

Sicilian mafiosi, *In the Name of the Law*.

Verga created a great work of art, but he has also created a country, an epoch and a society.'[7]

When these words were being published, Pietro Germi was a student in Rome's Experimental Centre for Cinematography with De Santis. For him as well, the idea of a cinema that could rediscover, along with Italian landscapes, an 'art inspired by a humanity that suffers and hopes', was tempting. The possibilities for such an art, however, were quite limited within the regime of Fascist cultural politics: there could hardly be human suffering in an Italy which Fascism said was the realization of all hopes. With the fall of the Fascist regime, all this became possible once again under the name of neorealism. For Germi, however, the return to Verga's Sicily, contemplated by De Santis as some sort of Italian-style western, was more than a possibility: it had become a necessity.

In 1948 the European Recovery Program, commonly known as the 'Marshall Plan', had begun to operate in Italy. Its aim was twofold: the first and better-known aim was to help rebuild the Italian economy and infrastructure after the destruction of the war; the second, less-noticed objective was to establish in Italy an American-style culture of liberal democracy to prevent not only the resurgence of Fascism, but the spread of communism, which had, in Italy, played a large part in the fall of the regime. A major component of the plan was thus the circulation of American cinema in Italy, which was distributed – a big gift to Hollywood – at the expense of American taxpayers through the Psychological Warfare Branch.[8] As explained in a report from the Rome bureau, cinema was 'useful above all in reinforcing the European admiration for the American standard of living'.[9]

While the influx of American-made movies set the conditions for the much-studied Americanization of Italy, it also created some concrete problems for Italian directors.[10] Following the strategic decision of the U.S. Department of State not to include the rebuilding of Italy's major studio – Cinecittà in Rome – in the Recovery Program, the Italian market was flooded by American products. In 1948, for the 344 American movies distributed in Italy, only 54 Italian movies were produced, a number that was drastically lower than the roughly 80 movies per year produced under the Fascist regime between 1939 and 1942.[11] It was only after 1948, when the new 'Andreotti Law' froze the profits of American movies shown in Italy and reinvested part of them in Italian productions, that an increase in Italian films (71 in 1949), and sufficient funds for the making of block-busters such as Germi's, became possible again. With box office sales at

$300,000, *In the Name of the Law* was the third-most-seen movie in Italy in the 1948–9 season.

The reasons for such success obviously go beyond mere financing. To compete with the hegemony of Hollywood, something more was needed. The American Production Code of 1934, which had made it impossible to show the Mafia in American movies, offered Germi an immense opportunity: not only was Hollywood legally incapacitated from providing more of the gangster movies which had made its fortune in the 1920s, but the Italian public was also hungry for the genre after twenty years of starvation under the Fascist regime.

Fascism and the Mafia

It should no longer be tolerated that a few hundred
criminals abuse, impoverish and harm a population
as magnificent as the people of Sicily.
– Benito Mussolini, *Writings and Speeches*

From the moment Benito Amilcare Andrea Mussolini became Prime Minister of Italy in 1922, he presented his Fascist movement as the party of law and order. It did not matter that his men circumvented the law, suspended the constitution, dissolved the parliament and assassinated their political adversaries. These were means towards a noble end: to eliminate criminality all over Italy; to transform a country of banditry and petty fraud into a cradle of heroic patriotism.

Stopping the advance of the Mafia in Italy, in all truth, was much needed. As the nineteenth century had closed in Italy with the Notarbartolo murder, the twentieth had opened with a show of force from the Mafia. The impunity of Palizzolo and Fontana proved that organized crime retained control not only of the island, but also, through institutional parties such as the Sicilian Autonomist Party, of Italian politics and the judiciary at large.

Around Palermo the Mafia, until then ecumenical in its political preferences, had started organizing around the parties of the Right. While infiltrations in the Socialist Party and in peasant unions were not rare, the Mafia could not tolerate any coming to power of the Left, which would threaten the wealth of both the big landowners and the *gabellotti*, whose power was on the rise. Whenever a mayoral election was in the balance, Mafia executions solved the situation with the physical elimination of left-wing candidates: Andrea Orlando and Luciano Nicoletti in Corleone, in 1905 and 1906 respectively; Lorenzo Panepinto in Santo Stefano, in 1911.

Notable in pre-war Mafia history is the case of Bernardino Verro, member of the Sicilian Socialist Party and organizer of the Peasants Cooperative Union of Corleone. In 1901, after a show of force of the Union, landowners had to concede to lower rates than usual for the lease of land to the peasants. Prefect Cesare De Seta wanted Verro investigated for 'promoting class hatred'; the Mafia clan of the *fratuzzi* (Brotherhood) simply sentenced him to death.[12]

Verro clung to life for more than a decade, first by leaving Sicily and then, after returning in 1906, by carrying a Browning automatic with him. In 1910, after barely escaping an assassination attempt, he left Corleone again. He also sent a letter to the police, informing them of the organization of the *fratuzzi* clan:

in the town, the *gabellotto* and Mafia capo, Michelangelo Gennaro; on a provincial scale, the *cricca* protected by the subprefect Spata, married to a woman from the Torina family of Caccamo, and therefore a descendant of a venerable Mafia dynasty, and by Vincenzo Cascio of the provincial administrative coalition. Clientelism and family tied both of them to Member of Parliament Avellone, who had testified on Palizzolo's behalf.[13]

This concentric organization of the Mafia, which from the local reached the highest seats of national power in an intricate web of familial and clientelistic ties, was not untypical. Nor was the inaction of the police.

In 1914, when he was the Socialist Party's nominee for mayor, Verro was obliged to return. His campaign, promising to fight the interests of the local Mafia, went exceedingly well.[14] Both *gabellotti* and landowners had reasons to fear a powerful union and Verro's cooperatives competing for the production and sale of agricultural goods. They mounted a campaign of innuendo to demolish Verro's character, accusing him of fraud and of being a mafioso himself. He was elected nonetheless. At this juncture, only one outcome was possible in Sicily: on 3 November 1914 Bernardino Verro was gunned down by two killers as he was returning home. The Browning automatic had malfunctioned. The Mafia had won yet again.

One more victory for the Mafia was the First World War:

> For the Mafia, the war had been good business . . . New
> possibilities had risen for illicit gain: Mafia activities opened
> to the black market and the exploitation of animal theft for the
> sale of horses to the army; open too was the immense traffic,
> through corrupt officers, for the sale of military exemptions
> and leave.[15]

At the end of the war, the only real threat to the Mafia came not from colluded governmental and judicial institutions, but the general strike of September and October 1919. Inspired by the insurrections in Russia, the 'red scare', as it was called in conservative papers, had acquired in Sicily the consistency of a movement for the conquest of the big latifundia. For the first time in its history, the Mafia and the land-based interests behind it were facing the danger of an epic defeat. The entire national situation did not look promising: all major factories in the industrial North had been occupied by workers, and the new Left-leaning Giolitti government in power had no solution in sight once its programme of moderate reforms had failed to appease the strikers.

In such a volatile climate the strategy of the Mafia, now on the defensive, was twofold: to push the rhetoric of a barely dormant Sicilian secession from Italy and, as the Palermo vice-commissioner intuited, to develop 'an organic plan for the elimination of every single leader of the Socialist party'.[16] Eliminations began in the small town of Prizzi, near Palermo. On the night of 22 September Giuseppe Rumore, secretary of the local union, was killed by two gunshots to the head. Other intimidations quickly followed: the kidnapping of trade unionist Giuseppe Cascio; the death threats delivered to trade unionist Giuseppe Zimmardi; the assassination attempt of Socialist vice-mayor Giuseppe Macaluso; and, finally, the murder of Socialist mayor Nicola Alongi – a 'dead man on leave', as he saw himself – on 29 February 1920.

Once the movement was beheaded in the countryside, Mafia attention could focus on the city, where the remnants of a Socialist Party and of worker unions (in the food, wine and naval industries) presented one last threat. At the height of a new strike of naval workers, on the evening of 14 October, Giovanni Orcel, leader of the metalworkers in Palermo, was stabbed to death.

It was no surprise, then, that two years later the newly elected prime minister Mussolini swore he would put an end to all such violence. It did not take long before the entire propaganda machine of the regime started hammering into Italian heads the idea that Fascism had in fact eradicated the Mafia once and for all. For the idea to remain persuasive, newspapers had to ignore any act of criminal violence. More relevant still for our story, by 1931, a special office of the Ministry for Domestic Affairs started reviewing no fewer than 18,000 books by Italian authors, as well as the entirety of the country's cinematic production. Any mention of the Mafia was censored: as the saying went, crime could not be conceivable in Fascist Italy. Few concessions were made for novels and films 'indicating that criminality and corruption exist only on foreign soil'.[17] Those Italians still eager to absorb Mafia stories, in short, could no longer count on the imitators of Verga.

Certainly propaganda alone could not suffice. One year after Mussolini had suppressed all opposition and assumed dictatorship of the country, a war against organized crime was officially declared. Operations began in earnest on 1 January 1926 when the police surrounded the town of Gangi, 50 miles outside Palermo. The town was cordoned off: access to roads, telephones and telegraphs was cut. Armoured vehicles stood at all cross-roads. Commanding the operation was Prefect Cesare Mori, sent to Sicily by Mussolini himself with the absolute power to annihilate the Mafia.

The first resounding success of such deployment of state power came in less than one day, with the apprehension of none other than Gaetano Ferrarello, the 'King of the Madonie', arrested in his farmhouse in the Madonie mountains. A rotund man of 65, Ferrarello had been on the run for almost half a century after having killed, Verga style, his wife and her lover. King or not, the uxoricide was not, after all, such a danger-ous mafioso. Mori, however, had learnt from his boss Mussolini that reality is what the media say it is. For a largely illiterate population such as the Sicilian one, in an island where radios were a luxury, he reverted to the old methods: to celebrate the swift arrest, Mori ordered the town crier to announce the glorious event at the sound of the beating drum:

Citizens of Gangi! His Excellency Cesare Mori, Prefect of Palermo, has sent the following telegram to the Mayor with the order to make his proclamation public: I command all fugitives from justice in this territory to give themselves up to the authorities within twelve hours of the moment when this ultimatum is read out. Once that deadline has passed, the severest measures will be taken against their families, their possessions, and anyone who has helped them in any way.[18]

On 10 January, seemingly satisfied with Ferrarello's arrest, Mori himself came to Gangi to celebrate. The town was festooned, and the local band played Verdi and military marches. On the walls were posters announcing Mussolini's 'heartiest satisfaction' on hearing of Mori's heroic deed: 'Fascism has cured Italy of many of its wounds. It will cauterize the sore of crime in Sicily – with red-hot iron if need be.'[19]

This and more such triumphs gained Mori the nickname of 'the Iron Prefect'; and gained to the regime the story, much amplified by the press, of the Fascist state's victory against the Mafia. As Mafia defector Antonino Calderone told Judge Giovanni Falcone in 1986, organized crime had indeed suffered at Mori's hand. The claim that the regime had eliminated the Mafia from Sicily by putting in jail a few wife-killers, however, sounds to historians more like a 'hollow boast'.[20]

It is more likely that the Mafia had a lesser role to play during the Fascist regime, since some of the 'services' it had traditionally provided were no longer needed. The Mafia had played two important roles in Sicily: protecting the estates of big landowners from socialistic demands for redistribution, and directing entire blocs of votes towards the elections of sympathetic candidates. In the new dictatorial regime, however, parliaments had been dissolved and the interests of landowners were better defended by the Fascist police and the young *squadristi* who enthusiastically hunted socialists with castor oil, iron clubs and, if needed, guns.

Some sort of elective affinity between the goals of Fascism and the Mafia, in other words, had created a regime of collaboration between the two sides:

> Several factors were responsible for the initial mutual tolerance demonstrated by Fascism and the Mafia. Above all else, Mussolini was determined to destroy any possibility of effective land occupations and to suppress banditism. Since he had not yet in hand the police-state apparatus which was to emerge only after 1924, he had during the first two years of his regime compelling reasons to enter into collaboration with influential mafiosi, men who were capable of enforcing law and order in the countryside.[21]

Such 'mutual tolerance' can be easily assessed by looking at the roll of Mafia men joining the Fascist party. The most emblematic was perhaps Alfredo Cucco, a bespectacled, hawkish-looking ophthalmologist from the province of Palermo, whose Mafia affiliations were hardly a secret in

Sicily. He became a Fascist deputy in 1924, and not even the dislike for his candidature expressed by the Iron Prefect himself could dissuade Mussolini from welcoming him into the party. Only in 1927, under Mori's insistent pressure, was he finally expelled, put on trial – and found 'not guilty'. The incident did not diminish Cucco's enthusiasm for Fascism in the least. In 1938 he was one of the 'scientific authorities' signing the 'Racial Manifesto' that opened the way for new racial laws that led to Auschwitz. In 1944, when the Allied troops occupied Rome, he escaped with Mussolini to Salò, near Milan, where an Italian Social Republic under Nazi protection was established. In 1947, after the collapse of the regime, he moved to create the neo-fascist Italian Social Movement (MSI).

The Iron Prefect was also tolerant of the Mafia. When Mussolini came to Piana dei Greci for his first official visit to Sicily, Mori's choice for the protection of His Excellency fell immediately on the powerful local boss:

Piana dei Greci was the center of a notorious Mafia gang headed by Don Ciccio Cuccia . . . Cesare Mori, recently appointed to the Palermo prefecture and . . . charged with making security arrangements for the trip to Piana, fixed it so that Mussolini and Cuccia would ride in the same automobile. His reasoning was that no one would dare touch Mussolini in the presence of so powerful a mafioso. As an added precaution Mori also provided a heavily armed motorcycle escort for the parade through Piana. All went well until the end of the procession when Cuccia turned to Mussolini and said: 'There is no need for so many cops (sbirri). Beside me your Excellency has nothing to fear because I give all the orders around here.' Turning to his men, Cuccia, in a voice full of authority, ordered: 'Nobody is to touch a hair of my friend Mussolini.'[22]

Offended by the incident, Mussolini, on his return to Rome, had Cuccia arrested.

Whatever this ambiguous relation of friendships and arrests may mean, what is certain is that neither crime nor the Mafia had ever really been eradicated by the regime. They were, like everything else in Italy, waiting to be reborn. When Fascism fell, the rebirth began. It was called 'reconstruction'. The publishing house Mondadori reconstructed the Italian Mafia genre with an immensely successful series of crime novels known as *gialli* because of their distinctive yellow covers.[23] Pietro Germi reconstructed an Italian cinema in crisis with a movie that exploited the Italian desire for Mafia stories after twenty years of deprivation. And the Mafia, slowly but surely, began to reconstruct itself.

Operation Husky

> Before Husky . . . they called them greaseballs.
> – Eric Dezenhall, *The Devil Himself: A Novel*

Of all the mysteries that have vexed military historians, one of the most notable is the military plan code-named 'Operation Husky' by Allied forces. In January 1943 Winston Churchill and Franklin Delano Roosevelt met with military advisors in Casablanca; Joseph Stalin, unable to participate, sent his trusted generals. It was clear to those involved that the German resistance could be penetrated from only two fronts: Normandy (Operation Overlord), which remained the strategic key for any final success; and Sicily (Operation Husky), which, isolated in the Mediterranean, offered few strategic advantages for an advance into mainland Europe, but where Germany's weakest ally – Italy – could be easily overcome. The problem was where to begin.

The Americans had initially opposed the idea of launching with Operation Husky since they saw a victory in Sicily, quite reasonably, as irrelevant. After further discussions, however, all three parties came to agree: irrelevant or not, the liberation of Europe would start with Operation Husky on 9 July 1943 and would continue with Operation Overlord, the D-Day for which would be 6 June 1944.

Why would military strategists agree on the necessity to begin the campaign from irrelevant Sicily? And why would they initiate liberation in Sicily so much in advance of D-Day, with the risk of keeping troops stationed in southern Italy for eleven long months? It is through unanswered questions such as these that Mafia history becomes the stuff of a perverted James Bond story. Narrated in works by such titles as *The Mafia at War* or *The Mafia and the Allies*, this story begins with what we can call – tentatively, in the absence of any reliable archive of the Mafia – 'the facts'.[24]

First fact: before commencing Operation Husky, the United States Secret Service contacted the Sicilian Mafia boss Charles 'Lucky' Luciano, possibly to request help in preparing Sicily for the landing. Luciano had been in Sing Sing Correctional Facility since 1936 on 62 counts of compulsory prostitution. These were the only charges that Special Prosecutor Thomas E. Dewey had managed to make stick on the notorious boss of bosses. After a quick ascent to power during the Prohibition era – he was said to have made over $12 million a year – Luciano had eliminated his own boss, Joe Masseria, and reorganized the New York underworld into five families, each with limited territorial competence. Tommy 'Three Finger' Lucchese was in charge of East Harlem and the Bronx, north of 107th Street. Carlo Gambino managed loan-sharking, illegal gambling, and protection money in the Brooklyn area. Joseph Colombo oversaw business in Brooklyn, Queens, and Long Island. Joe Bonanno controlled illicit traffic in Brooklyn, Queens, Staten Island and Long Island. Vito Genovese operated in Lower Manhattan, New Jersey and parts of Brooklyn and the Bronx. As the Mafia informant Joe Valachi told the u.s. Senate Committee after his arrest in 1959 – Terence Young's *Valachi Papers* of 1972 is a brilliant cinematic reconstruction of the testimony – the New York Five Families also had connections with the Chicago Syndicate, with which they formed 'The Commission' headed by none other than Luciano.

The u.s. Secret Service had already collaborated with Luciano, whose control of the New York waterfront was of strategic importance to prevent acts of sabotage of the u.s. fleet stationed in the harbour. Now, on the eve of Operation Husky, his help could be exchanged for a release from prison. The judge, apparently, did not consent. Luciano, however, was pardoned in 1946 – for unspecified services rendered to Naval Intelligence.[25]

Second fact: Colonel Charles Poletti, head of the 7th American Division for Civil Affairs of the u.s. Army, hired as his driver and interpreter during his days in Sicily his long-time friend Vito Genovese, who had left New York in 1937 to escape prosecution on Mafia charges. Poletti, who in his civilian life had occupied the position of Lieutenant Governor for the State of New York, was well known for his special treatment of mafiosi: he had 'signed the order to free such individuals as Francesco Gambino (serving a life sentence for murdering his cousin), Peter Tusa (life sentence for homicide), John Santapaola (thirty years for homicide), and others like Mario Pece, Maurice Buonuomo, [and] Anthony Gerardo'.[26] Poletti always denied his connection to the Mafia – in fact, he denied that the Mafia existed at all. This did not prevent him from nominating Michele Navarra, boss of Corleone, as transportation superintendent for western Sicily; Giuseppe Genco Russo, head of the Mussomeli clan, as

U.S. Attorney General poster offering a reward for information for the FBI in apprehending Jacob Shapiro and Louis Buchalter in 1937.

superintendent for public assistance; and Don Calogero Vizzini, boss of Villalba, as mayor of that town.

Calogero Vizzini, an archetypical figure of the 'humble' rural Mafia of the 1940s – 'it was not done for a Mafia chieftain to show off in the matter of his clothing or any other way, and sometimes, as in Don Calò's case, this lack of concern for appearances was carried to extremes'[27]– conveniently doubles as the main character of Operation Husky's Mafia legend. The historian John Dickie tells the legend nicely:

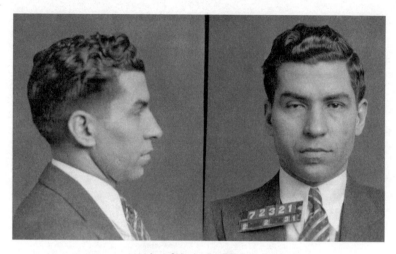

Mugshot of Charles 'Lucky' Luciano.

It is said that on the morning of 14 July 1943, an American fighter plane flew low over Villalba. It naturally drew the people out into the streets. When it roared down to rooftop level they could see, attached to its fuselage, a golden-yellow flag with a large L in the centre. As it passed over the house belonging to the parish priest, Monsignor Giovanni Vizzini, the pilot dropped a small package. But it was intercepted by an Italian soldier and passed on to the commander of the local *carabinieri*.[28]

The aeroplane returned the following day, and this time it evaded the undoubtedly zealous control of the Fascist police. The package it dropped was addressed to 'Zu' Calò', the name by which Calogero Vizzini was known locally. Inside the package was a letter, which read as follows:

> On Tuesday 20th Turi will leave for the fair at Cerda with the cows. I will set off the same day with the cows, the oxen, and the bull. Prepare the matches for the fruit and organize pens for the animals. Tell the other overseers to get ready.

The message was signed 'Zu' Peppi', namely Giuseppe Genco Russo, boss of Mussomeli.

Enigmatic signs are known to come from the sky, but this was a message coded in Mafia-speak. Someone was telling Vizzini that, on the twentieth day of the month, someone named Turi (another mafioso?) was to accompany the motorized divisions to Cerda. Vizzini had to leave on the same day with the troops, the tanks and the top commander (the bull). Places to camp (pens), eat (fruit) and collect weapons (matches) for the troops were to be prepared. The Americans, as a matter of fact, reached Villalba on the afternoon of 20 July 1943, and found 'fruit' and 'pens' already set and organized. On top of the first tank that entered Villalba was a yellow flag with an L in the middle: it stood for Lucky Luciano, who was inside the tank, having come to Sicily to shake hands with Vizzini.

Historians should certainly be sceptical of all this (not least because Luciano was allegedly still in jail): 'there was no American plot to enlist the Mafia as an ally in the invasion of Sicily', writes John Dickie, as 'it is hardly likely that the Allies would entrust the secret of Operation Husky, then the largest amphibious assault in history, to hoodlums.'[29] Other historians, however, are less quick to dismiss the involvement of the Mafia.[30] Was the Mafia the ace in the sleeve that convinced Churchill, Roosevelt and Stalin that Sicily could be easily won and kept so as to begin the real offensive in mainland Europe? Hard to know; what is beyond question is that the Mafia quickly resurfaced *after* Operation Husky, and that the Allied forces – not least because of Poletti's dubious nominations – 'were far from innocent in the Mafia's resurgence as a political force'.[31] As Salvatore Lupo comments: 'with the end of the war and the fall of Fascism, the Mafia returned to Sicily.'[32] And with the real Mafia, the one concocted by the cultural industry returned to Sicily too.

In the Name of the Law

What kind of a town is this anyway?
– *My Darling Clementine*, dir. John Ford

By transposing a Mafia story to a western key, Germi's In the Name of the Law (In Nome Della Legge) could kill no fewer than three birds with a single stone: capture the interest of Italian viewers for Mafia stories at a moment when the Mafia was visibly on the rise; provide a story of gangsterism – violence, thefts, homicides – that the American competition could no longer supply under the Production Code; and compete with Hollywood on its own ground: the western. As the film critic Guido Aristarco wrote in his review of the movie after its premiere, this was not exactly an 'imitation of the American western', but rather a creative elaboration that established 'analogies' between Sicily and the American frontier.[33]

What the analogies between Sicily and the mythical Far West could have been are not difficult to imagine: both were viewed as wild territories and both were to be conquered by courageous settlers or by intrepid functionaries of the State. In both places no law but the gun's was sovereign. In these frontier territories sheriffs were left alone with their courage, and so were judges like the one of In the Name of the Law (the character was inspired by the sheriff, played by Henry Fonda, of My Darling Clementine). Last but not least, Germi's mafiosi were like the 'Indians' of the western.

The mafiosi's first appearance high on a mountaintop on the far horizon, riding horses and brandishing guns, is such a brazen remark on the western that the word 'allusion' would not render justice to it. Mafiosi are a native Sicilian tribe in this movie – with their ethnic faces, their women in black shawls and their constant mentioning of 'traditions and customs'. Like the 'Indians' in the multiculturally sensitive version of the western, these Sicilians too kill with savage violence; and yet, like Geronimo, they are also led by a sense of honour, virile camaraderie and belonging to their land. This is what Judge Guido Schiavi (Massimo Girotti) learns by the end of the movie, just as John Wayne had learnt in so many movies before.

Judge Schiavi arrives in the small village of Capodarso (in truth, Barrafranca, a few miles from my own hometown), where he is soon confronted with a number of problems, the worst of which is a powerful local landowner, Baron Lo Vasto. We soon discover that the ambush shown in the opening sequence was to steal two of Lo Vasto's mules. When a local mafioso offers his help to rescue the animals, Baron Lo Vasto loses his temper:

> The Mafia?! You?! Give me a break! Here you have it: threatening letters, cut trees, blackmail, theft of cattle . . . And this morning my warden gets killed and two mules stolen. Am I am supposed to trust you now? Please! Don't make me laugh! Let Don Turi know that the Mafia is over. This is criminality, not Mafia! Tell him! And tell him too that from now on I will turn to the public authority for help!

The naive viewer would, at this point, conclude that Lo Vasto is the wronged hero of this story, and that the arrival of the sheriff in town –

The mafiosi prepare to attack the village of Capodarso, *In the Name of the Law*.

Judge Schiavi, to be sure – will unite the two in a duel to death against the Mafia. The naive viewer would be very wrong.

The telltale signs that our story is to move to a completely different path are already there for all to decipher: who has ever seen, in any respectable western, the sheriff partner with the wealthy owner of the saloon? In truth *In the Name of the Law*, like Verga's *Cavalleria*, is a tale of nostalgia: a longing for a beautiful original Mafia decayed into a mere criminality. 'The Mafia?! You?! Give me a break!': Lo Vasto's retort points to the sad fact that the original Mafia is no more, and only the theft of cattle remains. In the absence of a real Mafia, the 'public authority' has sovereignty over the territory – and such authority, Lo Vasto knows well, is in the pocket of barons like him.

The difference between an original Mafia and its modern decay into petty criminality is of course an old commonplace, which we know already from Pitrè: 'things have changed, and the word *mafioso* no longer has, for many, its original and authentic meaning.'[34] The entry of the sheriff/judge on this Sicilian stage functions then as some sort of messianic intervention that will restore the noble, original and authentic meaning of the Mafia: by the end of the film, he will have convinced the Mafia boss, until then at the service of the evil baron, to change sides. Baron Lo Vasto is starving the entire population of the town and the Mafia boss, like any good Robin Hood a proud, good-hearted outlaw, starts believing again: 'We are not criminals; we are men of honour.' He will help to bring the real criminal, Lo Vasto, to justice in the name of *a* law that becomes indistinguishable, needless to say, from the very name of the Mafia. People will no longer be starved in Capodarso, and will, undoubtedly, live happily ever after. One more feather can be added to the Mafia's cap.

Speaking of feathers, while Germi's problematic romanticization of the Mafia should certainly ruffle ours, the question remains as to why such romanticization was necessary at all. Why did Germi feel the need to imagine a good Mafia, and why was the Italian public so accepting of it? One possible if not particularly uplifting answer is that, already by 1949, the citizens of the post-Fascist Republic felt that the alliance of big business and 'public authority' to which Lo Vasto alluded had laid the basis for an utterly unjust society that starved the population. If so, a law protecting what is unjust ought to be broken in the name of a higher law. In the name of precisely such a law, the Mafia movie became an expression of a popular 'grudge against the police and government': 'the characteristic victims of the bandit are the quintessential enemies of the poor'; and the Mafia, in turn, transforms into the necessary fiction of 'the people's champions against the gentry' and against the gentry's State alike.[35] Germi's movie, in other words, calls upon the Mafia when it feels the need for a champion and protector of the people against abuses; his Mafia may not be able, in the end, to make a world of equality and justice, but it can at least right some wrongs 'and prove that sometimes oppression can be turned upside down'.[36]

Thus mafiosi appear for the first time in Italian cinema: 'as outlaws, but also as judges, with their own code of honour . . . They appear as mythical creatures, and such they will remain for several decades on the Italian silver screen.'[37] The western setting had allowed Germi to treat the Mafia as the western had treated the 'good savage': in this socially needed fable of innocent justice and honour – no matter if the fable was radically independent from what the real Mafia might have been. *In the Name of the Law*, in short, transposed 'the phenomenon of the Mafia, whose concreteness and materiality are . . . ignored, into a symbolic and emblematic plane'.[38] It made of the Mafia a myth.

The myth was an unprecedented success. In 1950, of the 104 movies produced in Italy, three repeated Germi's successful formula of the western Mafia: Aldo Vergano's *The Outlaws*, Enzo Trapani's *Turi the Bandit* and Camillo Mastrocinque's *The Ruthless*. The final pacification of Mafia and State, sealed by the shake of hands between boss and judge in Germi's movie, was reassuring for an Italy just out of the war and already torn by the political tensions between the two major parties, the Christian Democrat (DC) and the Communist. It was, undoubtedly, a happy ending that satisfied all – 'except the Sicilians', writes Sciascia, 'who had a very different experience of the Mafia and a divergent opinion of it'.[39]

Western *non troppo*: Rosi's *Salvatore Giuliano*

Robin Hood in England, Janosik in Poland and Slovakia,
Diego Corrientes in Andalus . . .
– Eric Hobsbawm, *Primitive Rebels*

It was not a Sicilian, however, who flipped Germi's romantic image of the Mafia on its head. Francesco Rosi was born in Naples, where a similar but distinct criminal organization, the Camorra, challenged the city. *The Challenge* (1958) was Rosi's first take on organized crime. His second – *Hands over the City* (1963) – was already a desperate cry for help; the challenge, Rosi seemed to suggest, had been lost. Organized crime, in a respectable double-breasted suit and with a seat in parliament, now had the city in its grip.

The Mafia, even more than the still marginal Camorra, was an appetizing topic for Rosi. The fact was that, for him, the mystery of the Mafia coincided with the mystery of post-war Italy: its endemic corruption; its political immobility (the Christian Democrat party would govern the country uninterruptedly from 1944 to 1992); its still unresolved southern question; and, last but not least, the reduction of Italy to a pawn of the Cold War. To solve one mystery meant to solve the other. Rosi tried to tackle the enigma of the Mafia four times: with *Salvatore Giuliano* in 1962, *Il Caso Mattei* (*The Mattei Case*) in 1972, *Lucky Luciano* in 1973 and *Cadaveri eccellenti* (*Excellent Cadavers*) in 1976. While none provided the final answer, they all pointed to the disturbing presence of the Mafia in all crannies of power in post-war Italy.

Salvatore Giuliano was Rosi's most ambitious Mafia movie. The figure of the protagonist was fascinating in his own right: born in the small town of Montelepre in 1922, Giuliano, aged 21, had become an outlaw after killing a policeman on 2 September 1943. The reasons for the homicide are unknown but, only two months after the Americans had landed in

Sicily, the killing of a policeman could still be imagined as an act of anti-Fascist resistance. At least this was how Giuliano liked to explain his first murder. More followed: from 1945 to 1950 his band had gained complete control of the entire western province of Palermo. Even this, he insisted, was in response to the cruelty and injustice of the Italian State. In 1946 he wrote a letter to President Harry Truman urging him to annex Sicily to the United States.[40] The idea was less bizarre than it sounds: Giuliano's request coincided with the desires of the Sicilian separatist movement at the time; and the United States, one must add, did not disdain the proposal, because of the strategic position of Sicily in the Mediterranean.

With an almost pathological need to control the stories around his persona, Giuliano had always 'made a point of cultivating a "Robin Hood" fable around himself'.[41] Throughout the 1950s 'the legend (otherwise entirely baseless) of Giuliano as the Robin Hood of Montelepre' circulated widely in Italy.[42] By 1956 the bandit's legend was an international affair. Gavin Maxwell's *God Protect Me from My Friends* recounted the deeds of the bandit as those of a Sicilian Robin Hood betrayed (hence the title) by his friend and lieutenant Gaspare Pisciotta. As a Robin Hood, historian Eric Hobsbawm contended, Salvatore Giuliano was particularly successful: 'Giuliano (with heavy protection) lasted six years, but at a guess a Robin Hood of some ambition would be lucky to survive for more than two to four.'[43]

Francesco Rosi's *Salvatore Giuliano* cuts into the flesh of the Robin Hood myth with cold, surgical precision. It opens with a stroke of cinematic genius: Giuliano lies dead in a courtyard. The peculiar angle of the camera, mounted high in a skewed perspective, offers a rather unnatural point of view. It is reminiscent, perhaps, of the ancient gladiator shows at the Colosseum, or of a balcony high up on a theatrical stage. The warrior is dead. A gun lies by his side. The dirt, the crumbling walls around the yard, the blinding sunlight of an overexposed photography, remind us again of a western setting, perhaps of a border town.

Germi's lesson has not been lost: a number of movies – including Carlo Lizzani's *Achtung! Banditi!* (1951) and Vittorio De Seta's *Banditi a Orgosolo* (1961) – made use of the western format to portray 'the position of banditry in the modern nation'.[44] Rosi's *Giuliano* is no exception. Wanted posters affixed to decayed buildings, silhouettes of bandits emerging from the hilltops, rides on horseback, flags waving on an Alamo of sorts, omnipresent guns – these all point to Germi's construction of the Mafia western. So does, at least on the surface, the invisibility of the bandit

Giuliano: he is 'rarely present on screen, and the only close-ups are of his dead body'.[45] As the Sicilian writer Leonardo Sciascia commented, Giuliano's invisibility seemed also an echo of Germi's Mafia myth: 'for the public this invisibility became . . . a mystical sign: Giuliano as the Idea of revolt against the State, of social revenge, of the redemption of the poor . . . the confirmation of a myth.'[46]

Those expecting the 'confirmation of a myth', however, had better look somewhere else. The truth is that Rosi was not intent on celebrating yet again the adventurous legend of the Italian frontier – a Far South of sorts with its tales of honourable mafiosi. His peculiar western wanted to show, rather, what lurked behind the glitter: ruthlessness and intrigue. As in the coeval spaghetti western, what moved the story of *Salvatore Giuliano* was neither honour nor tradition, but a most crude form of pragmatism untouched by ethical concerns: all is done here for a fistful of dollars.

The very invisibility of Giuliano was meant, from Rosi's perspective, not to 'confirm', but to liquidate any veneer of myth surrounding the legendary mafioso. He is invisible not because he is extraordinary and sublime but because for Rosi 'it was not Giuliano that counted, but the powers, the interests, the people that moved him . . . Relegating [Giuliano] to invisibility, Rosi made his accusation against the political class that moved him more harsh.'[47] Or, in Angelo Restivo's words:

Investigations and cover-ups begin as the body of Salvatore Giuliano is found by the police.
Francesco Rosi (dir.), *Salvatore Giuliano* (Galatea Film, 1962).

Rosi never shows him except as a corpse. By marginalizing in this way what is supposed to be the central figure in the story, Rosi purges the bandit legend of its inherent nostalgia, thus rendering the figure less the emblem of traditionalist values and more a kind of invisible 'force field' around which swirl the social antagonisms of the country.[48]

Making Giuliano invisible is one way in which Rosi tries to deny him and the Mafia any mythical status. There are more.

As the camera lingers on the courtyard where the body of Giuliano lies dead, we soon realize that we were wrong when we thought the unnatural perspective *seemed* to suggest a theatrical setting or a gladiator show. The scene *is* such a theatrical spectacle, through and through. As journalists with their cameras come in and out of the frame to take their shot of the dead bandit, the uncomfortable feeling that this is all a theatrical staging in which we are asked to play the role of credulous spectators grows. Giuliano's body faces down but his blood, instead of dripping to the ground, seems to have gone against gravity, up towards the top of his right shoulder. In fact, we do not even see Giuliano's face. The policeman looking in his pocket finds the ID 'of an as-yet unidentified person', not of the wanted bandit whose face any policeman must have known. Is this really Giuliano? Is this really where he was killed?

As doubts grow, a voice is heard. It speaks the cold, bureaucratic language of a police investigator, but with the automatism of a bad actor repeating a poorly rehearsed script:

VOICE: In the year 1950, on this fifth day of July, on the Via Fra' Serafino Mannone, in the De Maria courtyard, lies a male corpse, apparent age 30 years, lying in a prone position, with the left leg extended and the right leg bent at nearly a right angle. The right arm is extended with clenched fist, and the left is under the chest. The left cheek lies on the ground.
SECOND VOICE: You mean 'rests' on the ground.
VOICE: Very well. Correct that.

Of course it is not merely bad acting that is at stake here: what could the difference be, in a police report, between 'lying' and 'resting'? The suspicion grows that we are witnessing an institutional cover-up: the acting of a story already plotted and scripted. It is the story of Giuliano's legend and of his heroic death – 'resisting arrest' will be the official line. It is also the story, *mutatis mutandis*, of Germi's legendary post-war Sicilian Mafia in its fight against the State: to defend the poor against the rich. But this story, this legend, is for Rosi an institutional make-believe. The truth – about Giuliano and the post-war Mafia – lies elsewhere.

In search of this elsewhere, the western becomes something else. We could call this 'something else', in homage to Rosi's master and friend Cesare Zavattini, the 'investigative film'.[49] As an investigative film, *Salvatore Giuliano* begins at six minutes and 51 seconds into the (long!) movie with a place and a date displayed in large sans serif letters on the screen: 'Palermo 1945'. It is the first of the many flashbacks through which Rosi will lead his viewer, back to the rise of Giuliano. Crowds fill the streets, and signs of 'Long Live Freedom and Independence' are waved throughout. A voiceover, in the unmistakable diction of the documentary genre, gives the context for this scene of Sicilian celebration:

> Ever since the Allies' arrival in 1943, there had raged in Sicily a passion for separatism. MIS [Movement for Sicilian Independence] was the separatist party that wished to unite the region [with the United States of America]; and EVIS [Volunteer Army for the Independence of Sicily] was its military arm. The Americans, the English, landowners and the Mafia supported the movement. Many died in skirmishes between separatists and officers of the law. On September 30 1945 the first CLN [Committee for National Liberation] government ordered the arrest of the leaders of the independence movement: Finocchiaro Aprile and Varvaro.

We are at the end of the Second World War and a most unhealthy alliance has formed: EVIS, the Americans, the English, the landowners and the Mafia have agreed on a strategic objective – Sicilian separatism.

For EVIS and landowners, separatism means to bypass the national anti-Fascist alliance of communists and Christian centrists, who threaten land-based interests with their calls for land reform. For the English and Americans, separatism means to have a small nation, squarely in the middle of the Mediterranean, under their control in the opening moves of the incipient Cold War. For the U.S., moreover, Sicily can be a Puerto Rico of sorts – a faraway Mediterranean State of the Union. And then, in this setting for international intrigue, quite far from the popular legend of Robin Hood, Rosi finds the Mafia.

With the fall of Fascism, Italy's first Republic is born, along with the new mafia.
Scene from *Salvatore Giuliano*.

After Operation Husky, the list of Mafia men that Colonel Poletti had started to place in key administrative positions had swollen considerably. As Major General Francis James Rennell Rodd reminisced:

> With the people clamoring to be rid of a Fascist *Podesta*, many of my officers fell into the trap of selecting the most forthcoming self-advertisers, or following the advice of their self-appointed interpreters who had learned some English in the course of a stay in the USA. The result was not always happy. They invariably chose a local Mafia 'boss', or his shadow, who in one or two cases had graduated in an American gangster environment. All that could be said of some of these men was that they were as definitely anti-Fascist as they were undesirable from every other point of view.[50]

An OSS report dated 5 April 1945, entitled 'The Mafia Leadership Fighting Crime', describes the instrumental use of the Mafia to fight petty banditry and communist organizations in Sicily. It concludes:

> The Carabinieri and other public safety agencies were openly favorable to the Mafia leadership's interest in enforcing respect of the law and were avoiding any investigation into the killings of wanted criminals.[51]

What liberation meant for the Mafia was an unprecedented opportunity: the chance to assume direct and even legitimate power in Sicily with the Allies' benediction and prayer. The only remaining obstacle between the Mafia and the total control of Sicily was the central government in Rome. The solution to bypass that obstacle was simple for them: separatism.

This is the context that Rosi reconstructs in a few shots. As the scene of the festivities in Palermo fades out, the camera takes us to a private house where men are having an animated discussion about the future of Sicily. The meeting did indeed take place, on 6 December 1943, in the villa of Lucio Tasca, who had been chosen as the new mayor of Palermo by the Allies. There were about 40 people, including boss Calogero Vizzini, who had shocked poor Signor Tasca when he had put his revolver on the table: 'It bothers me when I sit.'[52]

The question in front of everyone was how to reach independence:

FIRST SPEAKER: We should have achieved independence before the war ended on the mainland. Then the government would have been faced with a fait accompli. Now it's useless. The situation gets worse every day. Either we give up, or we stage an insurrection right now.

SECOND SPEAKER: Who's going to stage the revolution? A bunch of kids?

FIRST SPEAKER: Right now there are 37 bands of outlaws in Sicily. Thirty-seven! They have enough weapons to fill an arsenal and they're not all escaped convicts. Most of them are victims of injustice, ignorance and poverty. They're just waiting for a chance to get back to civilian life.

SECOND SPEAKER: That's enough. You know most of us are against what you propose.

FIRST SPEAKER: Talking has got us nowhere. We set up an independent combat unit and absolve the party of all responsibility. Who did Garibaldi use to liberate Sicily from the Bourbons? He used the picciotti. And who were they? Escapees and bandits.

The dialogue in Rosi's movie faithfully represents the positions of Aprile and Varvaro: the Mafia, ennobled as a group of 'victims of injustice', and even more with the legend of their deeds during the Risorgimento, is the only path to separatism.

In the next scene Aprile and his men are in Montelepre to offer Giuliano the position of colonel of EVIS. This is the origin of post-war Mafia as narrated by Rosi. Whether Giuliano had initially operated in the context of what Hobsbawm calls 'social banditry' – 'a rather primitive form of organized social protest' of which Robin Hood is the archetype – it is at this stage of the story a moot point: Aprile's Sicilian separatism bends banditry and uses it for the interests of Sicily's leading classes.[53] Banditry, as Villari and Franchetti would have said, becomes the Mafia.

Nowhere is the distance between this Mafia and the Robin Hood myth more apparent than in the massacre of Portella della Ginestra, which takes centre stage in Rosi's account of Giuliano.

The Massacre of Portella della Ginestra

The first impression visitors get of Portella della Ginestra, a town enclosed between two mountains in the Albanian Plain near Palermo, is that of an endless field of yellow flowers. The evergreen shrub, which in the Arbëreshë dialect of the Albanians populating the valley is called Jinestrës, pollinates throughout the months of April and May, stunning the occasional traveller with a strong, pungent smell that is said to tame wild horses and rabid dogs. The Oxford English dictionary calls the shrub a 'broom', and its blossom 'flower of the desert'. The Italian writer Giacomo Leopardi dedicated his poetic testament to it – 317 verses in mixed measures celebrating the resilience of the delicate flower against the tragic indifference of a universe threatening its destruction.

It was on May Day of 1947 that the peasants from the plain, coming from the small villages of San Cipirello and San Giovanni Jato, gathered in Portella for the celebration. This year there were special reasons to celebrate: the Blocco del Popolo (an anti-Fascist 'People's Bloc' reuniting the Christian Democrats and the Communist Party) had won the Sicilian Parliament, and massive land reforms were on the horizon.

In a dramatic montage, Rosi shows the farmers arriving in the valley while Giuliano's men prepare the ambush: 'We're going to Portella della Ginestra to shoot at the communists.' The peasants enter the valley wearing their best clothes. Donkeys, mules and carts are decorated with ribbons. It is a festive atmosphere, no doubt. While families enjoy their picnic, the secretary of the local section of the People's Bloc starts his speech. Red flags are waving. The speech is suddenly interrupted by loud bangs. At first they sound to the people like fireworks for the celebration. Everybody looks around to find from where they are coming. They realize too late: from the hilltops, Giuliano's men are shooting in the crowd. Eleven bodies fall on the ground. The youngest two belong to seven-year-old children.

This spectacle of Mafia violence, however, does not distract Rosi from noticing the ruthless realpolitik that went into the planning and timing of the massacre. The message of Mafia intimidation sent with the guns of Giuliano was clear: its intended recipient was not so much the people reunited for May Day, but rather the Christian Democrats who had participated in the People's Bloc. What the guns spelled out was clear: 'We are ready to kill.'

The message was quickly understood: on 30 May, barely 29 days after the massacre at Portella, the Christian Democrats broke their anti-Fascist front and formed a new Sicilian parliament with the separatists. The next day the same happened at the national level. The separatists had made it to Rome. Having reached their objective, they now had little interest in pursuing the separatist agenda anymore. Rediscovering themselves as patriots of the Italian nation, they joined the ranks of the Christian Democrats:

The alliance between men of honour and DC politicians was hardly a secret. In the lead-up to the momentous polling day of 1948, Don Calò [Vizzini] and his *compare*, the boss of Mussomeli, Giuseppe Genco Russo, attended a sumptuous DC electoral lunch in Villa Igea, a Palermo hotel . . . The two mafiosi sat at the same table as some of the party's leading lights. In 1950, when Genco Russo's oldest son married, Don Calò was a witness at the ceremony, as was the DC president of the Sicilian regional assembly. Encounters like these were not shamefaced and secret. When politicians and bosses met in this period, they often intended to be seen together because their encounters advertised the solidity of the alliance between the informal power of the Mafia and the official power of the new political grandees.[54]

Ushering in a new era of political connections and collusion, Portella had announced the birth of a new Mafia. At the trial for the murder of Giuliano, Gaspare Pisciotta (played by Frank Wolff, the only professional actor in the cast) tells the judge that the separatist party of Aprile and Varvaro was behind the massacre. And now, he adds, 'They're in Rome with their seats in parliament!' No longer tied to the local and rural reality of pre-war Sicily, the Mafia had now national ambitions.

The Sack of Palermo

... the contradictory but undeniable process
of economic and cultural modernization ...
– Letizia Paoli, 'Broken Bonds: Mafia and Politics in Italy'

When Franchetti had observed it in 1876, the Mafia was already a modern
reality: modern in its 'industrial' organization and above all in its use of
parliamentary politics, which Turrisi Colonna and Gimmona had spear-
headed. Portella della Ginestra signalled that the process of modernization
had not ended in 1876. The massacre had been planned with the goal of
breaking the alliance of the People's Bloc so as to guarantee men of
honour a seat in both the local and national parliaments. A relationship
between the Mafia and representative politics, in other words, could no
longer be left to chance or to the goodwill of single politicians disposed
to deal with the Mafia. The relationship had to be rationalized so as to
become organic: rather than finding its allies in the parliament, the
post-war Mafia aimed to *be* in parliament itself – to become itself a party
or, as Salvatore Lupo writes, 'an integral part of the majority Christian
Democratic political party'.[55]

The *pentiti* of the 1980s ('repented' mafiosi in the wake of Tommaso
Buscetta's confessions) could go on and on listing names of mafiosi who,
following Portella, had entered the Christian Democratic party. Among
them were Giovanni Gioia, Mario D'Acquisto, Girolamo Di Benedetto,
Franz Gorgone, Sebastiano Purpura, Michele Reina, Ernesto Di Fresco,
Antonino Riggio, Francesco Caldaronello ... In the immediate post-war
period, such coincidence of interests and personnel between the Mafia
and Italy's leading party should have raised the Allies' suspicions. The
Christian Democrats, however, had chosen as their symbol a shield with
a cross inside; their crusade, it was implied, was against communism.
More concerned with a Cold War against the Soviets than with the Mafia,
the Americans were ready to overlook the dealings the party had with
organized crime. As Rosi's film suggests, the alliance of politics and
criminal organization solidified in post-war Italy, aided and abetted by
the winners of the Second World War.

Aprile and Varvaro had opened the way for the Mafia to enter Italy's
political system in first person. Salvo Lima and Vito Ciancimino would
soon become the new Mafia's most emblematic figures:

Lima and Ciancimino were an interesting pair. Ciancimino was a barber's son from Corleone who kept his close-clipped Sicilian barber's moustache and his country uncouthness long after he moved to Palermo at the end of the war and into politics. In 1984 he was the first public figure to be arrested, tried and eventually convicted as a mafioso. Twelve million dollars' worth of Ciancimino's personal assets were confiscated at that time. Lima on the other hand was almost too powerful to embarrass. Beyond a certain threshold, power erases embarrassment. He was a white-maned and silk-suited grandee, and when Salvo Lima walked into a Palermo restaurant, silence fell and people came to kiss his hand. The two worked well together in the interests of the friends and the transformation of Palermo in four years was concrete evidence of this. In four years of early teamwork, these two released 4,200 permits for new building in the city. Nearly three-quarters of these permits, over 3,000 of them, were given to five obscure figures, illiterate or retired, who were fronts for mafia interests.[56]

Through Lima and Ciancimino, the entente of Mafia and politics worked flawlessly in Palermo: mafiosi would buy cheap rural land, often made cheaper by intimidation. The political administration would then transform the same land into expensive building zones in exchange for kickbacks and votes.

The city of Palermo that tourists visit today is the blatant monument to the post-war alliance of the Mafia and DCs: a monstrous sprawl of asphalt and cement, high-rise after high-rise in a dull monotony that took the place of the few Art Nouveau buildings that had resisted the bombing of 1943, crumbling walls built with cement illegally mixed with sand, and a lack of basic urban services. This is what remains today of what was called 'the sack of Palermo': the signatures behind the sack are those of Salvo Lima, mayor of Palermo (1958–63 and 1965–8); Vito Ciancimino, councillor for public works until 1970 and then mayor; the 'King of Cement' Francesco Vassallo, in the construction business with ties to the families of Angelo La Barbera and Tommaso Buscetta; and Luciano Leggio who, with his trucking company, moved the tons of cement needed for the sack.

In some ways 'what befell Palermo in the post-war building boom was much the same as happened to cities all over the world': a construction industry looking for 'friends' in local and regional councils; councilmen ready, for a kickback and some votes, to pass information on which project can be approved and what bid can win; zoning laws becoming synonymous with land speculation; high-rise concrete blocks mushrooming everywhere; and, above all, the same incessant rhetoric on the virtues of 'modernization'.[57] In Palermo too, this modus operandi and rhetoric had its fervent supporters and its adversaries – within Mafia ranks as well.

Emblematic of this contrast was the dispute between Corleone's boss, Dr Michele Navarra, and his soldier Luciano Leggio. Born in a family of ten, raised in extreme poverty on a small livestock farm and known both for his limping and his ruthlessness, Leggio began his career in crime as a low-ranking member of the Corleone clan. His first climb up the Mafia ladder came with the murder, on 10 March 1948, of Placido Rizzotto, who was guilty of unionizing the peasants working on the boss's land. By 1958 the only person who stood between Leggio and the title of Corleone's boss was Dr Navarra.

The hostility between the two was, on the surface, a mere land dispute, like many in Sicily (as in the mythical Far West) that pitted farmers and cattlemen against each other over water resources. In truth the conflict was much bigger and entailed two different conceptions of the Mafia. Leggio was a proponent for the construction of a dam in the valley of the Belice river. The dam was part of a general project for the modernization of Sicilian infrastructure generously funded by the Sicilian Region and the national State. For Navarra, the problem was that the dam would put an end to his monopoly on the water that peasants needed for irrigation.

For Leggio, however, the dam was excellent business – not only for his trucking company, but for the Mafia in general, which he wanted to participate more actively in the speculation over state-funded public works:

> It was a clash between two opposed calculations, two social models, and almost two opposed visions of the world: the conservatism of the heirs of the old society of the latifundium . . . and the spirit of innovation of those who could see beyond the limiting horizon of the ancient parasitic activities based on agricultural activities. In a certain sense, this was clash between backwardness and modernization. Luciano had no doubts: Navarra had to be eliminated.[58]

Leggio's execution of Navarra – who was shot on 2 August 1958, with submachine-gun bullets – was in this sense symbolic of a modern Mafia, which not only preferred the machine-gun to the traditional shotgun, but was able to let go of any feudal sense of honour in the brutal slaying of the boss.

This was because modernization, for Leggio, was not merely competition over state resources and public works. It entailed an overall rationalization of the Mafia's entire organizational apparatus, from a semi-feudal system of vassalage to a modern international corporation no longer tied to a territory. In some sense, if Franchetti's Mafia was a paradoxical mixture of feudal and modern elements, Leggio intended now to solve the paradox in favour of a thorough modernization of the Mafia.

On 12 October 1957 Leggio took part in a gathering at the lush Grand Hotel et Des Palmes in Palermo that included a rather interesting group of fellows: the seat of honour was reserved for Lucky Luciano; following were Joe Bananas (Giuseppe Bonanno) and Frank Carrol (Francesco Garofalo) of the Bonanno family; Camillo Galante, Giovanni Bonventre and Joseph Palermo of the Lucchese family; Santo Sorge, Vito Di Vitale and John Di Bella of the Genovese family; and Vito Vitale of the Priziola family from Detroit.

The meeting was a key moment in the birth of a modern Cosa Nostra, whose structure was ultimately formalized in November at the villa of Joseph Barbara in Apalachin, New York.[59] At the bottom there were the 'families', cells controlling limited territories and composed of 'soldiers', capidecina or heads of ten-men units, and a managerial 'representative' assisted by an advisor or consigliere. At the intermediate level there were the mandamenti, or groupings of three or more families operating in contiguous territories. At the top stood the 'Committee' or Cupola, composed of the heads of each mandamento and presided over by a man of mutual trust.

Structural rationalization was quickly followed by the modernization of Franchetti's old 'industry of violence' into a fully fledged corporation specializing in the supply of socially desirable goods – notably prostitution, protection and heroin. Sicily offered this new Mafia supplementary business opportunities in the competition for public works, spurred by the funds of the Marshall Plan, and by the newly created Cassa per il Mezzogiorno (Fund for the South), instituted in 1950 for the modernization of infrastructures in the South.[60] To profit from the Italian euphoria for construction and modernization, Leggio's Mafia could rely, once more, on its strong ties with the party in power – the Christian Democrats.

The corruption of the DCs might have been more visible in Palermo; such corruption, however, extended to the whole island and up to the headquarters of the party in Rome. As Rosi made clear in his movie, the Mafia, including those who planned the massacre in Portella, now sat in parliament. In Rome, for instance, was Amintore Fanfani, leader of the DCs from 1954 to 1959. Under his leadership, the party underwent its wholesale modernization. Modernization meant one thing for Fanfani: party leaders had to be elected not by the leadership of the party but democratically by party members. Fanfani's strategy sounded democratic. It was, however, a scam. In Palermo, 'party members' were all the names – real and fictitious – to whom Fanfani's ally mafioso Giovanni Gioia had given a membership card: friends and relatives, but also dead people, characters from films and novels and other names just taken from the phone book. The sudden increase of memberships in Palermo meant one thing: Gioia and Fanfani could elect whomever they wanted to the party's leadership.[61]

Rosi's movie, the first public denunciation of the alliance between Roman politics and the Sicilian Mafia, could not but displease Fanfani, who had just been nominated Prime Minister as *Salvatore Giuliano* was undergoing its last cuts. For several months the censorship office, which Fanfani's party managed as if Italy still were in the grips of Fascism, kept the movie out of circulation. It was only a rebellion from within the Sicilian DCs that finally took Rosi's film out of the censorship office with a 'pass'. In 1961 Giuseppe D'Angelo, the governor of Sicily who belonged to the Aldo Moro faction of the DCs pitted against Fanfani, asked for a governmental investigation into the misdeeds of the Sicilian DCs. The investigation did not produce much but at least, on 28 February 1962, *Salvatore Giuliano* could finally have its premiere.

Boom!

'Boom! Boom! Boom! Boom!' were the sounds . . .
– Steve E. Wright, *Bloodline of a Mafia*

The movie premiered at Teatro Politeama in Palermo. Aside from the usual entourage of journalists and authorities, the theatre was filled by an unexpected crowd: the people of Montelepre, Salvatore Giuliano's hometown.

Since the beginning Rosi had wanted to involve the villagers actively in the movie. In neorealist fashion he did not trust professional actors, and preferred real people representing their own lived experiences. For the role of Giuliano's mother crying at the morgue over the dead body of her son, Rosi had chosen a woman whose son had been shot in similarly mysterious circumstances. For the scene of Montelepre's women protesting the arrests, Rosi again had villagers play the part:

> In an interview with Michel Ciment, Rosi explained that he wanted to film this scene with the actual women of Montelepre, but that as proper Sicilian women they didn't want to be on camera or be perceived as 'actresses'. He thus hired a large number of women from nearby Palermo – prostitutes, the only ones willing to do the job – and had them bussed over to the location. Once he began filming however, the women of Montelepre also took to the streets, refusing to be represented by others.[62]

Rosi also wanted to know directly from the people of Montelepre what they knew of Salvatore Giuliano – what they remembered or thought to remember.

Certainly, for a biopic such as this, extensive research in governmental archives and police records had been done (the scene of the trial, for instance, is a faithful reproduction of court transcripts). However, apart from the fact that Rosi distrusted the official record, not much could be found in it anyway: the circumstances of Giuliano's death were, and still are, held as a state secret for 'national security' reasons until 2016. The voice of the people, in short, needed to be heard, particularly since Rosi's belief was that cinema, as a social instrument, had to be in the hands of the very people it purported to represent.[63] This was not to be *his* movie: in a disdainful refusal of the *auteur* mystique, this was a collective 'narrative of the people'.[64]

The people of Montelepre, invited for the first (and last) time in their lives to such a gala occasion, must have certainly anticipated with eagerness the showing of *their* movie. Alas neither their expectations, nor Rosi's, were to be met:

> At the premiere at the Politeama Theater in Palermo, you could feel the disappointment of the public – more so of the people who had come from Montelepre . . . They were expecting a dramatic story packed with action and adventure; a story on the life and deeds of Giuliano that would celebrate his myth.[65]

Sure, disappointment for a myth dispelled must have had its role in Rosi's failed popular experiment. But the whole truth is that Italians in 1962, the citizens of Montelepre included, had little interest in the Mafia, politics or rural Sicily.

These were the years of Italy's so-called economic boom. Presaged in a reportage for The Economist in April 1958, the boom was the dawn of a 'new Italy . . . just dragged, kicking and screaming, into the twentieth century'.[66] In the span of only four years, Italy had quickly transformed its largely rural economy into an industrial and urban one. Indeed Italy's was 'one of the fastest industrial growths Europe had ever seen': production had increased at an annual rate of 8.4 per cent and by 1962 Italy alone accounted for 12 per cent of the total European industrial production.[67] Per capita income, which the United Nations calculated as 350,000 lire per month in 1951, within the range of 'underdevelopment', reached a more comfortable 571,000 lire per month by 1961.

As Italy continued to broadcast its glowing success through the new symbol of the boom – the television set – a sense of what poet Giuseppe Goffredo had called 'shame' had settled on the country.[68] It was shame for the recent past of hunger and hardship that the village of Montelepre, Sicily, still represented: the women in black shawls, the unpaved roads, the bandits . . . There was no desire to see on screen a Montelepre, no matter how true, that contradicted the common sense of the age: progress, development and modernity. What Italians wanted to see, instead, were the glittering images of the boom: Domenico Modugno's 'Volare' – 'in the blue painted with blue, so happy to be high up there'; Vespas and Cinquecentos; Fellini's La Dolce vita; television games, quizzes, prizes and ballerinas; and, above all, the now pervasive commedia all'italiana.

The country, in short, wanted cheerfully to enjoy the fruits of its recent wealth, not mourn with Rosi the abortion of the post-war Republic. Nor was it inclined, pace Rosi, to interrogate the sources of its modern comfort: how much of that boom was, like the building of modern Palermo, the legacy of Mafia affairs? In the same years that Salvatore Giuliano hit Italian theatres, Alberto Lattuada asked that very question in one of the most hilarious, but also most bitter, commedia ever concocted by Italian cinema: Mafioso. Aware of the epochal propensity of Italians for laughter, Lattuada was perhaps the first to realize that everything – the Mafia included – had to be turned into comedy in the Italy of the economic boom. Yet he was not willing to let laughter get in the way of a most serious, if at times cynical, analysis of modern Italy's wealth.

Palermo Cathedral, Sicily, c. 1943.

Sicilian Antonino Badalamenti (played by Alberto Sordi at his best) has made it in Milan, capital and epicentre of Italy's economic boom. The symbols of his success are for everyone to see: foreman in a modern-looking industry, he has a house filled with comfort (electric gadgets, from blenders to hairdryers, are anticipations of Jacques Tati's *Play Time*), a beautiful wife (of course blonde and northern) and two cute daughters (blonde too). On the eve of his departure for his native Sicily for summer vacation, he is summoned to the office of the factory manager, Dr Zanchi. Zanchi grew up in Trenton – 'Near Venice?' 'No, New Jersey' – where he had emigrated from Calamo, the imaginary Sicilian village where Antonino himself grew up, and where he is going to spend his family vacation. Zanchi asks Antonino – it is 'just a little favour' – to bring to Calamo a present from 'some common friends' to Don Vincenzo, the local 'notable'.

The reader of a book on the Mafia will be quite able to decode properly the words 'favour', 'friends', 'Don' and 'notable' without me having to spoil a most hilarious plot. The point is that, whether in a comedy or not, the Mafia of Lattuada's movie, like the coeval real-life Mafia, is a money-making machine which has spread its reach from Sicily to Milan, New York and New Jersey. If the Mafia had been for Germi the imaginary champion of a popular *ressentiment* against the State, in Lattuada's film the Mafia became the pretext 'to offer a dark commentary on the nature of modern capitalism', and an even darker one on Italy's economic boom.[69]

As a matter of fact this marriage of Mafia and business was before everyone's eyes by 1962. From Palermo to Milan, and from Milan to Wall Street (whose stock market was closely followed by the Gambino family), the Mafia had quite a few levers of power in financial markets.[70] The key figure of this financial Mafia was, beyond doubt, Michele Sindona, who we met briefly in chapter One, as the inheritor of Calvi's affairs with the Vatican Bank after Calvi was 'suicided' on London's Blackfriars Bridge. A Sicilian tax lawyer and accountant working in Milan for the Società Generale Immobiliare (Italy's nationwide real estate company), by 1957 he was already managing the profits of the Gambino family of New York and laundering heroin money for the families of Stefano Bontate (*mandamento* of Palermo), Salvatore Inzerillo and Rosario Spatola (*mandamento* of Corleone).

In 1958 Sindona managed to buy his first bank to ease his laundering operations, and then many more, including shares in the Vatican Bank (the pretext for the Vatican subplot of The Godfather Part III) and Long Island's Franklin National Bank. Giorgio Ambrosoli, the lawyer investigating Sindona, was murdered in Milan on 11 July 1979. Sindona was finally arrested in the United States by the FBI, convicted in 1980 and extradited to Italy where he was sentenced in 1984 to 25 years in prison. On 18 March 1986 he was poisoned by cyanide in the coffee served to his cell – meeting the same death as Gaspare Pisciotta, Salvatore Giuliano's lieutenant.

If the Mafia had started to wear a suit and a tie and play its fortunes in the stock market, that did not mean it had forgotten its old methods. On 30 June 1963 two cars parked in the suburbs of Palermo exploded, killing two bystanders and seven policemen. The bombs were likely intended for the Greco family, which controlled the areas of Ciaculli and Villabate where the explosions had taken place. It was the beginning of an internecine Mafia war – the so-called 'First Mafia War' – between the Grecos and, most likely, the family of Tommaso Buscetta. The police, in turn, declared a new open war against the Mafia. A different sort of boom was going to be heard in Palermo: 'In late 1962 and early 1963, explosions, car chases, and shoot-outs suddenly became regular events in Palermo.'[71]

Italians, however, seemed determined not to notice. All that Lattuada's movie had managed to accomplish was to open the way for the Mafia comedy. Its king was Giorgio Simonelli, and the Sicilian duo Franco Franchi and Ciccio Ingrassia (a cross between Jerry Lewis and Laurel and Hardy) were its jesters: *The Two Mafiosos* (1964), *Two Mafiosos in the Far West* (1964), *Two Mafiosos against Goldfinger* (1965) and *Two Mafiosos against Al Capone* (1966). The silent reign of *omertà* seemed at its end: the din of money, the clamour of the boom and, above all, raucous laughter were swallowing an old Mafia into the hubbub of the new. In the rumpus, the age of the Mafia western also came to a close: the frontier had been conquered. It was the beginning of the gold rush.

FOUR

The Godfather

Funny thing is, I've never been interested in the Mafia.
— Francis Ford Coppola, interview, *Playboy*

With Italy still chuckling at the *commedia* of the boom, the Mafia was resurfacing on American screens. There was, to be sure, little reason to laugh.

From May 1950 to May 1951 Senator Estes Kefauver's Special Committee to Investigate Organized Crime held public hearings in fourteen cities, calling more than 600 witnesses to testify. If a boom was ever mentioned at the hearings, it was that of the 'bombing, and other forms of violence to eliminate competitors and to compel customers to take articles sold by the mobsters'.[1] While Kefauver's report still believed in Pitrè's resilient myth that 'the Mafia was originally one of many secret societies organized in Sicily to free the island of foreign domination', it also made clear that a much less patriotic Mafia had landed in the United States. Senator Charles Tobey summed up the Committee's warning: 'Wake up, America!'

As a matter of fact America did wake up, every morning, to news of the Special Committee's investigation. Kefauver, and the Mafia along with him, had discovered the marvels of a new medium – the television – which, while commercially available since the 1920s, had become only recently a symbol of the post-war economic boom:

the three major networks then in existence, ABC, CBS and NBC, televised the hearings live in a rare coast-to-coast hook-up. The parade of shady characters – bookies, pimps, politicians and slippery lawyers – on TV screens captivated the nation, becoming television's first spectacular live public event, drawing an unprecedented audience of between 20 and 30 million viewers daily.[2]

The televised parade included the 'godfather' (the term having first appeared in Kefauver's report) of the Lucchese family, Tommy himself.

Don Vito of the Genovese family was also there; while he was appearing in front of the committee, he still managed to have Vincent Mangano killed and take his place as boss of the Gambino family. The killer of Mangano, the up-and-coming Albert Anastasia, also made an appearance on television: he announced his presence at the hearings, certainly to the displeasure of Genovese, as the new godfather of the Gambino family (only to be assassinated in 1957 while taking a shave at the local barber shop). The true star of the show, however, was beyond a doubt Francesco Castiglia, better known as Frank Costello.

A native of Italy, Francesco had risen to the top of the U.S. Mafia organization when Lucky Luciano, still in Sing Sing, had put him in charge of family interests. His origins had been as a low-rank soldier of the Morello family, whose misdeeds we followed in the 'Body in the Barrel' case solved by Lieutenant Petrosino. A meticulous military strategist, Costello gained Luciano's trust when he plotted the assassinations of the two men – Joe 'the Boss' Masseria and Salvatore Maranzano – who stood in Luciano's way to the top of the *cupola*: Masseria was gunned down at the Scarpato's restaurant in Coney Island on 15 April 1931 and Maranzano died in his Helmsley Building office in Manhattan on 10 September 1931, ambushed, à la Capone's St Valentine's Day massacre, by gunmen posing as IRS agents. As *consigliere* of the Luciano family, Costello controlled the slot machine and bookmaking operation. As boss, he expanded the gambling business with slot machines in New Orleans, casinos in Florida and Cuba, and illegal race wires in Los Angeles. Costello also cultivated political connections with City Hall to an unprecedented extent: William O'Dwyer, New York's 100th mayor, was a regular guest at his cocktail parties.

Caught by the IRS on charges of tax evasion (his wife had gone on a spending binge of some undeclared $570,000!), Costello had to appear in front of Kefauver's committee. While consenting to be televised, he stipulated that his face was not to be shown. Cameras focused on his hands, while the microphones broadcasted his peculiar voice (its unnatural timbre was the consequence of botched throat surgery), heavily accented in Italian:

> The eerie combination of Costello's hands and his accented, gravel-crunching voice cast him in a more sinister and mysterious role than showing his face on television. His hands became the frightening symbol of an otherwise unseen criminal empire.[3]

That very voice was said to be the inspiration for Marlon Brando's performance as the godfather in one of Francis Ford Coppola's most successful movies. The first appearance of Don Corleone in *The Godfather* – a hand moving slowly towards a chin in the dimly lit study – was also an allusion to the image of the Mafia that Costello had imprinted on the American public's imagination.

Twelve years later, the Mafia was on television again. Thirty-five-year-old Robert Kennedy had risen to the role of United States Attorney General, the country's top law-enforcement office. While his family was rumoured to have Mafia connections, Robert had set as a priority for his office to destroy not only the Mafia as an organization but also, more pressingly, its reach into politics and labour unions. A special unit of the FBI and a Senate Labor Rackets Committee were put in place. In 1962 a major breakthrough came for Kennedy: Joe Valachi, a small-time drug dealer and low-ranking soldier of the Luciano family, decided, for reasons that are still unclear, to become an informer.[4]

Through the month of October 1963 Valachi testified before Arkansas Senator John McClellan's Permanent Subcommittee on Investigations of the U.S. Senate Committee. The testimony was again broadcast live on television. Valachi introduced Americans to the initiation ritual of the pricked finger; insisted in using the term 'godfather' to indicate the head of each family; translated for the committee the locution 'Cosa Nostra' – 'our thing and our family', he said it meant; and, above all, testified to the existence of a Mafia without scruples which reached, as Kennedy and McClellan had always suspected, into all crannies of power.

Valachi's description of how the Mafia controlled business, politics and the unions presented America with a new problem: how to distinguish between legal and illegal business? As McClellan had feared:

> The testimony we have heard can leave no doubt that there has been a concerted effort by members of the American criminal syndicate to achieve legitimacy through association and control of labor unions and business firms. The extent of the infiltration poses a serious threat to the very economy of our country.[5]

The public following Valachi's testimony on TV was mesmerized and terrified at the same time. Joseph McCarthy's communist scare had been replaced by a new one. These were frightening times, indeed. On the evening of 22 November TVs reported on the assassination of President

John F. Kennedy, Robert's older brother. In Tampa Santo Trafficante, the local boss, was toasting: 'The son-of-a-bitch is dead.'

Three years after the broadcasting of Valachi's testimony, Hays's Production Code was definitively abandoned. If televisions could show, with Valachi, the real face of the Mafia and if organized crime had continued to exist and prosper despite the silence of Hollywood, what sense was there in operating under Hays's guidelines?

Thirty-eight years of the Production Code had left Hollywood, sieged by the spread of televisions and weakened by the competition of other countries' national cinemas, which operated without the same strictures. The crisis was worrisome: employment in Hollywood was down 42.9 per cent on figures from the 1920s; Paramount Pictures alone had had to fire 1,100 of its employees.

In 1968 a floundering Paramount needed to try something new. It nominated Robert Evans, ex-actor and fashion industry executive, as head of production. Evans, whose aggressive style was soon to be noted, could not have come to the new job at a better time: with the Production Code lifted, there was no doubt that what Paramount needed to remedy all its problems was a new Mafia blockbuster to revive the golden age of *Scarface*. Evans bought the screen rights for a manuscript titled *Mafia* from a barely known Mario Puzo for $12,500. A journalist for magazines such as *Male* and *Swank*, Puzo had already tried his hand at some ambitious novels. Their complete lack of success, and his growing debts (he was said to be a compulsive gambler), convinced him that it was time to put his writerly ambitions to the side and submit, like Giovanni Verga one century before, to the imperatives of a literary market in search of sensationalist Mafia stories. As Coppola said:

> Mario, who is a very fine writer, was going broke with several good novels out, so he set out to write the biggest bestseller in history. He was going to do anything he had to in order to get off the merry-go-round. So he wrote the perfect commercial book.[6]

Evans was not the only one in Hollywood thinking of a Mafia movie as the panacea for American cinema's trouble. In 1970, one year after the manuscript of the unknown Puzo had become a best-seller with the new title of *The Godfather*, Burt Lancaster's production company became increasingly interested in partnering with Evans for the production of a film

Frank Costello testifying before the Kefauver Committee
to investigate organized crime, 1951.

based on Puzo's novel. The only condition was that Lancaster would act in the film. He too needed a boost for his career.

Evans was not particularly keen on the idea – either because he did not think Lancaster was good for the part of the godfather or because, more likely, he did not want to share with anyone the profits of what already smelled like success. At any rate Evans had bigger problems to deal with, starting with the question of who could direct the film.

Peter Bart, executive at Paramount, had an idea: Francis Ford Coppola. Sure, if The Godfather was to make money, Coppola was perhaps not the ideal choice: until then, Coppola had directed only one low-budget B-movie (Dementia 13) and three studio films (You Are a Big Boy Now, The Rain People and Finian's Rainbow), which had been disasters at the box office. On the other hand, who besides an Italian-American could direct a film on the Mafia? Anyone who had no claim to an Italian heritage – Richard Brooks, Constantin Costa-Gavras, Elia Kazan, Franklin J. Schaffner, Fred Zinnemann, Lewis Gilbert and Peter Yates – had flatly refused to get into a potential wasp's nest of ethnic politics and recriminations.[7] Though not ideal, Coppola remained the best choice for a Mafia film.

Not that Coppola liked the idea:

When I was offered the project, I started to read the book and I got only about fifty pages into it. I thought it was a popular, sensationalist novel, pretty cheap stuff . . . I said, 'My God, what is this – *The Carpetbaggers*?' So I stopped reading it and said, 'Forget it.' Four or five months later, I was again offered the opportunity to work on it and by that time I was in dire financial straits . . . so I read further.[8]

But once Coppola, willy-nilly, had accepted, Paramount had still more troubles to solve.

A major one was the New York chapter of the Italian-American Civil Rights League (incidentally created in 1970 by crime boss Joe Colombo) which, after the announcement that a Mafia movie would be made, had promptly organized a rally in Madison Square Garden to protest 'the connection of Italians *equals* organized crime'.[9] Evans was prepared: an Italian-American director and an Italian-American screenwriter (not to speak of a cast overflowing with Italian-American names) were the guarantee that no offence was meant. Negotiations between Coppola and the League (Puzo had not been able to participate, as he was at Duke University's weight-reduction clinic, next door to my house) came to at least one agreement: there would be no mention whatsoever of the Mafia or Cosa Nostra in the movie, although concessions were made to name the 'Five Families'.

This masterpiece of political correctness obviously did not solve much. New York State Senator John Marchi still feared a mythification of the greatest scourge of the Italian-American community. Similar concerns were being expressed from many quarters. The movie proceeded into production anyway with a planned release date of Christmas 1971, though further touches, especially on Coppola's long takes, needed to be made in early 1972. When the movie finally premiered on 14 March, the success was beyond Evans's and Paramount's expectations: $81 million was cashed in on the first run. The polemics, however, did not end. As if to confirm Senator Marchi's fears, 'the film marked an indelible date in the history of cinema by contributing to the creation of a mythical image of the mafia.'[10] Accusations of immorality for romanticizing and mythifying the Mafia continued.

The very figure of the godfather Vito Corleone, a synthesis of real Mafia bosses Vito Genovese and Joseph Profaci (plus Frank Costello's hands and voice), was by Coppola's own admission a 'mythic' one: while the fictional Don 'is honorable and will not do business with drugs', his real counterparts, no doubt, 'did just that'.[11] Moreover the 'old Mafia' of Don Vito, contrasted in the movie with the new, corrupt one of the Sollozzos, makes of the Mafia a somewhat mythical tradition to be protected from modern perversions – very much according to Pitrè's paradigm. A 'beautiful' Mafia 'in the proper sense' is under siege; in modern times, 'the word *mafioso* no longer has, for many, its original and authentic meaning.'[12] It is then perfectly legitimate and reasonable to argue that '*The Godfather* has captured the essence of the Mafia myth. It has bought into it and sold it to the world.'[13]

Yet if a myth is at work in *The Godfather*, are we sure it is the myth of the Mafia? Coppola, for his part, denied the charge: 'it's a mistake to think I was making a film about the Mafia. *Godfather* I is a romance about a king with three sons.'[14] Strange as it may sound, Coppola's denial in fact seems applicable to all stories about the Mafia we have seen so far, as they are not so much reports on a real criminal organization but, if not myths, at least fictions – fictions that address very real social needs, desires, aspirations, fears and anxieties that go beyond the Mafia itself: Verga's need to regain a passionate life lost in the bureaucratization and modernization of post-independence Italy; Germi's desire to imagine a champion of the people against the post-war alliance of feudal aristocracy and State authorities; Rosi's aspiration to penetrate the veil of deceit woven by Italy's political system and its international allies; *Scarface*'s fear of Italian immigration and the miscegenation of Anglo-Saxon blood in America; Lattuada's anxiety vis-à-vis the capitalist modernization of the boom . . .

It is no surprise, then, that Coppola would see *The Godfather* as a 'myth', yes, but one concerning something other than the Mafia: the Shakespeare-like myth of 'a king with three sons', perhaps, in a tale of power, heredity and intrigue.[15] Or else a myth, in the tradition of the gangster film of the 1920s, of the great American Dream – but updated for the new circumstances.

'I Believe in America'

SOLLOZZO: I don't like violence, Tom. I'm a business man.
– *The Godfather*, dir. Françis Ford Coppola

'I believe in America.' With these words, pronounced over a dark screen, *The Godfather* begins. It is a tribute and an allusion to those movies – *Little Caesar* and *Scarface* above all – that made the gangster film the genre capable of narrating the Italian-American way of participating in the myth of the American Dream. Alluding to the same genre is the heavily inflected accent of the character pronouncing those words. The face of Amerigo Bonasera fades in – Amerigo like the explorer Vespucci who gave his name to the New Continent, and 'buonasera' as in 'goodnight'.

From the shadow, the imposing mass of Marlon Brando as Don Corleone emerges – first his hands, and then his mouth, famously filled with wads of Kleenex. He frowns, as if bored. In this first series of shots and counter-shots, the camera searches the expressions, sometimes fearful and sometimes satisfied, of the petitioners who have come to offer 'friendship' in exchange for a slice of that America in which they believe.

> Francis Ford Coppola could not devise a better stylistic solution to render explicit, from its very outset, the ideological stake of the film: throughout the 1970s, Coppola is the American director that more assiduously than anyone has dispelled mercilessly the myth of the 'American Dream'.[16]

There seems to be little doubt, given such an opening, that America is at stake in this movie. But which America? And which myth is being mercilessly dispelled?

In an essay of 1990, Fredric Jameson wrote that he believed this was the myth of American capitalism:

> When indeed we reflect on an organized conspiracy against the public, one which reaches into every corner of our daily lives and our political structures to exercise a wanton ecocidal and genocidal violence at the behest of distant decision-makers and in the name of an abstract conception of profit – surely it is not about the Mafia, but rather about American business itself that we are thinking, American capitalism in its most systematized and computerized, dehumanized, 'multinational' and corporate form.[17]

Jameson's intuition is quite convincing: Peter Bart of Paramount himself, through conversations with Coppola, had come to the conclusion that The Godfather was a movie 'with the Mob as a metaphor for capitalism'.[18] While 'capitalism' may not be a word much used in Puzo and Coppola's screenplay, 'business' most certainly is (48 times, to be precise). Don Vito,

Michael and Tom the *consigliere* all speak of 'the family business'; and the cliché 'it's not personal, just business' is repeated twice – both times to announce a murder.

As I have remarked in previous pages, the theme of business runs throughout the whole *Godfather* trilogy, and we saw that business was for Coppola both a personal problem (his artistic ambitions frustrated by Hollywood's money-making machine) and a social one (all that is truly valuable in life, as an old Michael Corleone realizes in *The Godfather Part III*, is sacrificed to monetary success). In this sense Coppola's ambiguous feelings of attraction to and repulsion for the Mafia could be understood as a metaphor of sorts for the contradictions of capital: it stands to signify Michael's impossible struggle to reconcile, for instance, the contradictory values of family and success; or Coppola's own impossibility to reconcile artistic ambitions with the success that only a Mafia movie could bring.

This ambiguity, this contradiction is, as we have already seen, the very narrative engine of the gangster film of the 1920s and '30s: the desire for success, a social imperative to make it, doubles into fear, the anxiety of failing or, even if succeeding, of being destroyed in the process. The final demise of the gangster as tragic hero, dying alone and shunned by society, was the sacrifice through which the classical gangster film ritualized this social oscillation between desire and fear.

To an extent, *The Godfather* pays tribute to the classic gangster flick: all the Corleones are, in a sense, classic tragic heroes. They always lose something dear in the process of making it to the top. On the other hand *The Godfather* certainly remains a most radical refashioning of the gangster genre in the history of cinema.

Such refashioning is needed for compelling reasons: historical conditions had changed greatly from the Prohibition and the Depression era. Bonasera's speech early in the movie suggests precisely that times are a-changing:

> I raised my daughter in the American fashion. I gave her freedom, but – I taught her never to dishonor her family. She found a boyfriend; not an Italian. She went to the movies with him; she stayed out late. I didn't protest.

Coppola insists with his interviewer from *Playboy*: 'we're living in a time when things are changing quickly. Zip, there went the Catholic Church; zoom, that was the traditional family unit you just saw go by.'[19]

On the one hand, The Godfather attempts to resist such changes. Against the disruption of traditional values, against the waning, precisely, of the Catholic Church, Coppola deploys here the old trope of the 'devout Mafia': the way in which the Mafia, starting with its initiation rituals, has always participated in 'collective religious ceremonies' under the banner of an albeit distorted Catholicism.[20]

The fact that mafiosi have traditionally professed their faith is not in itself surprising. Already at the turn of the last century, the French sociologist Émile Durkheim had linked the rise of homicide rates with the growth of those 'collective feelings whose interests reside in . . . religion': 'When it is a matter . . . of avenging a God, can the life of a man count in the scale? It counts indeed very little when offset against objects of such value and weight.'[21] Whether the particular mixture of religion and crime typical of the Mafia can be attributed to the particular pagan traits found in Sicilian Catholicism (the culturalist explanation), or whether religion functions merely as a form of legitimating crime in the name of a higher justice (the utilitarian explanation), it remains a fact that the Church and the Mafia have always been odd bedfellows. The boss Michele Greco liked to be called 'The Pope' ('U Papa). He was arrested while he was reading the Bible. The boss Antonino Mangano, instead, preferred the moniker of 'Our Lord' ('U Signiruzzu); it was he who decided, after all, who lived or died. The Mafia, as Alessandra Dino writes poignantly, 'believes that divine justice coincides with "the justice of the Mafia" and they are the "official interpreter"'.[22]

Punctuated by Catholic rituals – weddings, baptisms (and their atten-dant godfathering) – The Godfather is to this extent but a continuation of a typical motif of the Mafia film genre, which had faithfully represented this convergence of Catholic rituals and organized crime: the crucifixes of Scarface; the mourning rituals of Salvatore Giuliano; the churches and the statues of saints of Mafioso. By continuing in the tradition of the classic film genre, it is as if Coppola were trying to ward off the changes brought about by the new times – changes, as we have seen, that coincided with the new trends of American 'business'. In this sense Catholic rituals and iconography represent here an 'implicit moral rebuke . . . to American capitalism's systemic tendency to turn people against their deepest beliefs and commitments'.[23]

Needless to say, however, as much as Coppola tries to embrace this old world of religious rituals, as much as he tries to stick to the themes of the classic gangster films, traditional values are fast disappearing.

Michael's killing of his enemies while his godson is being baptized is a clear hint that 'business' is triumphing already, and that its 'systemic tendency to turn people against their deepest beliefs and commitments' has only a few obstacles left to overcome. By the time of the third *Godfather*, in fact, 'Catholicism is revealed as another racket, another set of opportunities to gain advantage by lying to yourself and to others.'[24]

Nor are Catholic rituals the only sort of tradition that Coppola tries to pit – always in vain – against the advancing new. Another is that of the family. 'A man who doesn't spend time with his family can never be a real man', says Don Vito. In the context of post-1968, when precisely the nuclear family was under attack, 'the conservative Family values of the Don constituted the kind of fantasy that Americans were likely to embrace.'[25] Paradoxically, however, it is in order to embrace the tradition of family values that Coppola needs to dispense with another tradition: that of the classic gangster movie. In fact, whereas *Little Caesar* and *Scarface* were ready to abandon family values – think of *Scarface*'s incest in a household run by a single mother – to embrace 'the principles of a Darwinian power struggle', with Coppola 'the Don exerts patriarchal authority over his Family. Those who work closest to him are not hired men but his own sons or adopted "godsons" all of whom respect him not as the leader of a corporation but as the upholder [of family values].'[26] It is around the theme of the family, then, that *The Godfather* begins to redirect the paradigm of gangster-cinema conventions towards a new direction: the parable of the Mafia movie is no longer *aspiration* for future reaches, but rather *nostalgia* for a lost world of which family values (rather than monetary values of exchange) are but a synecdoche. The loss of the beloved brother Sonny, as we already know, is only the first of a long sequence of losses that will punctuate Michael Corleone's entire saga, and which will culminate in the aching nostalgia of *The Godfather Part III*.

There is an even more radical change in respect of classic gangster-cinema conventions registered in *The Godfather*. For the American baby boomers of the late 1960s and early '70s who went to watch the film, the aspirations of Tony 'Scarface' Camonte had now been squarely realized. If Tony's dream was to change his shirt every day, that dream was now effortlessly attainable. In the vaunted affluence of mass-produced commodities, 'the cornucopian bounty of [the] system's surplus' – as the youth movement of the 1960s liked to say – were up for grabs.[27] In fact, even for the protagonists of *The Godfather*, a film set in the economic boom of post-war America, what used to be a dream had become reality: Michael

Corleone changes not only his shirts, but no fewer than 'five different ties throughout the film'.[28] The Christmas shopping flaunted in the first part of *The Godfather*, to the soundtrack of 'Have Yourself a Merry Little Christmas', becomes the emblem of a democratization of consumerism that, while underway in the 1940s, was certainly completed by the mid-1960s: 'everybody', says Michael, 'is goin' out to the mall.'

So, while Tony Camonte's gaudy excess created a distance between him and the viewer, Michael's bountiful shopping – at the promisingly-named 'Best & Co.' – instead 'entices the viewer to identify with . . . Michael'.[29] For this reason, the fate of the Mafia hero is no longer death (Michael will survive *The Godfather Part I*); nor is it individual isolation – 'to draw himself out of the crowd'.[30] In a society in which, as Marshall McLuhan lamented, 'the individual voice and singular point of view disappears into the chorus of a corporate and collective consciousness', even the tragic hero loses himself in the crowd.[31] No longer the sacrificial lamb of the society of the 1920s – 'The dilemma is resolved because of his death, not ours'[32] – he has finally become us:

> Although the tradition of the gangster film required a hero that we as an audience could clearly constitute as 'other' from us . . . *The Godfather* gives us a man that we want to be, or that we can't help being.[33]

The much-criticized sympathy Coppola's movie instils in us for his mafioso protagonist – our enjoyment of his power, our trepidations for his first homicide, our sustained empathy, the blunt fact that we like him – does not necessarily mean that we are abetting the Mafia here. More simply we are recognizing the hero's fate – having crowned the American Dream – as ours: 'I thought it was healthy', said Coppola, 'to make this horror-story statement – as a warning.'[34]

But where was the horror of this story, exactly, if success was now for everybody? Even for Italian-Americans, mafioso or not, the affluence of the post-war era was a done deal: 'America has made my fortune', declares Bonasera, an undertaker whose problem, from Don Vito's perspective, is that he never wanted to have anything to do with the Mafia. 'I understand', answers Corleone, 'you found paradise in America, had a good trade, made a good living.' Another successful businessman, and also not a mafioso, is the Italian-American Nazorine, owner of a successful pastry shop. In fact if the classic gangster film presented the Italian mafioso as the pathological perversion of the American Dream, Coppola presents instead the mafioso as the American Dream *tout court*:

> Right from the very beginning it became clear, as I was doing my research, that though the Mafia was a Sicilian phenomenon, there was no way it could really have flowered except in the soil of America. America was absolutely ripe for the Mafia. Everything the Mafia believed in and was set up to handle – absolute control, the carving out of territories, the rigging of prices and the elimi- nation of competition – everything was here. In fact, the corporate philosophy that built some of our biggest industries and great personal fortunes was a Mafia philosophy. So when those Italians arrived here, they found themselves in the perfect place. It became clear to me that there was a wonderful parallel to be drawn, that the career of Michael Corleone was the perfect metaphor for the new land. Like America, Michael began as a clean, brilliant young man endowed with incredible resources and believing in a humanistic idealism. Like America, Michael was the child of an older system, a child of Europe. Like America, Michael was an innocent who had tried to correct the ills and injustices of his progenitors. But then he got blood on his hands. He lied to himself and to others about what he was doing and why.[35]

The fact that America, like Michael, may have 'lied' is the first hint of a myth that Coppola wants to dispel. That Michael flatly lies to Kay, we do know: 'No!' he answers when asked if he has had his brother-in-law murdered! But what has America lied to itself and to others about? What horror stood behind what appeared, on the surface, as the full if complacent realization of the Dream?

'Leave the Gun, Take the Cannoli'

KURTZ: The horror . . . the horror . . .
– *Apocalypse Now*, dir. Francis Ford Coppola

The plot of *The Godfather Part I* is quite straightforward: after Don Corleone refuses to get in the drug business with the Sollozzo family, he becomes an obstacle for the remaining four families. He becomes the target for a failed assassination that leaves him hospitalized for some time, and then in frail health until his death. As Michael takes the Don's place, a war against the Sollozzos, which soon bleeds into a war against all other families, ensues.

The war theme is in fact a leitmotiv across the entire movie, starting with our first view of Michael – the war hero coming home at the close of the Second World War in military uniform and decorated for valour. Sollozzo talks of a 'full-scale war'; while Tom is determined 'to avoid a long, destructive war', Sonny is for an 'all-out war', and Michael takes Sonny's side, asking Tom to step down as the family's *consigliere*: 'You're not a wartime *consigliere*.'

In the post-war America of the 1940s, no such war ever tore the five families apart. Between the murder of Salvatore Maranzano in 1931 and that of Vincent Mangano in 1951, there seemed a peaceful coexistence between the families – each content in its territory. In his chronicle *The Rise, Decline, and Resurgence of America's Most Powerful Mafia Empires*, Selwyn Raab calls this period the 'Serene Times'. A new prosperity, and a new spending binge, were stirring the whole nation: new buildings were coming up like mushrooms around Hollywood, and casinos were opening at great speed – in Cuba first and, when Fidel Castro put an end to that, in Las Vegas: the new Mafia frontier and playing ground for the Jewish Mafia of Meyer Lansky (this will be the context for Coppola's *The Godfather Part II*).

The new and lucrative business of narcotics added to all this enough new resources for all to share and be happy. The families were prospering:

Shopping spree at the mall: Santa Claus is coming. Francis Ford Coppola (dir.), *The Godfather* (Paramount Pictures, 1972).

Frank Costello, Joseph Bonanno, Joseph Profaci, Vincent Mangano and Gaetano 'Tommy' Gagliano were running profitable businesses with little friction from the law and none from each other. While murders did not cease, they were usually authorized and amicably planned by the *cupola* itself: 'By the late 1940s, the Prohibition era of bloodshed and rivalries between the New York families was a distant memory.'[36] The war to which *The Godfather* alluded must have been a different one.

In an article written for *Vanity Fair* in 2009, aptly titled 'The Godfather Wars', Mark Seal recounted Marlon Brando's interest in the movie:

> Brando was intrigued, because he saw the project as a story not of blood and guts but about the corporate mind. As he said later, 'The Mafia is so American! To me, a key phrase in the story is that whenever they wanted to kill somebody it was always a matter of policy. Before pulling the trigger, they told him, 'Just business, nothing personal'. When I read that, [Vietnam War architects Robert] McNamara, [Lyndon] Johnson, and [Dean] Rusk flashed before my eyes.[37]

When the movie was released in 1972, Brando may not have been the only one to have those images flashing before his eyes.

Lyndon Johnson had declared the U.S. involvement in the Vietnam war on 24 November 1963 to be a just 'battle against communism'.[38] After the national shocks of My Lai (1968) and Cambodia (1970), and as the Pentagon Papers were being leaked (1971), Johnson's words started sounding to many in the U.S., including those involved in the growing anti-war movement, like a 'lie': what was truly at stake in the Vietnam war, Coppola believed, was not anti-communism, but 'a desire for world power'. As he told an interviewer from the *Chicago Sun-Times*, 'The Vietnam conflict was an example of one of the many similar, illogical, ludicrous conflicts that are cooked up on the world power front that our youth are sacrificed to.'[39]

The Vietnam war was a major concern for Coppola. In 1970, even before the Vietnam epics *Apocalypse Now* (1979) and *The Gardens of Stone* (1987) – a film that producer Michael Levy described as 'pro-military, anti-war' – Coppola had co-written the screenplay for *Patton* (1970).[40] The biopic was, on the one hand, a celebration of the Second World War hero. On the other, it was a reflection on what Coppola seemed to perceive as the horror lurking under the American Dream.

Meyer Lansky leaving court.

At his sister's wedding, Michael Corleone returns as a hero from
the Second World War, in *The Godfather*.

When Patton, played by George Scott (the psychopathic General
Turgidson of Stanley Kubrick's *Dr Strangelove*), appears for the first time
in the movie, he is dwarfed by a gigantic American flag. His figure is
minuscule, almost irrelevant – a pawn, like Rosi's invisible Giuliano, in
a much bigger game.

Patton's opening speech gives a first hint of the horror Coppola
seemed to be determined to show – a 'warning', as he put it – to America:

> Men, all this stuff you've heard about America not wanting to
> fight – wanting to stay out of the war – is a lot of horse dung.
> Americans traditionally love to fight. All real Americans love the
> sting of battle. When you were kids, you all admired the cham-
> pion marble shooter, the fastest runner, big league ball players,
> the toughest boxers. Americans love a winner and will not tolerate
> a loser. Americans play to win all the time. I wouldn't give a hoot
> in hell for a man who lost and laughed. That's why Americans have
> never lost and will never lose a war, because the very thought of
> losing is hateful to Americans. Now, an army is a team – it lives,
> eats, sleeps, fights as a team. This individuality stuff is a bunch
> of crap . . . Now, we have the finest food and equipment, the
> best spirit, and the best men in the world. You know, by God,
> I actually pity those poor bastards we're goin' up against. By
> God, I do. We're not just gonna shoot the bastards, we're going
> to cut out their living guts and use them to grease the treads of

our tanks. We're going to murder those lousy Hun bastards by the bushel . . . Wade into them, spill their blood, shoot them in the belly.

It is not, for Coppola, that Patton was a criminal: he *was* a hero fighting a good war. It is not, either, that the American troops in Vietnam, or even Kurtz of *Apocalypse Now*, were criminals: as Coppola insisted, 'the Army is not making the policy.'[41] Coppola seems to tell the same war story time and again: in *Patton*, *Apocalypse Now* and *The Gardens of Stone* – in fact, in *The Godfather* films as well – a hero is taught, as an American, to win and not to tolerate a loser (poor Fredo!). When the hero does just that, he is then called a criminal: 'And they call me an assassin', says Kurtz/Marlon Brando, sounding again like Don Vito. 'What do you call it when the assassins accuse the assassin? They lie. They lie and we have to be merciful for those who lie. Those nabobs! I hate them. How I hate them!'

Patton's words, like Kurtz's, could just as well have come out of Michael's mouth. He has to win, and the fact that he does makes him a hero. Calling him an assassin, a mafioso, is just a lie – the lie of those nabobs who pretend they are different. Because, says Coppola:

> What's the difference between the United States putting a guy like Trujillo in power so our companies can operate in the Dominican Republic and the Mafia's handing the Boston territory to one of its *capos*? Then, after twenty years, either guy gets a little uppity and either organization feels free to knock him off.[42]

What's the difference, indeed? Just as Johnson sends the American youth to Vietnam to kill and be killed in the name of a 'battle against communism', so does the mafioso Barzini of *The Godfather* send his henchmen to the New York streets; 'after all', he says with a sneer, 'we are not Communists.'

The gangster hero of the 1930s had to die in order to be recognized as the pathological degeneration of the American Dream. Michael, gangster hero of the new times, refuses this ultimate sacrifice. He is no pathological degeneration; he *is* the American Dream, the very horror that lurks at its roots, and can no longer be exorcised as something different:

> MICHAEL: My father's no different than any other powerful man
> . . . Like a senator or a president.

General George Smith Patton IV addresses the troops, Franklin J. Schaffner (dir.), *Patton* (Twentieth Century Fox, 1970).

KAY (*laughing*): You know how naive you sound?
MICHAEL: Why?
KAY: Senators and presidents don't have men killed . . .
MICHAEL: Oh, who's being naive, Kay?

Filmed at a time when senators and presidents do indeed kill – 'my government chooses to send the Army into some absurd military conflict in a desire for world power' – and when senators and presidents have, in fact, been killed too, Michael's words start to dispel the myth and uncover the lie.[43] In fact it is not Michael who has been lying throughout, but Kay; naive Anglo-Saxon Kay, who repeatedly lies to herself and to us by pretending that those Italians, those Corleones, are something exotic and out of the ordinary. She is the one refusing to see the real horror, and prefers to believe, with false innocence, the convenient lie:

CONNIE: Michael! You lousy bastard, you killed my husband! You waited until Papa died so nobody could stop you, and then you killed him . . .
CONNIE (*to Kay*): Why do you think he kept Carlo at the mall? All the time he knew he was gonna kill him . . . That's your husband! That's your husband!
KAY: Michael, is it true?
MICHAEL: Don't ask me about my business, Kay . . .
KAY: Is it true?
MICHAEL: Don't ask me about my business . . .

KAY: Oh, no!
MICHAEL: Enough! All right! This one time – this one time I'll let you ask me about my affairs . . .
KAY (*whispering*): Is it true? Is it?
MICHAEL: No.

Kay wants to believe the blatant lie because much of her comfort – her Christmas shopping, her own, personal economic boom – has its origin in crime.

If *The Godfather Part III* was nostalgic for a putatively 'original' Mafia not yet corrupted by business, *The Godfather Part I* suggests instead that the Mafia is the origin of all 'business'. Michael's intention to make the Corleone business entirely legal – 'in five years, the Corleone Family is going to be completely legitimate, trust me' – like Don Vito's aspirations for his son – 'Senator Corleone, Governor Corleone, or something' – point to the thin line that separates criminality from business or politics. At the origin of what is legitimate, in some Shakespearean sense, there is always a crime. Senators Kennedy and McClellan were right after all: how can one distinguish legitimate from illegitimate if what today is legal is only yesterday's murder and theft? Yesterday's robber barons have become today's respectable businessmen; yesterday's wars have become America's diplomatic power. At the origin, there is always brute force. This, in short, is the horror that Kay refuses to see by hiding behind a lie.

And this is the horror that Coppola's movie wants to make visible on the screen. With the Statue of Liberty in the background – tired symbol of the American Dream – Rocco shoots Paulie three times. The horror, however, must be hidden soon by the lie of everyday normality. Rocco takes a packet from the car. It is most elegantly wrapped: 'Leave the gun, take the cannoli.' They are, we can be sure of it, the best cannoli that money can buy.

The Rise of the Corleonesi

Father . . . I want to kill you.
– The Doors, 'The End'

The rather depressing message of *The Godfather* – that crime is the original accumulation of wealth and power out of which legal business and politics grow – was, in Coppola's own words, only a cautionary tale: 'I don't at all feel that America is doomed', he said. 'I thought it was healthy to make this horror-story statement – as a warning, if you like – but, as a nation, we don't have to go down the same road.'[44] In order for the warning to work, however, identification with the Don – he is our American Dream – had to be followed, in the most classic of ways, by repulsion. We should not want to go down the same road, indeed; nor should Michael, the war hero, go down the same road as the Mafia.

Filmed in the wake of the youth protests and anti-Vietnam demonstrations of 1968, *The Godfather* begins with good omens. Young Michael seems quite determined not to follow in his criminal father's footsteps. Like the protagonist of a song by The Doors – 'The End', a veritable anthem of the 1960s, which Coppola chose as the soundtrack for *Apocalypse Now* – the young Corleone returns home to kill, symbolically speaking, his father: 'Kay, my father's way of doing things is over', are his words; 'he's finished. Even he knows that.'

Michael belongs to a generation that sees things with young eyes. Child of the sexual revolution (the 1960s often intrude in the post-war setting), Michael mocks his father's moral prudishness with Kay, his fiancé:

MICHAEL: Ya' know, if we go to my father's house we can't push the beds together.
KAY (*laughs*): Why not?
MICHAEL: Because they're in separate rooms.
KAY (*laughs*): Well, all right then. Then we won't go. We won't tell your father.
MICHAEL: Okay.
KAY: You know, we'll just get married first, and we'll tell him later.

The problem is that the young generation, like Michael, seems to have betrayed the promise to take a different path. After the attempted murder of Don Vito, Michael's visit at the hospital is the first hint of the coming metamorphosis: 'Just lie here, Pop. I'll take care of you now. I'm with you now. I'm with you'. From war hero, he is becoming, slowly but surely, a mafioso like his father. Futile are Kay's recriminations and her appeal to promises that have been made: 'But you're not like him, Michael. I thought you weren't going to become a man like your father. That's what you told me!' By the end of the movie, there is no hope in sight. Michael has become his father. The last words of the film, pronounced by Clemenza kissing

Sightseeing in New York: Rocco Lampone pops Paulie Gatto, the traitor, with three shots to the head, *The Godfather*.

Michael's hand, leave no doubt; like his father before him, Michael has become 'Don Corleone'.

As Coppola explained in an interview, it was certainly not easy for the young generation to change the 'system' put in place by their fathers:

> Well, people like myself, who decide that it's necessary to work within a system in order to be able to change it or eventually to go off on their own to subsidize the kind of work they believe in, inevitably become changed by the process . . . I know a lot of bright young writers and directors in Hollywood who are very successful – some of them I gave jobs to four or five years ago – and they're making a lot of money; but they are no longer talking about the things they used to talk about. Their conversation now is all about deals, about what's going to sell and what isn't. And they rave about their new cars and their new hundred-thousand-dollar houses. They don't even see or hear the changes in themselves. They've become the very people they were criticizing three years ago. Like Michael, they've become their fathers.[45]

To go down a different road, another new generation was now needed. The cautionary tale of *The Godfather* was to prepare the new generation to take action, not to repeat the horror of the fathers – nor of the sons of '68, allegorized by Michael.

While Coppola was hoping for change in the United States, things were changing quite swiftly in Italy instead, where *The Godfather* became the most-seen movie of the 1972–3 season: $250,000 worth of tickets were sold in the city of Palermo alone. As *The Godfather* was screened in Palermo's theatres, the 'First Mafia War' was ending (see chapter Three). The Sicilian Cosa Nostra had reached peace by forming a triumvirate of Palermo's families: Stefano Bontate of the Palermo *mandamento*, Gaetano Badalamenti of the Cinisi *mandamento*, and Luciano Leggio (or his lieutenant Salvatore 'the Beast' Riina when Leggio was on the run) of the Corleone *mandamento*. The Mafia peace maintained by the triumvirate had jump-started big business again (with heroin now thriving), and public works were assured by the three men's political referents. Bontate counted Salvatore Lima, architect of the sack of Palermo and now congressman in Giulio Andreotti's DC government in Rome, among his friends, while Badalamenti and Leggio shared the favours of Vito Ciancimino, the other mind behind the sack and now mayor of Palermo.

It seemed a peaceful coexistence. The share and distribution of political 'friendships', however, already foreshadowed a problem: there was no doubt that the power Bontate could yield, with the help of the Honourable Lima in Rome, was beyond the reach of Badalamenti and Leggio. The triumvirate looked more like an isosceles triangle with Bontate on top. Triangles, in the Mafia as in love stories, are notorious for being the cause of much strife and jealousy.

The Corleonesi were not the kind of men willing to permit anyone – let alone rich, young and urban Bontate – to be on top. Sure the Bontate's money and military power were still unmatched in Sicily. The Corleonesi, humble men from the provinces that they were, started building both. They began in 1971 with a series of kidnappings, including that of the son of Francesco Vassallo, a close friend of Bontate and Lima. It was a symbolic act of power and defiance on the part of the Corleonesi; neither Bontate nor Lima could do anything to free the hostage. Kidnapping, however, had also a more pragmatic objective: to raise money and, with money, weapons and armies to engage Bontate in a war to the death.

FIVE

Prime Time

Almost anything goes now that *The Sopranos*
has been deemed fit for primetime.
— Peter Stock, 'No Standards to Violate', *Society Magazine*

On 23 April 1981 – the day of his 42nd birthday – as he was driving home in his flashy Alfa Romeo Giulietta, Stefano Bontate was machine-gunned in Palermo, the very city he thought he had under his control. With Luciano Leggio in jail, Salvatore Riina was left to plan the attack. The hit man was Giuseppe Greco, the most lethal killer of the Corleonesi. His ferocity was betrayed only by his nickname: *Scarpuzzedda*, 'little shoe'. With small feet, Greco had lots to compensate for with violence.

On 11 May *Scarpuzzedda* struck again: Salvatore Inzerillo, a close ally of Bontate and relative of New York City boss Carlo Gambino, was hit by a hail of lead that rendered his face unrecognizable. Neither the bullet-proof car he had purchased after Bontate's murder, nor his connections to Gambino, could save him: the Corleonesi, armed with AK-47s purchased with the returns from the kidnappings of the 1970s, could not be stopped by anyone or anything. Derogatorily called 'the peasants', rough and uneducated, they had never set foot in the classes of eloquence and rhetoric at the University of Palermo and certainly did not excel in the art of negotiation. They were quite convincing nonetheless, and managed to reach their objective – absolute control of the Sicilian Mafia – through the methodic decimation of their adversaries – whether real, perceived, suspected or even remotely possible.

Between 1981 and 1983 there were at least 400 Mafia killings in Palermo, and at least as many again across Sicily. They were mostly the work of Riina's Corleonesi, determined to erase any trace of the Bontate and Badalamenti families from the face of the earth. Their lethal reach went beyond Sicily: the dismembered body of a nephew of Badalamenti's turned up in a field in Germany; Inzerillo's own brother, who had fled Sicily for the U.S., was found dead in New Jersey. Among the very few who managed to escape the slaughter were Tommaso Buscetta, arrested by the FBI in New York in 1970, and Salvatore Contorno, the 'butcher' of the Bontate family. As *pentiti*, or 'repentant' collaborating witnesses against the Corleonesi, they became important informants for prosecuting magistrates. While they survived in witness protection programmes, all their relatives were methodically exterminated. When Contorno was asked by his judge to explain who were the winners and the losers of the Mafia War, he truthfully declared: 'The winning and losing clans don't exist, because the losers don't exist. They, the Corleonesi, killed them all.'[1]

The Corleonesi did not stop with the elimination of the Bontate and Badalamenti families. Having completed that mission, it was now time to dispose of those who had helped them in their climb to the top – lest they could claim a share of their power and control. Rosario Riccobono and twenty of his associates, who had slaughtered a number of Bontate's friends on behalf of Riina, were quickly dispatched to a better place; Filippo Marchese, whose speciality was to dissolve in acid the enemies of the Corleonesi, was strangled and put in acid too – as though in a parody, most likely unintentional, of Dante's *contrappasso*. One hundred and sixty mafiosi vanished in 1982 alone.

At the height of the new Mafia War, in March 1982, the *carabiniere* (military policeman) General Carlo Alberto Dalla Chiesa, who had singlehandedly dismantled the Italian terrorist group the Red Brigades, was sent to Palermo to put an end to the bloodbath. If he could defeat terrorism – people said – he could certainly do the same with the Mafia! Alexander Stille describes the arrival of Dalla Chiesa in the city of Palermo, now firmly under Riina's reign of terror:

> The mafia greeted Dalla Chiesa in predictable fashion. On April 30, just before he was supposed to take over his new position, mafia killers murdered Pio La Torre [member of the parliamentary Anti-Mafia Committee]. Dalla Chiesa spent his first day on the job at La Torre's funeral – a sinister augury for the future.[2]

The augury was intended. One hundred days later Dalla Chiesa was murdered along with his wife by a firing squad led by the seemingly indefatigable *Scarpuzzedda*.

The Corleonesi must have had a taste for symbols. Killing a national hero, a high-ranking officer representing the authority of the State in Sicily, could only have one meaning: the Mafia was at war with the State

– and the State was next to powerless in this war. It was, therefore, no surprise that Palermo's archbishop, Cardinal Salvatore Pappalardo, speaking at the funeral, could compare his city to Sagunto, destroyed by Hannibal during the Punic Wars: 'While Rome thinks what is to be done, the city of Sagunto is conquered by the barbarians! This time, it is not Sagunto, but Palermo. Poor Palermo!'[3]

Just in case Riina's message had not been clear, the Corleonesi were thoughtful enough to leave no room for interpretation. On 29 July 1983 chief prosecutor Rocco Chinnici, who was investigating the banker Michele Sindona's political connections and his money-laundering schemes between Sicily, the U.S. and the Vatican, was blown up by a car bomb parked in front of his building. Killed with Chinnici were his two bodyguards and the concierge. Fourteen bystanders were injured – the first collateral casualties in an all-out war.

Just before being killed Chinnici had signed arrest warrants for Dalla Chiesa's suspected murderers, including one for Greco. Chinnici was convinced that the homicide was not merely a symbolic message, but the practical elimination of an adversary that had come too close to a truth that connected Sindona's Mafia dealings with high-ranking officers of the DCs in Rome. He made no secret of his suspicions in the report that accompanied the arrest warrants: the murder of Dalla Chiesa, he wrote, 'transcends the typical goals of a criminal organization'. This was a 'political homicide; a homicide, in other words, in which Mafia interests converge with the murky interests of those in the government of the Republic'.[4]

As was revealed soon after Chinnici's murder, a police informant – the Lebanese drug trafficker Bou Ghebel Ghassan – had warned, only a week before, that 'a Palermo magistrate' was being targeted for assassination in retaliation for the arrests. Nothing, however, had been done by the authorities to protect Chinnici, the most obvious target for an assassination. As soon as the press got hold of this, outrage ensued. Throwing more wood on the fire, the weekly magazine *L'Espresso* published extracts of Chinnici's diary in which fellow judges and prosecutors of Palermo were privately named as Riina's men: 'If something bad happens to me, two men are responsible: (1) That great coward [prosecutor] Ciccio Scozzari; and (2) the attorney Paolo Seminara.'[5] Palermo's court was soon nicknamed *la procura dei veleni*, the court of poisons. There were good reasons for the sobriquet.

In such a toxic atmosphere, Antonio Caponetto, the prosecutor in Florence, was sent to Palermo to take Chinnici's place. Caponetto had no experience whatsoever with Mafia cases – and one wonders if he had been chosen precisely because of this – but he was nonetheless an honest man. The first thing he did in office was to create a special pool of judges with years of expertise in Mafia cases. Headed by Caponetto, the judges Giovanni Falcone, Paolo Borsellino, Giuseppe Di Lello and Leonardo Guarnotta formed the first 'anti-Mafia pool' that the history of the Italian judiciary had ever known.

Falcone was the first judge of the pool able to cast a glimmer of hope in this otherwise despairing situation. The 'boss of the two worlds' Tommaso Buscetta, who had been arrested by the FBI after his escape from Riina's killers (and after a daring stunt in Brazil), had decided to talk. He had started to collaborate with FBI director Louis Freeh and assistant U.S. attorney for New York's Southern District Richard Martin in 1980. He had helped them by unravelling the traffic of heroin from Palermo's refineries to New York pizzerias (the so-called 'Pizza Connection') controlled by the Inzerillos. As Martin said, Buscetta 'gave us the basis for the RICO [Racketeer-Influenced and Corrupt Organizations Act]'.

Buscetta was now willing to talk to Falcone, a Sicilian like him from the poor neighbourhood of La Kalsa in Palermo:

> I trust you, Judge Falcone, and I trust deputy police chief Gianni De Gennaro. But I don't trust anyone else. I don't believe the Italian state has the real intention of fighting the mafia . . . I want to warn you, Judge. After this interrogation you will become a celebrity. But they will try to destroy you physically and professionally. And they will do the same to me. Never forget that you are opening an account with Cosa Nostra that will only be settled when you die. Are you sure you want to go ahead with this?[6]

Falcone was sure, and the information he got from Buscetta was worth the risk.

Buscetta informed Falcone of the real nature of the Mafia War that the authorities were trying to contain, without ever truly understanding; he knew of Riina's designs to take the directorship of the Mafia away from Palermo, and he knew the Corleonesi well. More importantly Buscetta's direct knowledge of the Mafia stretched back to the 1950s, when Lucky Luciano had given it the structure that it still had in the 1980s. What came to be known as the 'Buscetta theorem' was arguably the biggest breakthrough in the entire history of the Italian anti-Mafia, comparable only to the RICO legislation in the U.S. Since the meeting of 1957 at the Grand Hotel et Des Palmes in Palermo (discussed in chapter Three), the Mafia, as Buscetta's theorem demonstrated, had not been a vague entity or loose grouping of independent actors, but a strictly structured organization. Soldiers, *capidecina*, *consiglieri* and *mandamenti* were all coordinated by a central *cupola*, which took all strategic decisions. The theorem allowed the judiciary to add a brand new offence to Italy's criminal code: Mafia association. If the Mafia was a structured organization, everybody who was a part of it was equally responsible for any crime committed by any other member of the association.

The theorem started bearing fruit: by the autumn of 1984 the police inspector Antonino Cassarà, one of the very few men trusted by Falcone in the 'court of poisons', had signed 366 arrest warrants. However, a top-secret memorandum sent by Ralph Jones, U.S. consul general in Palermo, to the embassy in Rome and the State Department in Washington, hinted that something was still missing in Buscetta's revelations:

> Magistrates in Palermo have issued 366 arrest warrants against mafiosi of every type . . . based in large part on the unprecedented confessions of the mafia boss Tommaso Buscetta . . . The arrest warrants struck exclusively members of the military arm of the mafia . . . No politicians were arrested. An indictment was issued against the former mayor of Palermo, Vito Ciancimino [Christian Democrat], who is the puppeteer who maneuvers various members of the city council . . . The PCI [Partito Comunista Italiano] may try to play the 'mafia card' against Foreign Minister Giulio Andreotti, whose faction, which has for some time tried to cover its left flank by cooperating with the PCI in the regional government, is considered by many the most closely tied to the mafia on the entire Sicilian political scene.[7]

The indictment of Ciancimino, a close ally of Lima (with whom he had orchestrated the sack of Palermo), was, to be sure, no small thing: as Consul Jones suspected, it could potentially end up involving high-ranking DC officers in Rome – way up to the cunning Giulio Andreotti.

At home in the high chambers of the Vatican among popes and cardinals, Andreotti was equally at ease with Sicilian mafiosi. A week after Ciancimino's indictment translated into his arrest, Buscetta rendered the following statement to Falcone:

The cousins Ignazio and Nino Salvo are 'men of honor' of the family of Salemi and were presented to me as such by Stefano Bontate, when I came to Palermo in 1980. The friendship between Bontate and the Salvos was very close and, as I observed, they saw one another frequently . . . The Salvos' role inside Cosa Nostra is modest but their political importance is enormous. They have direct relationships with well-known members of parliament, some of them from Palermo, whose names I would prefer not to reveal . . . I also met with Nino Salvo in Rome. Salvo had to come to Rome for questioning by a prosecutor and since I was in Rome at the time, staying with Pippo Calò, I met with him and with a member of parliament.[8]

When, on 12 November 1984, Falcone ordered the arrest of Nino and Ignazio Salvo, the name of Andreotti was found on the pages of Ignazio's personal agenda.[9] It was not difficult for Falcone to figure out the well-known member of parliament whose name Buscetta preferred not to reveal; however, without Buscetta's corroboration, Andreotti, then Foreign Minister of Italy, remained untouchable.

In the meantime Buscetta had opened the floodgates to welcome a swarm of *pentitismo*. All those mafiosi – in truth, few had remained alive – who had an axe to grind with Riina's Corleonesi joined the choir. On 1 October 1984 Falcone began meetings with the other survivor of Riina's bloodbath: 'I intend to collaborate with the justice system telling everything I know about Cosa Nostra', Salvatore Contorno told Falcone, 'because I realize that it is nothing but a band of cowards and murderers.'

More warrants were issued, and then more arrests, with convoys of the police's motorized unit – the 'flying squad' – speeding with their sirens howling through the streets of Palermo. Riina was not impressed; after killing two members of the flying squad, he aimed higher. On 28 July 1985 the police commissioner Giuseppe Montana, commander of Palermo's flying squad, was ambushed by two men as he was spending the afternoon at the marina with his girlfriend. On 6 August the time came for Antonino Cassarà, deputy chief of Falcone. As his wife watched from the balcony, his body, and that of his bodyguard Roberto Antiochia, were riddled with shots from nine AK-47s in the street below.

Outrage in the streets of Palermo was palpable when the authorities came to Cassarà's funeral, Salvatore Lima above all. Yelling 'Bastards!' and worse things frankly untranslatable from Sicilian, Lima's car was attacked by the infuriated crowd, spitting, screaming and kicking. Lima could not set foot out of the car, and the convoy of four bulletproof vehicles that had accompanied him had to turn back and escape from Cassarà's funeral. With Palermo in uproar, its new mayor, Leoluca Orlando, a Christian Democrat himself, pleaded with his party to investigate, once and for all, its complicity with the Mafia. The answer he got back – 'the Mafia does not exist' – convinced him that a new party had to be created. He left the DCs in 1991 after years spent struggling with its leaders.

Satisfied, perhaps, that Falcone and the anti-Mafia pool had learned their lesson, Riina now turned his attentions towards the best men of his own clan – those whose ambition could perhaps, one day, challenge his leadership. In September *Scarpuzzedda* was shot to death by two of his supposed friends, Vincenzo Puccio and Giuseppe Lucchese, on direct order from Riina. Puccio, arrested in 1986 on unrelated charges, was beaten to death in his cell at the Ucciardone prison in Palermo on 11 May 1989 by fellow inmates Antonino and Giuseppe Marchese. When Giuseppe, fearing for his own life, became a *pentito*, he confirmed that Puccio's sentence had been passed by Riina.

The crescendo of Riina's brutality was marking a significant shift not only in the public's perception of the Mafia, but in the Mafia's self-perception. The legends of Robin Hood-like Mafia justice, including the myths of honour, loyalty and family, had been essential in maintaining cohesion within the Mafia ranks. The sense of *omertà* as an almost chivalric virtue in defence of a secret brotherhood, and even a public acceptance of the Mafia as an honourable society, largely depended on the credibility of those myths and legends. The occasional murder of a Mafia man or boss had consequently to be justified with reference to that mythological apparatus: he had brought dishonour to the family; he had offended the innocents; he was a rat or a coward. The traditional Mafia had always walked this thin line with care, making sure brutal force was accompanied by the creation of consent. Honour and respectability, no matter how 'perverted' (as Franchetti would have said), played a rather important role in the consensus-building rhetorical machine of the Mafia. They legitimated violence as a means, a necessity, to a noble and just end.

Riina's psychotic killing of anybody in his way, his disregard for friends and loyalty and his total lack of interest in the collateral casualties of his war were now quickly eroding the entire rhetorical apparatus that the Mafia had belaboured for over 100 years. What had honour to do with the killing of women and children whose only fault was a blood relation with Buscetta or Contorno? What kind of family was this Cosa Nostra, in which the loyalty of a *Scarpuzzedda* was rewarded with death? What kind of brotherhood was this, in which friends betrayed friends and no one knew where the bullet was coming from? As *pentito* Contorno put it, the Mafia was nothing more than 'a band of cowards and murderers'.

Falcone, who had never bought into the myths of the Mafia to begin with, had no intention of being intimidated by cowards and murderers. In February 1986 the trial he had put together with Cassarà's help, and in collaboration with the anti-Mafia pool, began. Known as the Maxi Trial, it included 474 defendants, among whom were Leggio and Riina (the latter, on the run, was tried *in absentia*). Under the spotlight of the national and international press, the trial was the emblem of an Italian state under siege: a fortification in reinforced concrete modelled upon the bunkers of the Second World War was built inside the Ucciardone prison. Judges and jury went in and out of the *aula bunker* – the 'bunker courtroom', as it was called – under unprecedented military surveillance. Tanks were stationed at the street corners of the Ucciardone. The verdict of the Maxi Trial was announced on 16 December 1987: 114 acquittals, but a total of 2,665 years of jail for those found guilty, Riina and Leggio included.

For every step forward the anti-Mafia movement made, however, two steps back would regularly follow. If the killings of the Corleonesi were not hindering progress, it was the Italian state that would seem to be acting on Riina's behalf. In 1990 the Court of Appeals reversed the sentences of the Maxi Trial: it had refuted Buscetta's theorem and with it much of the work done by Falcone. As long as Riina could not be proven to have materially killed anybody, there was no 'Mafia association' that the Court of Appeals would recognize as evidence of a crime. A final verdict on the cases now depended on the decision of the Court of Cassation, Italy's Supreme Court. Then, its chief prosecutor, Antonio Scopelliti, was murdered in August 1991. The truly discouraging news for Falcone, however, was that the court was to be presided over by none other than Corrado Carnevale, a close friend of Salvatore Lima – aptly nicknamed 'the verdict slayer'.

Carnevale had already annulled a total of 500 sentences involving Mafia cases, saving 134 lifers from prison (including the killers of Chinnici), and helping even more convicts by suspending a total of 700 years of jail time. He firmly believed – or so he wrote in his sentences – that the Mafia was a 'fairy tale' and that Buscetta's theorem was the fancy of Falcone's imagination. Drug trafficking in Sicily? That did not exist either. Take, for instance, the emblematic case of the Bolognetta trial. After months of wiretappings, the police had recorded a conversation between known mafiosi mentioning an imminent delivery of 'pizzas and shirts' in Bolognetta, a small municipality twelve miles southeast of Palermo. Presuming – quite correctly – that pizzas and shirts were code names for heroin and cocaine, the police had caught the mafiosi with kilograms of drugs still in their hands. It was an easy case to try – until Carnevale slew the guilty verdict, that is. He explained that there was no reason for the police to assume that 'pizza and shirts' referred to heroin and cocaine, no matter that their assumption had, in fact, been proven correct. Their search and seizure was illegal, and the drugs, 'technically', did not exist! As reporter Attilio Bolzoni wrote in *La Repubblica* on 23 June 1988, for Carnevale, 'technicalities exorcise the facts'.

Carnevale's presidency of the Court of Cassation was undoubtedly bad news for Falcone's Maxi Trial. It was enough to fill the prosecutor's role – vacant since the murder of Scopelliti – with a more 'friendly' figure who could give Carnevale enough excuses to slay yet another verdict. No doubt some political pressure could have fixed everything in the best possible way for the mafiosi awaiting final judgement. The world, however, had changed more rapidly than Carnevale and Riina had realized: it was not only the outrage of the Italians and the scrutiny of the press that made Carnevale's game more difficult to play, but a seemingly unrelated event that had happened on the other side of the Iron Curtain, which completely reshuffled the whole political chequerboard of Italy's power games.

With the fall of the Berlin Wall in 1989, the international role the Christian Democrats had played since the end of the war suddenly lost all meaning. The u.s. and other NATO members no longer had any interest in keeping the DCs in power as a bulwark against communism. Italians themselves were not quite sure what an anti-communist party could still offer in a post-communist world. The party's notorious corruption and Mafia collusions, once tolerated by many in Italy and abroad for the sake of anti-communism, could not be allowed to continue any longer. As Andreotti himself declared in an interview to *El País* in July 1988, 'if the Berlin Wall had not gone down, nothing would have happened.'[10]

Instead much started to happen. At the regional elections in 1990 the DCs were haemorrhaging votes. In the North, a new localist party, the Northern League, threatened the DC hegemony – previously unassailable throughout the history of the Republic. In Sicily, Palermo's mayor Leoluca Orlando left the DCs to create a new anti-Mafia party, La Rete (the Network).

More worrisome for the DCs, the investigations that would culminate in the massive 'Clean Hands' inquest of 1992, which indicted Giulio Andreotti 'for having contributed in a non-occasional manner to protecting the interests and reaching the aims of the criminal association known as Cosa Nostra', were already underway. The DCs, in short, had other fish to fry than the Maxi Trial.

Under pressure from Falcone, and with the DCs in disarray, newly elected Minister of Justice Carlo Martelli of the Socialist Party removed the 'verdict slayer' from the Court of Cassation on suspicion of 'external cooperation in the crime of Mafia association'. On 31 January 1992 the Court of Cassation overturned the Court of Appeal's verdict and confirmed 60 convictions. Among them was Riina who, in *absentia*, was sentenced to life in jail.

Riina's answer came without delay. On 12 March Salvatore Lima, the DC senator who, in the eyes of the Corleonesi, had not done enough to prevent the verdict, was killed. A gunman approached his car on a motorbike, first shooting the wheels and then, when Lima tried to escape on foot, shooting him in the back and then again, delivering a fatal shot to the neck. Lima's car was on its way to Palermo's Centrale Palace Hotel, where a reception for Lima's party leader, now Prime Minister Giulio Andreotti, had been scheduled for the afternoon:

> People were struck by the shrunken, terrorized and humiliated figure the prime minister cut when he came down for Lima's funeral. The minister of justice at that time, Claudio Martelli, remembered two years later how Andreotti looked after Lima's murder. 'His face had an even waxier look than usual. He was terrified, either because he didn't understand, or maybe because he did.' Huddled in his heavy overcoat, Andreotti looked like an aged tortoise retracting into its shell.[11]

If Lima's assassination had settled the Corleonesi's account with the DCs, an open debt remained with the anti-Mafia pool. On 23 May 1992 over 400 kilograms (900 pounds) of TNT killed Judge Falcone, his wife and three bodyguards on Highway 29, a few kilometres from Palermo. Two months later on 19 July, another judge of the anti-Mafia pool, Paolo Borsellino, was the victim of a car bomb parked near his mother's house.

Even the final arrest of Riina on 15 January 1993 was not enough to stop the violence. Organized as a military army, the Corleonesi could simply replace one captured general with another. The system continued to function. The new boss, as bloodthirsty as the previous one (wanted for 300 homicides), was Leoluca Bagarella. He liked to be addressed as 'the Godfather' and fashioned his style upon Marlon Brando's Don Vito Corleone. The *Godfather* theme was played at his wedding party. On 14 May 1993 Bagarella tried to have TV anchorman Maurizio Costanzo killed with a bomb explosion in Rome; Costanzo had expressed delight on TV regarding the arrest of Riina. On 27 May a car exploded in Via dei Georgofili in the centre of Florence. Five bystanders were killed and 40 more were wounded. Another bomb killed five in Milan's Via Palestro on 27 July. On the same day bombs exploded at the churches of San Giovanni in Laterano and San Giorgio in Rome. A few months before, Pope John Paul II, during his visit to Sicily, had spoken of the Mafia's 'culture of death, profoundly inhuman, anti-evangelical', warning that 'one day, the judgement of God will come!' What came, instead, after the bombs in Rome was the homicide on 15 September of Palermo's anti-Mafia priest Pino Puglisi, while on 31 October football fans barely escaped a massacre when a bomb failed to explode at the Olympic Stadium in Rome.

The Mafia was at war – with everybody, and with the State in particular. The stake of this war, as it was hypothesized by an investigation launched in Florence in 1998 (and continuing with a trial still underway in 2014), was to force the Italian state to negotiate directly with the Mafia. Riina himself wrote the terms of the negotiation in a famous *papello* (Sicilian for 'list of requests') delivered to Vito Ciancimino.[12]

This is only a piece of the gloomy context in which the Italian cultural industry was forced, by a tragic succession of facts, to rethink the Mafia movie: much more blood and many more bombs could easily be added to the list. Unsurprisingly not only Germi's Robin Hood fantasies, but Coppola's romantic portrayal of the Corleone family, were entirely unpresentable to an Italian public truly frightened by the spectacle of sheer terror that the Corleonesi were staging. The real Mafia had colonized the entirety of prime-time television with news of murders and interviews of hopeless magistrates. The likes of Bagarella, fashioned as Don Corleone, seemed to have colonized the Mafia genre too. It was time to take both prime time and the genre away from them.

The Octopus

Remember, 007, you're on your own!
– *Octopussy*, dir. John Glen

On 11 March 1984, at the height of the war between the Corleonesi and the Anti-Mafia, Italian public television (RAI) began broadcasting a new weekly drama series that would continue – a rare case of longevity for any TV serial – until 2001. It was aptly titled *La piovra* (*The Octopus*). With Roger Moore still topping the box office with his gallant adventures to uncover the international jewel-smuggling operation headed by the mysterious Octopussy, the Italian *Octopus* was of a very different nature. As the jacket of the U.S. DVD edition explains, 'the title of this classic Mafia thriller says it all, evoking the image of a secret criminal culture extending its tentacles into every layer of society.'

The secret service; the press; business, legal and illegal; banking; construction and high finance; politics; and even police and the magistrature – everything and everyone is in the grips of the Mafia's tentacles. *The Octopus* begins in a small, unnamed city resembling Trapani in western Sicily. From Trapani it moves in concentric circles that chronicle the Mafia's expansive reach into Rome, Parliament, Milan, Turin and ultimately across three continents. As the local police commissioner is killed in the opening episode, his substitute, Corrado Cattani (played masterfully by Michele Placido), arrives in Sicily; he soon understands, like 007 before him, that he is on his own. No one can be trusted. The hero is all alone against a Mafia conspiracy of unthinkable proportions.

A product of its time, *The Octopus* is a radical rethinking of the Mafia genre. To begin, the context of the 1980s, with the Corleonesi's seemingly unstoppable war, offered new elements that could never have been fathomed before. The connection of the Mafia with politics and banking, which even in *The Godfather Part I* remains somewhat abstract, had acquired a different consistency with the investigation of Sindona's affairs and Ciancimino's arrest. The series is almost didactic in its portrayal of how the Mafia secures a public contract or speculates in the financial market. Drug trafficking had also become a more palpable reality on which the film could now dwell; drug addicts are not only present in many scenes, but even figure as protagonists. Cardinal Pappalardo's 'Sagunto Speech' offered additional elements to portray the changing role of the Church in the Anti-Mafia struggle. The 'court of poisons', too, was faithfully represented in The Octopus to create, for both the police commissioner protagonist and the viewer, a thrilling atmosphere of distrust. The flying squad convoys, the mass arrests and the ambushes with AK-47s added new dynamic possibilities to the traditional car chases and gunshots.

The major innovation of The Octopus is, however, a relatively simple one: for the first time, we as viewers are asked to identify with an anti-Mafia hero, namely Commissioner Cattani. Strange as it may seem, until that point the very opposite had been true. The heroes whose suffering or success we felt as our own were all mafiosi: Verga's Turiddu, Hawks's Scarface, Germi's bandits, Coppola's Corleones and even Rosi's Giuliano, a victim of a power that transcended him as it transcends us. The constant risk of such identification had been of falling into a mythification of the Mafia; the innovation of The Octopus tries to prevent just that. As Nando dalla Chiesa, son of the general killed in 1982, once wrote: in the 1980s 'the Mafia film becomes the anti-Mafia film'.[13]

In fact by the 1980s it was not only film that had taken the anti-Mafia path. The question of whether art could oppose the Mafia (or at least not be complicit in its glorification) touched, by now, all possible genres. At the theatre, a series of anti-Mafia plays were performed, beginning with Leonardo Sciascia's L'Onorevole (His Excellency) and his rewriting of I Mafiosi della Vicaria. Sciascia had started writing anti-Mafia novels as early in the 1960s, and the two plays had in fact been penned in 1966. Although the Teatro Stabile in Catania had refused to perform them in the 1960s, by 1980 L'Onorevole toured Italy with some success.[14] In the same years Letizia Battaglia used photography to document the horrors of the Mafia while songwriter Fabrizio de André sung scathing words against boss Don Raffaele Cutolo in the song 'Don Raffaè', and Otello Profazio was touring Sicily, in the folk tradition of the cuntastorie (the kind of story-teller remembered in Pasquale Scimeca's film Placido Rizzotto), reminding everybody that 'the law of the Mafia is the shotgun.'

Even painting, with the work of Gaetano Porcasi and the various Arte contro la Mafia festivals springing up all over Sicily, would soon discover the possibilities of art pitted against organized crime. No wonder that Sciascia himself, in a shocking article published in Il Corriere della Sera of 10 January 1987, feared that the anti-Mafia movement was becoming a kind of careerism.[15]

The director of the first four episodes of The Octopus, and arguably the originator of the anti-Mafia film genre, was Damiano Damiani, an exponent of Italy's so-called *cinema democratico*.[16] In his history of Italian television, Aldo Grasso describes 'democratic cinema':

> Its physiognomy is given by its dialogue and the construction of its stories: indignation, desire to denounce the corruption of institutions, a good ability to give consistency to conspiratorial theories, and the certainty that, if you think the worst, you may end up being correct in Italy. Its material is taken from the news that you read in the papers every day. Character traits, however, definitely belong to the American cop movie.[17]

Perhaps the most typical example of democratic cinema is Damiani's *Perché si uccide un magistrato* (How to Kill a Judge, 1975). While not his best film, it is the interesting story of Giacomo Solaris, a fictional director of Mafia movies (played by Franco Nero, unforgettable face of the spaghetti western tradition, up to Quentin Tarantino's *Django Unchained*). The sort of questions he asks himself throughout *How to Kill a Judge* – all variations of the fundamental one: 'How is the Mafia going to use my films?' – are symptomatic of democratic cinema's awareness of the social responsibility of the medium. More specifically, these questions focus on the possible uses organized crime can make of the Mafia genre to acquire legitimacy or, as in the case of Solaris's movies, to discredit a judge before killing him.

The *cuntastorie* or story-teller, once a ubiquitous figure in Sicilian popular piazzas, sings and narrates mafia stories, Pasquale Scimeca (dir.), *Placido Rizzotto* (Arbash, 2000).

Damiani had begun directing films on the Mafia as early as 1968, when he had adapted Sciascia's novel Il giorno della civetta (The Day of the Owl, 1961) for the big screen. Like Sciascia, he was less intent on glorifying the Mafia through spectacular killings and fast-paced action than on showing – anticipating the logic of The Octopus – 'the way in which the Mafia works by expanding its reach'.[18]

With Sciascia, Damiani also shared a taste for a particular kind of fictional character – one that has been called, quite appropriately, 'the doomed detective'.[19] In The Day of the Owl, Police Commissioner Bellodi is defeated in the end by the Mafia through a false witness who provides an alibi for those involved in the murder Bellodi had successfully investigated. The same fatalistic paradigm is at work in Sciascia's other Mafia novels. In A ciascurio il suo (To Each His Own, 1966), which Elio Petri made into a movie in 1967, Professor Laurana, who has untangled the truth of a Mafia murder, is himself murdered. Il contesto (Equal Danger, 1971), adapted by Francesco Rosi as Cadaveri eccellenti (Excellent Cadavers) in 1976, also ends with the assassination of a police inspector.

The epithet of 'doomed detective' fits Commissioner Cattani of The Octopus like a glove. Like Sciascia's characters – and, most sadly, like many of his real-life counterparts – he achieves some modest success in one scene only to suffer, in the next, the most catastrophic of defeats. Trying not to spoil the series for my reader, let me just say that his defeats are much more tragic, bloody and even shameful than any Greek tragedian could have possibly conceived. He is betrayed, beaten up, humiliated and offended like a mouse in a cat's paws. As many have commented since, if the risk with the traditional Mafia film was the mythification of the Mafia, the risk with democratic cinema was giving 'the image of an omnipresent, omnipotent mafia', one 'whose force cannot be controlled'.[20] Cattani was not only on his own, but was doomed to perennial defeat.

I must confess I did not understand then, and cannot understand even now, the great popularity of The Octopus. In a country of 60 million inhabitants, 8 million watched the first episode, and over 15 million were tuned in by the sixth. Why were we all glued to the screen when Cattani, the hero with whom we all had identified, was brought into one circle after another of pure Mafia hell? No doubt the episodes are excellently directed, have exceptional casts, and dispense the many pleasures of action à la Dirty Harry. But could you imagine Clint Eastwood always being humiliated in the end – always the loser?

Lest this was a case of collective masochism on our part, the only rationale I can come up with to explain the immense success of *The Octopus* is that it was the first prime-time entertainment in the entire history of the Italian media – not the news, not the debates and not the Mafia serials that had preceded it (*Alle origini della mafia* – *At the Origin of the Mafia*, 1972 – was the first) – which informed Italian citizens of all 'the intrigues, the crimes, the connivance of untouchable personalities within the Mafia'.[21] While the daily papers and TV news barely hinted at the intrigues in parliament and 'the court of poisons', while all those who could give proof of those intrigues were being systematically eliminated, from Chinnici to Falcone, *The Octopus* showed us, albeit in the guise of fiction, what Italy had indeed become. It helped us make sense of the reality of what British journalist Tobias Jones famously called 'the dark heart of Italy'.[22] And if *The Octopus* did not provide us with a happy ending, it at least gave us a moral lesson: in the face of defeat, we were still asked to take poor Cattani's part, not to leave him all alone and doomed. For the final triumph of Good against Evil, our indignation was needed – and *The Octopus* elicited indignation at conspicuously high dosages.

In this sense the wager of democratic cinema had worked. There was no return to the Mafia myth after *The Octopus*. All that remained was the tragedy of martyrs like Cattani, ready to sacrifice everything in their struggle against a dark conspiracy. So, while Leonardo Sciascia kept writing stories without hope, Italian cinema transformed the Mafia genre into what has been called a 'memorialist impulse'.[23] It started erecting films, as it were, as monuments to the victims of the Mafia. Giuseppe Ferrara's *Falcone* (1993) was the monument to the victims of Highway 29. Marco Amenta's *La siciliana ribelle* (*One Girl Against the Mafia*, 2008) chronicled the martyrdom and death of Rita Atria, the daughter of a Mafia man who defied the family to collaborate with Judges Falcone and Borsellino. Marco Tullio Giordana's *I cento passi* (*One Hundred Steps*, 2000) immortalized anti-Mafia activist Peppino Impastato, killed by the Mafia in 1978 (see Preface). And Pasquale Scimeca's *Placido Rizzotto* (2000) became the memorial to the syndicalist of that name killed by Leggio.

As a matter of fact, the wager of democratic cinema had worked so well that by 2001, when *The Octopus* was in its tenth season, Prime Minister Silvio Berlusconi and his political allies did their best to stop the series once and for all. The occasion had come from an interview that actor Remo Girone had released before the beginning of the new series, and more precisely by his statement that the tenth season of *The Octopus* was dedicated 'to the heroism of all those policemen and magistrates who are today under attack'. For those of us accustomed to the nth season of *Law and Order* or to the deeds of Scotland Yard, this could have passed as an almost trivial, certainly opportune dedicatoria. But in an Italy still ravaged at the turn of the millennium by the aberrant encroachment of Mafia on politics, scandal it was. Franco Corbelli, the spokesperson of Berlusconi's House of Freedoms coalition, was certain that the 'attackers' mentioned by Girone were to be found in his own caucus. He demanded that public broadcasting stop immediately, as *The Octopus* was, in his words, 'a political attack against the House of Freedoms, against the judicial principle of innocence until proven guilty, and against the most influential leaders of our coalition, Cavaliere Berlusconi, his Mediaset Televisions System, and his newspapers'.[24] Berlusconi was, in fact, while Prime Minister, also the manager of three private television stations competing with public broadcasting for market share. Through his media empire, he had launched a frontal attack against the whole judicial system of Italy, and in particular against those magistrates who had put him under investigation.

Berlusconi's legal troubles had begun as early as 1993, when Mafia defectors had reported alleged negotiations between Cosa Nostra and Berlusconi's party (Forza Italia), which had, in effect, replaced the DCs after 1989. The fact that Berlusconi's majordomo was Vittorio Mangano, a man of honour from the Porta Nuova family, did not make things better for the flamboyant knight (*Cavaliere del lavoro* was Berlusconi's picturesque title, of which he was stripped only in 2014 after he was found guilty of tax evasion). In 1999 Berlusconi's right-hand man and lawyer, Marcello Dell'Utri, was sentenced to two years and three months in prison; according to the prosecution, 'there was an attempt to make [Berlusconi's] Fininvest group into a company friendly to the criminal association.'[25] Awaiting judgement on appeal, Dell'Utri became a fugitive when he fled to Beirut on 8 April 2014, presumably in an attempt to reach some non-extradition country in Africa. He was seized four days later thanks to an Interpol arrest warrant issued from Rome.

While Mangano's and Dell'Utri's (alleged) Mafia connections did not help, Berlusconi's more immediate worries in the late 1990s were the investigations into false accounting, fraud and bribery that the 'Clean Hands' team of magistrates had begun against him. The investigations would bear fruit only in 2014 when, on 15 April, Berlusconi was finally sentenced for committing tax fraud – to . . . house arrest and community service! At any rate – forgive the exasperated digression – what disturbed

Berlusconi about *The Octopus* was precisely what Girone had suggested: that the TV series' intention was to celebrate the heroism of magistrates. Hoping to escape prosecution, Berlusconi wanted those same magistrates depicted in the worst possible light. To hinder their investigations, he unleashed all his media and political power in an all-out campaign against the whole judiciary, who were guilty, in his eyes, of over-reaching and being politically biased.

In truth it might not have been only Girone's defence of magistrates against those attacks that irked Berlusconi. Since its first season in 1984, *The Octopus* had been a none-too-veiled allegory of a precise political faction. As Tobias Jones reminds us,

> The Christian Democrats were . . . described by Leonardo Sciascia as 'invertebrate, available, conceding, and at the same time tenacious, patient, grasping; a type of octopus which knows how gently to embrace dissent to return it, minced, into consensus'.[26]

As Berlusconi's Forza Italia party had taken the place left vacant by the death of the DC octopus, it may be no surprise that the object of the series' implied criticism had shifted accordingly. The tenth season was notable for a particular speech delivered by the evil arch-mafioso Tano Cariddi (played by Girone). Cariddi announced here a change of strategy for the Mafia after the Corleonesi wars of the 1980s:

> CARIDDI: No more blood, no more unnecessary deaths. This violence has only made our opponents stronger. We do not need to go to war against the State. Something else must be our goal. Let's use the laws that already exist and approve more that fit our interests. Sicily must be what Switzerland was for industrial capital and what tax havens are for financial capital. Our land should become the safe haven of the new globalized economy, freed from the laws of nation states. It will be sufficient for our island to become a free port.

As the daily *La Repubblica* did not fail to notice on the occasion, the mafioso's strategy

> is exactly the programme for Sicily presented in parliament by the party of Cavaliere Silvio Berlusconi. In 1996 his men called

the project 'Fredrick II'. The strategy was to boost the Sicilian economy through the creation of offshore fiscal havens and the institution of a Sicilian free port. Who can be surprised if the Cavaliere, or whoever speaks on his behalf, will be very, very irate?[27]

As a result of the polemics (and given Berlusconi's control of public broadcasting as prime minister), the final season of *The Octopus* was broadcast in 2001. Berlusconi's television stations were eager to fill the void: in 2007 a new series titled *Il capo dei capi (The Boss of Bosses)* – not to be confused with the biopic of the same name on Paul Castellano – aired on the Berlusconi-owned Canale 5. It was the mythic, almost hagiographic biopic of Salvatore Riina from his humble origin to his arrest. Without the complications of democratic cinema, the Mafia could still sell.

In truth, however, *The Boss of Bosses* did not sell that well. Whether Berlusconi liked it or not, *The Octopus* had changed the Mafia film in Italy forever.

Organized Prime

About 17 spots have been made so far.
Among them are ones named 'Bada Bing' and 'Cannoli'.
Twelve car dealers in seven states have used them so far.
The ads also appear on fliers, YouTube videos and billboards.
And for the little ones? The children's network Nickelodeon
is making a kiddie TV movie about the Mafia.
– Dona De Sanctis, 'It's *Only a Movie*', in *Italian America* (2006)

Corleone boss Leoluca Bagarella was not the only mafioso trying to live his life to the soundtrack of the *Godfather* theme: Coppola's movie had also made a splash in the underworld of the United States.

After seeing the picture in 1972, a young wannabe, Salvatore 'Sammy the Bull' Gravano, who one day would acquire Mafia fame, was exultant. 'I left that movie stunned,' Gravano reminisced. 'I mean, I floated out of the theater. Maybe it was fiction, but for me then, that was our life. It was incredible. I remember talking to a multitude of guys, made guys, everybody, who felt exactly the same way. And not only the Mob end, not just the mobsters and the killing and all that bullshit, but that wedding in the beginning, the music and the dancing, it was us, the Italian people!'[28]

The 'wannabe' in question was a rather peculiar character for an American Mafia story. Salvatore Gravano was not the poor immigrant that, like Scarface or Vito Corleone, had found in the Mafia a way for social advancement in the typical Horatio Alger pattern of rags to riches. Instead he was the son of that part of the Italian-American community that, like Amerigo Bonasera, had made a good life for itself in America: a dress factory, a brick row home in Bensonhurst and even a vacation cottage in Long Island.

Crime, for him, had nothing to do with social climbing. It was a different kind of passion. That passion began manifesting itself in 1952 when Salvatore, aged seven, started stealing cupcakes from a local grocery – not for need, but just for the fun of it. Once caught he escalated his reckless behaviour, becoming a feared street gangster in Bensonhurst. He was 'made' in 1968, as an associate of the Colombo family.

Despite lending his services in larceny, hijacking and armed robbery, the kid from the rich block did not quite fit the profile. His commitment, however, was beyond question. He was quickly promoted to racketeering, loan-sharking and homicide: 'I felt a surge of power', he later reminisced: 'It's just that killing came so easy to me.'[29] It came, in fact, as easily as in the movies. Because that was the Bull's true passion: to live as if in a Mafia movie. Cosa Nostra, for him, had never been the road to the American Dream, but rather the pathway to a life of Hollywood stunts.

That cinema and real life were for him a veritable melting pot, we know from his daughter Karen:

> Once we were at a movie theater in Phoenix, he pulled a gun from his pocket and was poised to use it on a guy who seemed to be following us. I didn't know what was happening. We were just leaving the movie theater when he had grabbed me by my arms and ordered me to keep walking. I watched in horror as he put his hand on the revolver stuck in the back of his pants.[30]

Gravano thought cinematically: the anticipated scene came straight out of the John Dillinger mythology. He must have imagined himself as a new Dillinger, stepping out of the Biograph Theater in Chicago after watching *Manhattan Melodrama*, only to be shot by the FBI. It would have been as beautiful as *Public Enemies*, with Johnny Depp playing the part of

Dillinger – or of Gravano? Truth be told, it was not the FBI ambushing him, but the theatre manager asking for an autograph – better than nothing, arguably, for the Hollywood-struck Gravano!

Gravano would eventually crown his dream of becoming a true Mafia-movie star in 1998 when *Witness to the Mob* came out (with Nicholas Turturro in the part of Gravano) to celebrate the Bull's talent for murder: the slayings of his best friends, his wife's brother and his own boss. Gravano seemed, however, quite conscious of the fact that his middle-class origins were not exactly the material for Hollywood. By the mid-1980s he was already looking for a more proper character to cast in the role of Mafia hero in a classic quest for the grand American Dream. He found that hero in John Gotti. Gotti, more than Gravano, 'was like a movie star'.[31] Aptly born in the poverty of the Italian-American Bronx, Gotti had risen to some prominence in the Gambino family, trafficking drugs out of the Ozone Park neighbourhood of Queens. He had ambitions. He was ready to become the new Scarface. Like Tony Camonte, he needed now to take the place of his boss. And *that* movie was scripted entirely by the Bull.

Gravano planned the murder of Paul Castellano, Gotti's boss, in a stunt worthy of Hollywood. First, along with Frank DeCicco, Joseph Armone, Robert DiBernardo and Gotti himself, Gravano chose a name for the conspiracy:

> the five conspirators . . . picked a symbolic name for their cabal as if they were reenacting a scene in an espionage novel or movie. Each would represent a finger of a lethal hand called 'the Fist'.[32]

Gravano then formed a firing squad of eleven to ambush Castellano.

In the tradition of gangster cinema, the location for the shooting was a restaurant – Sparks Steak House on East 46th Street between 2nd and 3rd Avenues (presumably a barber shop might have worked too). By 5 p.m. on 16 December 1985 (Christmastime, as in *The Godfather*'s Sollazzo war) the firing squad, properly costumed in white trench coats, Russian-style fur hats (don't ask me why) and walkie-talkies, had taken position around Sparks: two shooters at the restaurant's entrance, seven more at the corners of 46th Street, and Gravano with Gotti in a car parked at the corner of 3rd Avenue. As Castellano's car approached the front of the restaurant, the shooting began. Castellano fell like Don Vito in *The Godfather Part 1*. Gravano and Gotti's car approached the dead body for a close-up then panned away, so to speak, heading back to Brooklyn. On the way, news of the murder could be heard on the radio. Even Coppola could not have staged it better! As James Poniewozik wrote in *Time* magazine, 'the mafia gave the movie material. The movies gave John Gotti a script.'[33]

That script produced the greatest media sensation ever. Every event in Gotti's life after the Castellano murder was grist for the media: his annual income of $500 million; his $2,000 Brioni suits (hence the nickname 'Dapper Don'); his Mephistophelian smile; his mocking offers of espresso to undercover FBI agents tailing him; his intimidation of witnesses; his escape from a bomb that bosses Anthony Corallo and Vincent Gigante had set for him; his racketeering trials . . . He was the new Al Pacino living the life of luxury shown in De Palma's *Scarface*. Sure Capone had liked the press, Costello and Valachi the TV, but none of them could possibly have equalled Gravano's creation: Dapper Don John Gotti. As an editorial of *Media Industry Newsletter* contended:

> 'Scarface' could not match the 'Dapper Don' in telegenics, nor could any other mobster for that matter. Which is why, following Gotti's death, retired FBI agent Bruce Mouw (whose forensics helped convict Gotti for the 1985 murder of Paul Castellano) gave this 'epitaph' to *The New York Times*: He was the first media don.[34]

Media interest in Gotti was fully reciprocated. *Time* magazine once put an Andy Warhol portrait of him on its cover, and the media-hungry Gotti promptly hung a framed copy in his office. As Andrew Maloney, the attorney who prosecuted and finally put him in jail, once said, John Gotti 'was made to order for the press. The way he looked, dressed, his arrogance toward the law. The press was manipulated by him and turned him into a folk hero. Almost everyone forgot or downplayed the fact that he was a vicious murderer.'[35]

On the other hand, maybe the press did not downplay his vicious murders after all: maybe those, too, were like a movie for the press. Because, with Gravano and Gotti, Mafia life was becoming indistinguishable from Hollywood spectacle. A murder like Castellano's was a spectacle too. FBI wiretaps recorded endless discussions between Gotti, Gravano and their associates, critiquing the cinematic qualities of the re-enactments of the Castellano murder that had been broadcast on television. Moreover:

Rudolph Giuliani, the former New York City mayor (and Mob-movie fan), said in his gangbusting prosecutor days that you could tell the difference between surveillance tapes recorded before and after the Godfather movies came out: the hoods started speaking like characters in the films. The movies that mobsters made possible ended up remaking the mobsters.[36]

Cosa Nostra had morphed into a real-life show.

When Gotti's son John Jr got married, the wedding became the pretext for a *Godfather* re-enactment. The movie *Gotti: In the Shadow of the Father* (with John Travolta in the role of Dapper Don), the second biopic after *Gotti* (1996), exploited this parallel quite intentionally:

> The *Godfather*, of course, begins with a wedding, but in Junior's film, called *Gotti: In the Shadow of the Father*, the wedding is Junior's. It took place at the Helmsley Palace in 1992, and in honor of the day, Leona Helmsley draped a twenty-foot Italian flag outside the hotel. Gotti's best man was his first soldier, who was later murdered. Every New York family had its own table, each mobster dressed in a tux. There was lobster and Cristal. Gangsters handed Junior envelopes of cash – a haul of $348,000 – and then lined up at Senior's table to pay homage, all the while plotting to settle scores. 'That scene will be in there,' said Gotti confidently. 'We want something Godfather-esque.'[37]

Even during the much-publicized trial, there is no doubt that 'the media played up mob leader John Gotti's case like it was something out of *The Godfather* movie saga.'[38]

John Gotti was certainly not the first American mobster with a media life (and afterlife); he was the first, however, who had almost erased the thin line separating the real Mafia from the fictional one. 'The "real" – mafia sociologists were remarking in the years of Gotti's ascent to fame – is difficult to discern from the fictional.'[39] By the time Gotti had risen to the stardom of the Dapper Don, what was real had become next to impossible to distinguish from the images produced by the cultural industry: 'It is impossible to ascertain the truth', argues one study on the media representations of the Mafia's facts and fictions; 'what remains and is perpetuated is myth.'[40] The long sequence of Mafia films based on 'real events' – *Goodfellas* (1990), *Bugsy* (1991), *Casino* (1995),

Donnie Brasco (1997) – staged real life just as Gravano and Gotti, in real life, were staging Hollywood. Real-life television could start from there: *The Rise and Fall of a Real Life Mafia Don* (on Gotti) became, in 1996, the highest rated 'real-life' film in H B O history to date. After this came the Mafia reality show – Victoria Gotti's own *Growing Up Gotti* and, more recently, *Mob Wives*.

The soundtrack for Gotti's ascent to fame, and for his staging of a Mafia between 'the real' and 'the fictional', was no doubt gangsta rap. The music world had always had a fascination with the Mafia that went beyond Nino Rota's 'Godfather Theme'. Ballads on Salvatore Giuliano and other bandits were always part of the Robin Hood folk tradition of southern Italy. As early as the 1940s, rumours of Frank Sinatra's involvements with boss Willie Moretti occupied the gossip columns of so many papers that the singer Johnny Fontane of the first *Godfather* was taken by some to be an allusion to 'the Voice'. Even jazz was not shy in capitalizing on the theme of the Mafia: Joey DeFrancesco's album *Goodfellas* (1999) is a case in point. During John Gotti's reign, however, it was rap music that saw in the Mafia an immense repertoire to cultivate.

To be precise, I am talking here of rap music outside of Italy. In Italy, in fact, the wave of anti-Mafia begun with democratic cinema was far from receding. Still in 2014, when an album of traditional Mafia ballads titled *Il Canto di Malavita* (*Songs from Criminal Life*) was released, it provoked such an outcry that many distributors preferred not to sell it in its country of origin. Even rap, accordingly, took in Italy the route of anti-Mafia songs: 99 Posse's 'All'antimafia' (To the anti-Mafia); Frankie hi-nrg's 'Fight Da Faida' (Fight against the Mafia Feud); Mass MC's 'Der Pate' (The Godfather); Bisca's 'Profumo di maggio' (The Smell of May, on Peppino Impastato's murder); Almamegretta's 'Sudd' (South) . . .

In the U.S., instead, the Mafia seemed to fit the quintessential image of rap's 'badman tradition': Snoop Doggy Dogg's hit album *Tha Doggfather* (1996); The Gambino Family rap group in New Orleans; the recording studio Murder Inc Records run by Latino gangsta rap artist Irv Gotti (actually Irving Lorenzo) in Queens; Lil' Kim's album *La Bella Mafia* (2003), dedicated to 'the whole Gotti family'; rap artist Scarface (Brad Terrence Jordan) . . . What did African-American and Latino rappers see in the Mafia? Perhaps they saw in it precisely what Italian rappers saw in the anti-Mafia: a form of artistic militancy against social norms and the status quo. Whereas the battle cry of Italian rappers – Almamegretta's 'resist', for instance – was directed against the collusion of Mafia and politics ('senators and mafiosi' in 'Sudd'), in the U.S. the same 'resistance' took instead the form of the Mafia badman:

> The badman plays on all of white America's fears . . . and, most frighteningly (for the mainstream), is imagined as individually triumphant in the battle with white America rather than falling victim to lynching or castration. The badman does not remain within the realms of acceptable black behavior established through community norms, but he is heroic by virtue of his very lawlessness in a society where law has often proven the definitive sign of African American inequality, either by means of legal or judicial injustice.[41]

It may certainly be ironic that this black appropriation of the figure of the white (and often supremacist) mafioso could only fold into yet another re-appropriation: Gotti, the real mafioso, was made into a cultural icon precisely by these fictional appropriations of his real persona.

What such blurring of the lines between reality and fiction ultimately meant is perhaps still open to interpretation. For some it meant that the real Mafia, with Gotti, was at its twilight. Gotti's arrest, the RICO statute, FBI crackdowns from New York to Florida and growing numbers of mobsters defecting into government witness programmes all exposed an unprecedented vulnerability of the American Mafia. Cosa Nostra, losing its hold on real America, was perhaps preparing its afterlife in another, fictional world of pure sensationalism.

Gotti himself seemed to subscribe to such an interpretation: 'You'll never see another one like me.' Precisely like the great tragic hero of the American gangster film, Gotti, by now a character from a film himself, had to meet his scripted destiny and bring down with him the whole Mafia that he had so glitteringly represented. 'At the dawn of a new century', writes Selwyn Raab, through Gotti's demise, 'the American Mafia was portrayed as a crushed Colossus.'[42] Upon Gotti's death on 10 June 2002, the usually restrained *New York Times* wrote a 3,000-word obituary. It too concluded that, with Gotti's death, the Mafia was also over. Its place had been taken by a spectacular show: Dapper Don was for the *New York Times* 'a relic of earlier days, before the Mafia became the sordid and self-conscious crew portrayed on *The Sopranos*'.[43]

The Sopranos

CARMELA: Everything comes to an end!
– *The Sopranos*, dir. David Chase

Whether the Mafia of the late 1990s was truly a 'relic' or not, there is no doubt that the television series that began the new millennium – the HBO show that 'changed the face of American television' – was quite a 'self-conscious' reflection on the Mafia's fate, both on and off screen.[44]

Self-consciousness, most obviously, is the cipher of *The Sopranos*' psychoanalytic subplot. The pilot episode opens memorably in the office of psychiatrist Jennifer Melfi. Through the legs of a female nude – a strange nativity scene bringing us into the world of *The Sopranos* – we glimpse a plump yet strong man, middle aged, pruriently turning his eyes towards us. Slowly he focuses on the statue's naked breasts. Mafia boss Tony Soprano – uncomfortable in the therapist's chair – has come for a consultation. He suffers panic attacks but, try as he might, 'can't talk about [his] personal life'.

What anxiety afflicts the mobster? In the face of Tony's hackneyed 'very strong resistance' to therapy, perfervid Dr Melfi does not give up: the contours of a rather traumatic family romance soon enter the clinical picture – and, with it, the very picture we are watching.[45] Reminiscent perhaps of the Addams Family (Judith Malina, the Addams' Grandma, reappeared after all as Aunt Dottie in *The Sopranos*, while Uncle Junior *does* look like an incorrigible Uncle Fester of sorts), the Sopranos are a distressing bunch indeed: a psychotic uncle, an out-of-control nephew (Christopher), a perennially discontented mother straight out of the Bates Motel and then the usual middle-class, suburban angst of 'kids taking drugs and getting in trouble, marriage and divorce, infidelity, broken friendships, depression, illness'.[46] There are plenty of good reasons, no doubt, for Tony to panic.

There is an even bigger reason, however, which has little to do with Tony's admittedly dysfunctional family:

TONY: Lately I'm getting the feeling I came in at the end. The best is over.
MELFI: Many Americans, I think, feel that way.
TONY: I think about my father. He never reached the heights like me. But in a lot of ways he had it better. He had his people, they had their standards and pride. Today, what have we got?

Tony Soprano at Dr Jennifer Melfi's office, David Chase (dir.), *The Sopranos* (HBO, 1999).

Longing for a better time when the forefathers had it better; a sense of loss, meaninglessness and a lack of direction: *The Sopranos* begins where *The Godfather Part III* had ended – from Vincent's nostalgia for grandfathers making three bucks a week; from Mary's cry, 'Only in America!', echoed now by Melfi's sad realization, 'Many Americans, I think, feel that way.' It is the sense of an ending.

'46 Long', the second episode of *The Sopranos*, opens on a similar note. Tony Soprano and his gang are watching TV. The show is continually interrupted by snide commentaries, impersonations of Michael Corleone – 'Just when I thought I was out, they pull me back in' – and (peculiar) reflections on the rise of Mexican organized crime. Through the vicarious eyes of the Sopranos, we are watching an interview with Vincent Rizzo, former soldier in the Genovese family turned government witness and – it goes without saying – best-selling Mafia author. The topic at hand is the present state of the Mafia:

ANCHORMAN: John Gotti. Life in prison, no chance of parole. We've seen prosecutions in Florida and elsewhere of top Mob figures . . . What's the situation on the ground today, right now, in the Mob?
RIZZO: The party's over . . . It's not like it was . . . you know, the heyday? You know, the Golden Age . . . or whatever, of the Mob? That's gone. And that's never coming back.

Tony, seemingly irritated, shoots a rubber band at Rizzo's face on the TV. His associate Paulie also grows impatient: 'They pay this *chiacchierone* by the word?!'

Why such impatience, one might ask, and why such irritation? Truth is, the *chiacchierone*, the chatterbox, might have touched a raw nerve. Once more the disturbing sensation of having arrived too late settles in. The Mafia is indeed a 'relic', to use the word of the *New York Times*. Or, as *Television Quarterly* put it in its commentary on the episode,

> [in late-1990s America] the power of the Mafia, though still con-siderable, has long been on the wane. Recent estimates of the current membership of the Mafia indicate that there are no more than 1,000 made members of the mob, down from a high of about 5,000 in the nineteen-fifties. In fact the number of actors who have played or are currently playing made members of the mob prob-ably far exceeds the men who were or actually are members.[47]

Tony and Paulie too are the leftovers of a bygone era – anxiously, self-consciously so. After Tony tries to hide his therapy sessions from his crew across twelve long episodes (psychoanalysis is not becoming for a mafioso), we discover, in the thirteenth episode, that he's not the only one who sought counselling. 'Look', reveals Silvio Dante, 'this thing of ours, the way it's going . . . be better if we could admit to each other . . . these are painful, stressful times.' How can one still be a mafioso in the year 1999 when the situation on the ground is so dire? And, for that mat-ter, how could one play a made member or launch a Mafia series when the Mafia's Golden Age, 'or whatever', is gone, never to return? No won-der David Chase, the series creator and head writer, thought 'there's an overwhelming sadness about *The Sopranos*'![48]

A trouble shared, Dr Melfi must have thought, is a trouble halved. In 1999 this sense of an ending, this panic in the face of doom, is not the Mafia's own: 'Many Americans, I think, feel that way' too. If Melfi's scarcely encouraging words sound like yet another allusion to the cen-tral theme of the American Mafia movie – the American Dream and its aftermath – it is because, in a sense, they truly are. Scarface had a dream, and so did Michael Corleone, who wanted to escape the 'business' of America for a nobler, 'old' Mafia of idyllic Sicily. Now that the Mafia of *The Sopranos* has become conscious of its own demise, it is clear that dreams, alas, are not what they used to be.

Of course 'dreams in *The Sopranos* are the rule rather than the exception.'[49]
No other series in the history of television ever made such a consistent use
of dream sequences – dreams of talking fish, butterflies and dead people.
In the psychoanalytic setting of *The Sopranos*, Dr Melfi makes the trite
observation that 'Freud says dreams are wishes' (4.11). The banality of the
therapist's remark completely misses, as it is often the case, the real problem:

TONY: Well, I had a dream the other night . . . I was riding in a
Cadillac, like my father used to have. Carmela was driving, and
I was in the back passenger seat . . . I don't know where we were
going. No place. 'Cuz we never seemed to get anywhere. Kinda
like this therapy . . . That's all of it. Oh, and . . . my friend had a
caterpillar on his head. It turned into a butterfly.
MELFI: Has your friend recently changed?
TONY: Not a friend. Associate. And no.
MELFI: What do you think the dream means?
TONY: Can't you tell me what the fucking thing means?

Ready, like the caricature of the therapist she is, to over-interpret an
alleged deep symbolic meaning hidden in a butterfly, Melfi completely
misses the literal point: as Tony bellows, 'Oh, fuck the dream, it's just a
dream!' It is just a dream, quite disturbingly, in which nothing can be
wished anymore. Going to 'no place', driven in the back seat, Tony is left
with dreams that, in a sense, cannot dream of anything anymore: they're
just dreams.

That 'we never seemed to get anywhere' is not merely his personal
problem, but the very fate of America and its Dream: this was a point Tony
had already tried to make to Dr Melfi in the first season (1.7). Here too,
Melfi had missed the point:

TONY: You're born to this shit. You are what you are.
MELFI: Within that there's a range of choices. This is America!
TONY: (*scornfully*): Right, America!

Forgetting that 'Many Americans . . . feel that way', and pathologizing
Tony instead, she remains incapable of seeing that his panic belongs to
the whole nation.

It is in those same years, as a matter of fact, that Tony's begins to be
called 'the Prozac nation' – and not for nothing:[50]

The Sopranos fit in with the current fin de siècle melancholy that seems momentarily to have gripped our culture. It is the feeling that our best days are behind us that permeates books like Tom Brokaw's best selling *The Greatest Generation* and *The Greatest Generation Speaks*, James Bradley's *Flags of our Fathers*, or films such as Steven Spielberg's *Saving Private Ryan*.[51]

Whence such a sense of despair? Sociologists could quickly answer: 'social mobility', a concept established by the sociologist Pitirim Sorokin in the 1920s as the precondition to realizing the American Dream, had brusquely come to a halt in the America of the 1990s. 'The proportion of families to remain in the same quintile', reported one *Encyclopedia of Social Problems*, 'increased from about 35 percent in the 1970s to about 40 percent in the 1990s.'[52] Characters of *The Sopranos* may concur: Christopher's aspirations to be 'made' into a mafioso flounder because – Tony informs him – 'the books are closed. They're not accepting any new members' (1.2). As for Tony, he was still lucky enough to having made it into a McMansion (it was featured in *Architectural Digest*).[53] The future of his children, Anthony Jr and Meadow, however, remains less certain. Worries about college and job prospects bring Tony together with 'the vast majority of Americans at the time' who had started to worry about the lack of social mobility.[54]

The Sopranos, as a consequence, is brimming with hints of the epochal decline and fall of the American Dream. If the *Godfather* saga had pictured the dark side of the American Dream while it was still triumphant, Tony now witnesses its progressive corruption: the Monica Lewinsky scandal (1.11); 'those Enron-type connections' (4.1); and the war in the Middle East 'routinized' in the fourth season.[55] What is worse is that this sense of general decay cannot simply be blamed on Washington or al-Qaeda. There is, for instance, a telling episode (5.10) in which Tony, ostensibly a patriot, wishes for a moment that security at American ports and water-fronts were more secure to prevent terrorists from smuggling in a biological weapon or a bomb. The thought does not last long: the idea of speculating on American weaknesses, no matter the destinies of the national commu-nity, brings him back to himself. We are, after all, in the land of self-made selves. He will steal a cargo shipment.

As Tony progressively abandons 'standards and pride', and even his patriotism, for personal gain, we are also, uncomfortably, like Tony at Dr Melfi's office, forced to register the naked truth:

the moral failure behind all of Tony's professional successes – from his destructive business activities to the direction his spoiled, sulky children are taking in life – suggests that America has failed in its original idealistic undertaking: to balance its vaunted individualism with responsibility to the larger community – local, national, and global.[56]

Tony's hypocrisy is everybody's hypocrisy, and the Mafia movie, by the 1920s, had already alerted us all of the imminent danger: the myth of the self-made individual is hardly reconcilable with the needs of any larger community. The Dream has now come to an end, revealing itself ultimately unable to 'balance' anything at all.

Virtually all characters in *The Sopranos*, while boasting moral superiority vis-à-vis the mobster, participate in 'the sniveling hypocrisy of mainstream middle-class Caucasian professionals (clergy, teachers, lawyers, therapists, politicians, doctors)'.[57] They are only too happy, while criticizing him, to take advantage of Tony's wealth and power: Dr Melfi has a parking ticket annulled (1.4); Anthony Jr's teacher gets back his stolen car (1.3); Carmela, Tony's wife, confesses to her priest that she has always turned a blind eye to her husband's real 'business' for the sake of a life of luxury (1.5); Father Intintola himself knows well who Tony is but he is happy enough to be a *schnorrer*, as he puts it: a freeloader in the Soprano household.

Film critic Dana Polan seems to have made it his mission to argue – convincingly – that such hypocritical betrayal of all 'standards and pride' occurs not only in the lives of the characters, but in the lives of the viewers. For the urban professional class with disposable income for pay-per-view television, the suburban Italian-American setting of *The Sopranos* displayed 'kitsch, tastelessness, [and] political incorrectness' as something to laugh about from a presumed distance. The show offered:

> the urban sophisticates a chance to slum, an opportunity to throw off propriety and flirt thereby with a scandalous and even dangerous world. In this respect, it probably is important that *The Sopranos* offer stereotypes of Italians: the show can thereby engage in political incorrectness for liberals who want both to feel above such attitudes *and* to find relief in a context in which they are not responsible.[58]

Yet vicarious identification with Tony's obscenities and tastelessness is always accompanied in *The Sopranos* by the show's much celebrated irony, its so-called status as 'quality television', which creates a distance between viewer and character.[59] In other words the classic dynamic of identification and (ironic) repulsion, which characterizes the American gangster genre, is at work here too.

Here too, as Sandra Gilbert puts it, the Mafia, 'the Sopranos R us.'[60] And if the viewer of *The Sopranos* was not much better in the end than the mobsters on the screen, even worse was the cultural industry's tongue-in-cheek exploitation of the franchise: HBO added an extra season – a sixth – to the planned series and syndicated the entire show (A&E won the auction). It also created Sopranos bus tours, cookbooks, do-it-yourself manuals, coffee-table guides, an anthology of scripts, a trivial pursuit game, a pinball machine, a video game, a Tony-and-Carmela line of clothing (it did not go well), and – inevitably – deluxe DVD sets. Oh, and I forgot the publishing of *The Tao of Bada Bing! Words of Wisdom from The Sopranos!* As Michael Corleone would have said, 'it's all business':

> HBO's own marketing of *The Sopranos* and its ancillary products thus targeted . . . a savvy audience which replaces aesthetic refinement and critical depth with a bleeding-edge creativity in which morality and meaning matter only insofar as they remain saleable.[61]

Just as the mobster brackets 'standards and pride' for the sake of business, so does a whole society suspend 'morality and meaning' for sales, or for the thrill of 'bleeding-edge' TV entertainment. It is no wonder that, without standards, pride, morality and meaning, the American Dream could survive no longer. As Tony railed, 'Oh, fuck the dream, it's just a dream!'

Once again the American Mafia movie has become an allegory for an entire nation, but this time for a nation that is in crisis. As Anthony Jr summarizes in the series finale, tellingly titled 'Made in America':

> You people are fucked. You are living in the dream . . . Don't you see it? Bush let al-Qaeda escape the mountains. Then he has us invade another country. It's like America . . . I mean, this is still the place where people come to make it. And what do they get – bling! And come on for shit they don't need and can't afford.

The waning of the American Dream, and the progressive realization that 'we' are complicit in its evanescence, seem, then, a sufficient cause for Tony's panic:

> This is one of the reasons given for Tony Soprano's anxiety attacks in the television series. The 'business' of the Mafia is taking over from the 'value system' . . . Just like Michael Corleone, Tony is unsure whether it is his failing . . . or a modern society . . . that is causing the stress.[62]

Tony is like Michael Corleone; *The Sopranos* like the much-quoted *Godfather* saga; the Mafia like Coppola's America.

Sure; but if so, we would be no further than we were with the *Godfather* and Michael Corleone: business is inescapable and everyone is doomed to submit to it, even if that means making yet another Mafia movie. And this is precisely the problem of *The Sopranos*. Besides a dysfunctional family, besides the death of a dream and the inescapable fate of 'business', there is in fact a newer and more ponderous reason for panic: all narrative possibilities for a Mafia movie are now exhausted. All has been said and done. How can one still be a mafioso in the year 1999? Or, *mutatis mutandis*, how can one keep a Mafia series running from 1999 to 2007? Is it possible to do anything other than repeat *The Godfather*? Both Tony and Chase seem to feel 'that they've literally arrived late on the scene of history and that there's nothing affirmative left to be said'.[63] They are, so to speak, the emblem (or symptom) of the Mafia genre's own exhaustion.

As early as 1967 the American novelist John Barth had presaged the advent of a new age – it was to be called postmodernism – in which nothing new could be said or done. He called the literature of this age

> 'the literature of exhausted possibilities' – or, more chicly, 'the literature of exhaustion'. By 'exhaustion' I don't mean anything so tired as the subject of physical, moral, or intellectual decadence.[64]

By 'exhaustion', Barth meant that narrative had to make do with the fact that it 'has pretty well exhausted the possibility of novelty'. What remained for narrative to do was to quote, cite, allude, repeat self-consciously what had already been narrated; to add 'footnotes' or 'postscripts' to previous stories.[65]

In this sense Tony Soprano and his gang are the emblematic characters of the exhausted Mafia genre: the exhaustion of the (American) utopia doubles in *The Sopranos* – and here is its greatness – into the exhaustion of the very narrative genre that had accompanied it. There is no doubt that 'self-consciousness, then, is a conspicuous feature of Tony Soprano's world even aside from therapy.'[66] It would be wrong, however, to assume that here self-consciousness concerns, as in the Italian democratic cinema of the 1980s, any sort of moral dilemma: does film fight or abet the Mafia? Does it help or hinder the Italian-American community? As with John Barth, we are not concerned here with 'anything so tired as the subject of physical, moral, or intellectual decadence'. In an epoch that has suspended, precisely, morality and meaning for bleeding-edge entertainment, self-consciousness is simply the anxiety of having nothing more, nothing new to tell about the Mafia and its great tragic hero. The only remaining question is how to create entertainment when all narrative possibilities are exhausted and the very myths that had sustained those narratives – the Mafia, the American Dream – are relics of a bygone era.

As John Barth had predicted, repetition is then the only option. To begin, characters seem doomed to play characters of other movies: Christopher plays Clemenza from *The Godfather Part I* – 'Louis Brasi sleeps with the fishes' (1.1); Silvio Dante plays Al Pacino – 'Fuck, is that Pacino or is that Pacino? Spitting image!' (1.2); Paulie's car horn plays the *Godfather* theme (1.11); and everybody relentlessly watches and comments on the whole *Godfather* saga (Part III sucks, everybody agrees), in addition to William Wellman's *The Public Enemy*, Martin Scorsese's *Goodfellas*, *Mean Streets* . . . In fact entire sequences of *The Sopranos* can only repeat similar ones from other movies. While Meadow sings in the choir, Brendan Filone is being killed (1.3). But haven't we seen the same in *The Godfather*, when the Sollozzos are being killed as Michael's godson is being baptized?[67]

The discourse on the Mafia is truly saturated and exhausted. This is the problem that makes Tony self-conscious. It is not only cinema that has said it all. Televisions run Mafia classics again and again, discuss the Mafia, interview mafiosi and the police and report on Cosa Nostra. At the dinner table, Dr Melfi discusses recent studies on the relation between psychoanalysis and the Mafia (1.8). At the golf course, the Mafia and John Gotti are topics for discussion between one round and another (1.10). Even in the ivory tower, university professors give lectures on the Mafia (4.3). The Mafia is talked about, represented, narrated everywhere.

This, it seems to me, is the fundamental trauma that Tony Soprano submits to Dr Melfi's analysis; the same one that David Chase lays on the Freudian couch of our viewership. Everything that could be said about and done with the Mafia film has been said and done. In this very sense, both Tony and Chase 'come in at the end'. As panic grows, a compulsion to repeat settles in symptomatically. Dana Polan singles out 'cyclicity and repetition' as the very narrative style of The Sopranos, in which characters and situations, while at times striving to change, never do:[68]

> In this respect, it is tempting to read the non-ending ending of the series . . . as, in fact, offering a closure of sorts, even if no end to the narrative was shown. In this view, there is no need to show what might happen next, since in a sense we know already what life had been like, is like, and will be like, for each character: Tony thus will always be seeking quiet moments with his family, even as he knows that menace could come from anywhere and at any time; Carmela may try to find furtive moments of independence, but ultimately she will always be there to stand by her man; Meadow will always be a bit unskilled at things like parallel parking and will always be coming to family events from her own life elsewhere; A. J. will always have limited career ambitions (or, rather, he will have ambition but not the follow-through) and will settle for whatever brings him immediate material comfort.[69]

While such cyclicality is certainly the inheritance from soap operas and the picaresque novel, and while it undoubtedly fits the arrested development of its characters, it remains above all the clear symptom of a narrative exhaustion: allusions, citations, recombinations and pastiche become the solutions for a Mafia TV show self-conscious of the impossibility to add anything new. What the heck: even the mobster at the psychiatrist's office has been done in Analyze This!

As Vincent Rizzo had said, 'the party is over', and as Tony confirmed, 'I come in at the end.' Like Barth's 'literature of exhaustion', 'The Sopranos' present their problem as a merely narrative one nothing to do with the tired question of moral or intellectual decadence. This is, after all, prime-time TV entertainment and nothing more. All is for leisure, amusement and recreation. Or is it? If this were a merely narrative problem, why does The Sopranos hint so continuously to a real America outside of the show?

Why do 'Many Americans, I think, feel that way'? And why does Tony so scornfully retort to Melfi's optimistic 'This is America'? with 'Right, America!'

In the real America, this sense of an ending could after all have spelled rather good news for the decline of the American Mafia. It was also, however, a rather alarming symptom for what the Mafia had always meant on the screen. Since the time of Hawks's *Scarface*, the Mafia had represented the desires and fears of a whole nation. Cast in the figure of a character at the margin of society – the gangster as outcast and outlaw, and ethnically marked as Italian – such desires and fears could then be ritualized from a safe distance. Despite fears, there was something to desire. Even in the *Godfather* saga, while the 'new' Mafia resembled 'business' more and more, there was always an 'old' Mafia, an elsewhere, a utopia to desire – Sicily, Don Tommasino, Apollonia's love, the family. The problem with *The Sopranos* is that there is nothing more to desire – even dreams, as Tony knows, are just dreams. Life is what it is, and repeats as such in a routinized social immobility and stagnation. 'The books are closed. They're not accepting any new members.' The end of social mobility coincides with the exhaustion of the Mafia film. When nothing can change, when the rags-to-riches plot is belied by social immobility, the tragic hero is no more. Exhaustion is not a mere narrative problem after all: the Mafia genre is exhausted, not because all has been said and done, but because the desires and fears that gave life to it are themselves exhausted.

In 2009 the *Wall Street Journal* published an article titled 'Will this Crisis Produce a Gatsby?' Its author, Sean McCann, looked back at the Great Depression of 1929: 'America became less equal and less fluid in the 1920s, as the era's prosperity increasingly benefited the wealthiest. By the end of the decade, the top 1 percent of the population received nearly a quarter of the national income.'[70] That situation, McCann argued, had galvanized novelists and film-makers in America to search for an emblematic figure – a Gatsby – capable of representing the crisis and somehow re-imagining the American Dream. Why, he asked, had the same not happened at the turn of the millennium, when a very similar crisis was gripping America? The fact is that the new crisis already had its Gatsby – but one self-conscious of the fact that a Gatsby had already come before him, and had eventually failed in reviving the American Dream. That new Gatsby was Tony Soprano, a man in the garbage business quoting from a Mafia repertoire that, with no desires or fears to represent anymore, had become ironic waste. His life, after his desperate attempts to represent the mafioso as yet another great tragic hero, could only end with the famous black screen that concluded the saga.

Many viewers were disappointed by the finale of *The Sopranos*. They expected closure: Tony killed at the restaurant, or Tony triumphing over his enemies. Either ending, many argued, would have given a final meaning to the whole saga and was therefore better than an inconclusive, meaningless blank screen. Yet, neither dead like Scarface nor refusing to die like Michael Corleone, Tony Soprano had only this one last chance to say and do something new with the Mafia movie. He simply disappeared, accepting the fate of a Mafia movie that could no longer mean anything at all. He disappeared because he had, after all, nowhere to go. This he learnt early on from a dream, an omen which a therapist, too zealous in her search for lofty meanings, had simply misunderstood: 'I don't know where we were going. No place. 'Cuz we never seemed to get anywhere.'

SIX

Avatars

Just as the American Cosa Nostra, battered by the RICO statute, seemed to have nowhere to go, so too in Sicily had the Mafia entered a period of decline. The Corleonesi's all-out war against both the State and the public at large had, in the end, backfired. Public opinion could no longer tolerate the escalation of brutality, and the State had to respond with a turn of the screw on Mafia operations. The special unit of the military police designed by Falcone and Borsellino and finally instituted in 1991, the Anti-Mafia Investigation Department (DIA), was showing an unprecedented zeal in its investigations. After Salvatore Riina's arrest in 1993, Leoluca Bagarella, his successor, was captured in 1995.

To prevent jailed bosses from communicating with the outside, *carcere duro*, a regime of total isolation for Mafia associates, was instituted in 1992 with article 41bis of the Italian criminal code. Riina had been reported as having sent coded messages from prison to other Mafia chiefs in handwritten notes, *pizzini*, as he called them in his half-baked Italian, disguised as comments about football or motor racing. Now in total isolation, without even the possibility of making phone calls and communicating with his lawyers, Riina and Bagarella bitterly complained of being 'tired of being exploited, humiliated, oppressed and used like goods exchanged among the various political forces'.[1] Despite national and international protests – which included Amnesty International and the European Court of Human Rights – 41bis was there to stay. The State and its institutions, simply, could not give the impression of compromising with the Mafia.

After Bagarella, his successor, Bernardo 'the Tractor' Provenzano, was arrested by the DIA in 2006. On the run for 43 years, the Tractor – a fitting name for one who, in the words of an informant, 'mows people down' – must have intuited that Riina's excess of violence was not too good for business. Provenzano's guidelines for the new Mafia were: a moderate use of violence; cooperation with still corruptible state institutions; and, above all, systematic infiltration of public finance. While it would be impossible to estimate how many mafiosi started wearing business suits to mix undetected within Italy's (and not only Italy's) stock markets, Bagarella's reforms were too little, too late. The police and the judiciary were now relentless in their determination to bring the Sicilian Mafia to its knees. By 1995 roughly $150,000 in property and assets had been confiscated from Riina alone. In the following years, that sum increased exponentially as more and more Mafia assets were frozen or sequestered.

Suffering repeated military, judicial and economic losses, the Sicilian Mafia was under siege. Proving yet again Villari's and Franchetti's adage that the Mafia is not brigandage, the crisis of the Sicilian Mafia could be measured through the parallel resurgence of petty criminality – theft and burglary – in the Sicily of the new millennium.[2] The poorest strata of the population that until then had been on the payroll of the Mafia were now on their own.

It would have been overly optimistic to presume that the Sicilian Mafia was finished. As Tommaso Buscetta said before dying of cancer in 2000, 'Giovanni Falcone and I deluded ourselves that this time the Mafia would be defeated.' Four years later, the historian John Dickie was also not ready to celebrate final victory:

> The 'rustic chivalry' myth is dead. The secret that the Sicilian mafia managed to keep for so long, the secret of its existence, is out, and out for good. But through all that time, forces much more formidable than myth have kept the mafia strong.[3]

It would be one more delusion to think even today that the Sicilian Mafia is no longer.

While the Sicilian Mafia remains in a mode of 'submersion', however, its avatars have not only taken its place and visibility in the new world order, but have even appropriated its myth and its very name.[4] In an interview released to the French newspaper *Le Monde* on 12 February 1993, then-President of Russia Boris Yeltsin described his own country as 'a powerful bulwark of the Mafia. We are surpassing countries like Italy, which have been historically on the forefront. We have Mafia structures that are corroding Russia at its core.'[5]

The following year the Italian judge Luciano Violante, President of the Anti-Mafia Commission from 1992 until 1994, published a volume tellingly titled *It is Not the Octopus: Twelve Theses on the Italian Mafias*. Alarmed at the imminent danger of organized crime in a nuclear powerhouse such as Russia, Violante could no longer talk about *the* Mafia, but of mafias in the plural.[6] These included not only the Russian 'mafia', the Latin American drug cartels, the Chinese Triad, and the Japanese Yakuza, but also the Italian 'Ndrangheta (from the region of Calabria) and the Neapolitan Camorra, all pushing their way onto the world stage of organized crime. In the years of globalization, the Mafia itself, warned Violante, had become globalized.

To be sure, none of these new mafias was the real thing. They had grown independently from the original Mafia, with no historical and structural connections with the Mafia of Palizzolo, Fontana and Riina. They were no longer, as Violante's title hinted, the Sicilian-trademarked Octopus. They were not part of Luciano's, Gambino's and Gotti's Sicilian-American *cupola*, either. They were, however, even more terrifying than the Mafia that had taken its first steps in the lemon groves around Palermo:

> the Mafia by today's standards of criminal activity seems almost a model of romantic banditry. The contemporary criminal world now consists of even more frightening criminal groups, such as Colombian narco-terrorists who don't hesitate to massacre innocent families and whole villages, or the Russian Mafia, which not only traffics in traditional criminal items such as drugs and prostitution, but has been known to steal and sell missiles and submarines, and – if John le Carré's recent novel *Single and Single* can be trusted – even blood plasma.[7]

While Violante's book was making waves in Italy, on 20 November 1994 the United Nations conference in Naples was devoted to the threat of these emerging global 'mafias'.

Just as the original Mafia of the 1870s was the by-product of the restructuring of Italy into a modern nation-state, these new ersatz mafias also came to life when state institutions, businesses and private property were being restructured the world over under the impact of globalization. Under the impulse of economic liberalization, new opportunities have arisen for criminal organizations. The opening of borders – the European Union, the North American Free Trade Agreement and the fall of the Iron Curtain – have made trafficking of illegal drugs, prostitution and the laundering of money easier than ever before: 'Free trade measures may be good for the global economy, but the subsequent growth in cross-border traffic has made it simpler for smugglers to hide contraband among legal goods.'[8] Furthermore economic reforms implemented under the banner of deregulation and free trade have often disrupted local economies unable to compete with the big multinationals, and have forced some of them to shift production to the manufacturing and distribution of illegal goods. If Mexican corn (to mention one country that saw a vertical increase of organized crime activities following NAFTA) could no longer compete in the global market, both fields and labour force had then to be converted for the production of opium and marijuana. The Russian 'mafia' came into being when a new post-communist nation was born after the demise of the Soviet Union; in China, the Triad re-emerged when Jiang Zemin's 'capitalist turn' led the country to join the World Trade Organization in 2001; in Japan, it was the economic crisis of the 1990s that led to the forging of new relationships 'between the liberal democratic party, the business world, and the underworld of the yakuza'; and in Latin American countries, with the increasing traffic of people and drugs as a result of NAFTA, the new mafias appeared as 'the dark side of globalization'.[9]

In Italy as well, organized crime had morphed, as Violante had intuited, into something else. Headquartered in mainland Italy, between the Neapolitan neighbourhood of Secondigliano and Casal di Principe near Caserta, its name dating back to the eighteenth century, the Camorra that moved into the twenty-first century, however, was a postmodern reality through and through: just as the postmodern tragic heroes of *The Sopranos* could only be a copy of the originals from classic gangster cinema, so the Camorra, a 'mixture of archaism and postmodernity', eminently capable of adapting 'to the regime of deregulation (and, in certain contexts, to the plain absence of rules) that characterizes today's global economy', was an avatar of the traditional Mafia.[10]

Gomorrah

Fake Mafia or real Mafia, I had no way of knowing.
Neal Stephenson, *Zodiac*

Near the beginning of Matteo Garrone's film *Gomorrah* (2008), a boy brandishes a toy gun: 'Who do you think I am? I am number one . . . I am Tony Montana . . . Colombians everywhere . . . The world is ours!'

Another boy feeds him the words, as if from a script. The two boys are Marco and Ciro, protagonists of one of the five plot lines intersecting in the movie. Their ambition, which sets their story in motion, is to become 'made' men in the Camorra. They stand in a now-dilapidated villa whose overdone architecture – doric columns a-plenty, a sweeping internal foyer, a hexagonal pool and baroque double stairways curving in a delusion of grandeur – seems to have come out of the garish fantasies of some pre-Gotti gangster in an American movie.

The words, the *script* that the two boys are rehearsing, come from the last sequence of Brian De Palma's *Scarface* (1983), the remake of Hawks's masterpiece from 1932 that, along with Coppola's *Godfather*, had managed to redefine an entire genre. In the last scene of the movie, Tony Montana (Hawks's Italian Camonte had become a Cuban refugee in De Palma's film, and his name was changed accordingly) is attacked in his own villa by the Colombian cartel: 'Who you think I am? I kill all you fuckin' assholes. I take you all to fuckin' hell!' Montana dies the death of the tragic hero: he falls, gun in hand, in the hexagonal pool. On top of it, a neon sign ironically glitters: 'The World is Yours.'

In fact the villa where the two boys of *Gomorrah* are acting out their fantasies of Camorra heroism is an exact copy of the one Scorsese had built for his movie.

This was not its first replica. In 2006 guests at the Electronic Entertainment Expo had been welcomed into a full-size copy of Tony Montana's villa. Here they could sit at a table to play Vivendi Universal Games' *Scarface: The World Is Yours*. In yet another reproduction of the villa – a digital one – players could assume the role of Tony to fight a bunch of Colombian hit men appearing like angry birds from all corners of the screen to kill him.

The curiosity of the villa in *Gomorrah*, however, is that it was not a stage set built for the movie. Camorra boss Walter Schiavone had actually erected the real thing in Casal di Principe in the 1990s. Legend has it that Schiavone had seen *Scarface* so many times, and had identified with Al Pacino's impersonation of Scarface to such an extent, that he gave a copy of the DVD to a local architect and commissioned from him a country house just like Tony Montana's. People in Casal di Principe knew the building as 'Hollywood'. Schiavone, to his chagrin, had little time to enjoy his fantasy. He was arrested in 1999 on murder charges and the villa, expropriated by the authorities, was converted into a physiotherapy centre for the disabled (Italian courts seem not to lack a sense of humour) in 2008.

Garrone's use of 'Hollywood' in the scene of the two aspiring Camorra associates was thus very well timed, as filming took place just before the villa's planned renovation. After democratic cinema, Schiavone's architectural insanity was a particularly effective visual reminder: cinema can easily be appropriated by criminals insofar as it enhances their legend. At a time when Mafia mobsters liked to be called Scarface (Pasquale Manfredi, for example), and when busts of Tony Montana could be found in the private homes of Mafia bosses (as, for instance, in the home of drug lord Carlo Padovani), virtually all Italian directors venturing in the territory of the Mafia movie, Garrone included, were aware of the danger: 'when Scimeca went on site in Sicily to film *Placido Rizzotto* . . . he found that the current Mafia just loves people coming to make films about them'; and when Marco Tullio Giordana began shooting *One Hundred Steps*, he soon realized that 'mafiosi are very happy to be represented in cinema.'[11]

As Antonino Tricomi summarized:

> mafiosi know that in our contemporary society one has to be constantly 'on stage', and that the media representation is more important than reality, to the point that the former replaces the latter. Therefore, they do aestheticize power by transforming it into a ritualistic spectacle.[12]

So when Garrone went to Scampia to film *Gomorrah* in the housing project of Le Vele, he had to face a major problem: 'often', he admitted, 'it's

Children at play, Matteo Garrone (dir.), *Gomorra* (Fandango, 2008).

Tony Montana's palace, Brian De Palma (dir.), *Scarface* (Universal Pictures, 1983).

cinema that helps to shape these people's taste, and not the opposite . . .
Even if the film denounces a given 'reality', it moves in a different direction.'[13] The danger was particularly present in the specific case of *Gomorrah*
since the movie, in a tribute to the neorealism of Francesco Rosi's *Giuliano*,
was to recruit non-professional actors from the low ranks of the real
Camorra to play their own part. Could the movie make them into stars?
Could it turn in the wrong direction indeed?

To prevent precisely such a turn, Garrone, a director well known for
his impeccable aesthetic sensibility, built a movie that cautiously resists
anything glamorous or spectacular. Shot in 4:3, *Gomorrah* resembles a
drab TV documentary: no widescreen, and no magic of cinema. The hand-
held camera increases the documentary effect and lack of aesthetic quality.
Gunfights, while brutal, remain quite unspectacular. After a Tarantino-
like beginning – the opening solarium sequence – falsely promising
fast-paced action, gore and violence, the movie quickly slows down,
proceeding at an often intolerably slow pace. Garrone's intention soon
becomes clear: the solarium sequence, like Schiavone's 'Hollywood',
alludes to the delusions of grandeur Camorra men have about themselves. It represents their own self-fashioning according to the models
provided by the cultural industry's transformation of crime into a spectacle: they *want* to be athletic, tanned heroes moving in fast-paced action
towards a life lived as a spectacular adventure.

What they truly are, instead, is pretty much defined by the images
(the photography is rigorously unglamorous throughout) of the dilapi-
dated locale where the rest of Garrone's movie unfolds. *Gomorrah* takes
place in the Neapolitan housing project of Le Vele:

a concrete ziggurat . . . of walkways suspended under a cloudy, peaked skylight. The walkways run between rows of apartments that are decaying at best, and at worst have had their facades ripped away, exposing a damp and crusted back wall that is reverting to the condition of a cave . . . Monumental Italian ruins, in the contemporary version.[14]

The housing project is where the Camorra finds its foot soldiers. They are mostly young children like Marco and Ciro, since jail time is shorter for children caught by the police. They deal drugs and kill in exchange for a second-hand motorcycle or a fistful of euros or, sometimes, just for the glory of being made men.

The young outlaws are managed by senior leaders, who live in the same squalor. They have no better opportunity in life than what the Camorra offers. Chronic unemployment and a total neglect on the part of the State make them a cheap labour force for anyone willing to give them a chance; the Camorra gives them one. Deliberately working against the conventions and expectations of the gangster genre, Garrone portrays them all as being as hopeless and unglamorous as the place they inhabit. 'Sweaty, dirty, badly dressed, overweight, unhealthy (one of them suffers from throat cancer and speaks with an artificial voice aid in a way which is grotesque and ominous)', they are 'a direct antidote to the glossy outlook of much of the film production on the subject of organized crime'.[15]

So by the time we get to the end of the movie, Marco and Ciro's illusions of a 'glossy' criminal life à la Scarface become utter, tragic disillusionment. They have defied the direct orders of their captains. Like Scarface, they want it all, they want to be number one. They must now be punished. They are killed – not in a spectacular battle against Colombians in the lavishness of a magnificent villa, but matter-of-factly, on a charmless sandy shore littered with garbage. The beach, which in much Italian cinema since Fellini's La Strada (1954) had been the archetypical 'locus of redemption', becomes 'an apocalyptic landscape . . . a cataclysmic vision of mountains of garbage'.[16]

Whereas the killings in the early solarium scene were fast and action-driven, the death of the youths (quite allegorical, if one thinks of the metaphor of youth as a symbol of hope in early post-war Italian neorealist cinema) comes slowly and without a proper climax. Marco and Ciro are just shot down. Their weapons – the very symbol for their having 'made

Beautifully tanned mafiosi at the solarium, *Gomorra*.

it' into the Camorra – are taken away from them. A bulldozer lifts their bodies to dispose of them – waste, like anything else, in the real world of the Camorra. It is as if, with them, Garrone wants to dispose of the very genre of the gangster movie. That genre, like the boys who had tried to shape their lives within it, is itself waste – a point that Tony Soprano, the garbage man from New Jersey, had also recently tried to make. Will we be able, after *Gomorrah*, to see a gangster flick again? Can one of any significance be produced still? Garrone, like David Chase, may well have wondered this, and so should we.

But if Garrone's *Gomorrah* is ultimately another reflection on the Mafia film in the epoch of its exhaustion (or at least of its ethical danger), Roberto Saviano's book – also called *Gomorrah* (2006), and from which the film selected a few paradigmatic plot lines – is altogether a different story. Saluted by the *New York Times* as 'the most important book of the year', Saviano's *Gomorrah* marks the return, in grand style, of the 'Mafia' to the written page.[17] Not since the time of *Cavalleria rusticana* had writing on the Mafia gained such powerful expression and, with more than 50 translations and millions of copies sold, deserved success.

In the 1870s Giovanni Verga had found in the Sicilian Mafia a mythical, ancestral sense of honour that he saw as lacking in the petty routines of Italy's middle-class existence. The Mafia, as he put it, had offered him 'a certain perspective' from where to lament, 'at a distance' from the general decay, the twilight of a bygone era of passions.[18] In 2006, by which point cinema had canonized Verga's Mafia into a routine of heroic actions that real mafiosi routinely appropriated to legitimate their (routinely brutal) actions, Saviano is in search again of a 'distance' – but distance, this time, from the very myths of Verga's Mafia now codified by cinema. Behind those myths is a reality, Saviano trusts, which words ought to uncover. As he writes after a visit to poet Pier Paolo Pasolini's tomb:

> I felt like finding a place where it was still possible to reflect without shame on the possibility of the word. The possibility of writing about the mechanisms of power, beyond the stories and details. To reflect on whether it is still possible to name names, one by one, to point out the faces, strip the bodies of their crimes, and reveal them as elements of the architecture of authority. To reflect on whether it is still possible to sniff out, like truffle pigs, the dynamics of the real, the affirmation of power, without metaphors, without mediation, with nothing but the cutting edge of the word.[19]

Once cinema's imaginary seems to have been completely taken over by real criminals, once cinematographic references create mythologies of imitation for real criminal organizations, the only 'distance', the only 'place of reflection' that remains for Saviano is 'the cutting edge of the word'. Beyond moving images is the word, able to cut the real from the fictive, the truth from the myth.

Saviano's *Gomorrah* reclaims such an ethical 'primacy of the word' as a form of militancy against the myths of Mafia cinema. The book is moved by a 'powerful desire to place the word at the center of a struggle against the mechanisms of power. Words against cement mixers and guns . . . The word, with its only armor . . . A word that is a vigilant witness, that never stops seeking the truth.'[20] So, word upon word, *Gomorrah* becomes

The death of youth, *Gomorra*.

a new page written in order to understand the workings and the darker side of globalized capitalism:

> It seemed to me an amended chapter of Marx's *Capital*, a paragraph added to Adam Smith's *The Wealth of Nations*, a new sentence in John Maynard Keynes's *General Theory of Employment, Interest and Money*, a note in Max Weber's *The Protestant Ethic and the Spirit of Capitalism*. A page added or removed, a forgotten page that never got written or that perhaps was written many times over but never recorded on paper.[21]

But what does organized crime have to do with capitalism that *The Godfather* had not already told us? Was not Coppola's saga already hinting, precisely, at the globalization of the Mafia as a capitalist (or 'business', to use Coppola's own word) network?

One important novelty registered by *Gomorrah* is that the criminal protagonist of the new globalized world is no longer the Mafia. Saviano's point is an easy one: the constant attention on Cosa Nostra and the Mafia has let the Camorra grow unnoticed and undisturbed into a monster of unprecedented proportions. The Mafia's crisis, simply put, was the Camorra's opportunity. In fact it was the very event that initiated the decline of the Mafia that triggered the Camorra's ascent: with the fall of the Berlin Wall, the Neapolitan families promptly transferred funds and made huge investments in Prague and Brno. By the early 1990s all criminal activities in the Czech Republic were controlled by the Secondigliano clan, which from there quickly moved to enter the market of unified Germany. While for the Sicilian Mafia of Riina the fall of the Berlin Wall had meant the weakening of its DC political protection, for the Camorra, it was simply a lucky chance. New markets were opening new commercial networks around the globe.

Before Western leaders understood the potential of these new possibilities, and before multinational corporations could make their move, the Camorra was already there. Taking advantage of the political and economic crises of Romania, Poland and the former Yugoslavia, it offered loans to finance the reconstruction of infrastructure and the rebuilding of defence. In exchange it gained control of arms depots and, most importantly, privileged entry into the new markets.

The Eastern European market was only the beginning. At the dawn of the twentieth century the Camorra controlled, through the port of Naples, traffic of unimaginable proportions. It was not simply drugs or contraband: in the new millennium, as Saviano put it, 'consumer goods have replaced the nicotine habit.'[22] Quicker than anybody else in recognizing the potential commercial success of the rising star of China, the Camorra soon capitalized on the enormous traffic to and from Eastern Asia. COSCO, the largest Chinese state-owned shipping company and the world's third-largest fleet, has its major European operation in the port of Naples – one of the world's largest: with over 900 m (3,000 ft) of pier, just under 140,000 m² (nearly 1.5 million ft²) of cargo room, and roughly 150,000 containers passing through every year, the COSCO terminal in Naples accounts for almost all the traffic in transit between Europe and China.

'Everything that exists passes through here', writes Saviano: 'there's not a product, fabric, piece of plastic, toy, hammer, shoe, screwdriver, bolt, video game, jacket, pair of pants, drill, or watch that doesn't come through here.'[23] What China builds and Europe consumes goes through Naples: 'the clothes young Parisians will wear for a month, the fish sticks that Brescians will eat for a year, the watches Catalans will adorn their wrists with, and the silk for every English dress for an entire season.'[24] And the Camorra stands patiently at the dock, shaving off its share from the wealth of nations. An estimated 60 per cent of all the goods passing through Naples bypasses official customs inspection. Fifty thousand shipments are contraband, 99 per cent of which comes from China. Amounting to an estimated 400 million euros in taxes evaded each year, this back and forth of cargo ships under the control of organized crime puts in the Camorra's coffers around 36 million euros of revenue per day, according to the anti-fraud unit of the Italian Customs Agency.

On top of this are the gains the Camorra extracts from the manufacture and wholesale of the prestigious products 'made in Italy'. Secondigliano, not Milan, is the true, if unsung, capital of the Italian fashion industry. 'Made in Italy' is made in Secondigliano. Here the most sought-after garments carrying the logos of Italian elegance are tailored before reaching every corner of the globe. The elegance of Hollywood stars is manufactured here by unseen workers. One such worker is Pasquale, whose story climaxes in one of the most unforgettable pages of *Gomorrah*:

Pasquale had turned on the television and was flipping channels, but all of a sudden he froze. He squinted at the screen, as if he were nearsighted, though he could see perfectly well. No one was talking, but the silence became more intense. His wife, Luisa, must have sensed something because she went over to the television and clasped her hand over her mouth, as if she'd just witnessed something terrible and were holding back a scream. On TV Angelina Jolie was treading the red carpet at the Oscars, dressed in a gorgeous garment. One of those custom-made outfits that Italian designers fall over each other to offer to the stars. An outfit that Pasquale had made in an underground factory.[25]

Underpaid, unrecognized by the world and unappreciated, Pasquale could not work as a tailor anymore after seeing the Oscars on television. He became a truck driver for a local clan. He remained, for Saviano, the hidden face of globalization: 'no one would have believed that Angelina Jolie would go to the Academy Awards wearing an outfit made . . . by Pasquale. The best and the worst. Millions of dollars and 600 euros a month.'[26]

In Secondigliano, for even less than Pasquale's 600 euros a month, workers toil at breakneck speed over sewing machines, manufacturing garments that will be sold in the luxury market under the most fashionable of Italian labels. Officially, as Saviano puts it, 'these factories don't exist, and neither do the employees.'[27] Unofficial – in other words, illegal – labour is the fuel that nourishes the global markets. No safe conditions, no minimum wages and no benefits translate into low labour costs, and low labour costs, in turn, into cheaper products – into the dream, that is to say, of democratized conspicuous consumption. The Italian Pasquales, with their skills, could certainly demand more. But many Secondiglianos are spread around the globe, many reservoirs of destitution and despair ready to offer labour and human lives at the lowest cost and for the most precarious working conditions. Work would simply disappear from the area and reappear in China or Bangladesh. Everybody in Secondigliano knows the logic of globalization better than any Chicago economist.

The way these factories work is perhaps unique. Major name brands come from Milan to Secondigliano to auction contracts. For a fixed price these name brands need a certain quantity of clothes in a certain number of weeks. There is no actual bidding on the price; the Milanese firms determine it. Each factory can decide whether to accept the deal or not, and all those that accept are given the necessary materials for free. The winner of the auction is the factory that delivers first. All others can keep the fabric and the already-manufactured clothes, but will receive no pay. The fashion houses will retail their pieces at such high prices that the material lost is not even a consideration.

The role of the Camorra at this stage of production is to offer loans to Secondigliano's manufacturing factories – for salaries, equipment, maintenance and shipping costs – with interest rates of 2 to 4 per cent. Why does organized crime play such a role in the production of the made in Italy? Where are the banks? 'No one', remarks Saviano, 'should have an easier time obtaining bank credit than these companies, who produce for the Italian fashion world, for the market of markets. But they're phantom operations, and bank directors don't meet with ghosts.'[28] What the Camorra gets in return, besides interest, is the material and finished garments that fashion houses have left behind to the losers of the auction. These garments will then be recirculated through the fake-goods market.

Their fakeness is, in fact, of a mind-boggling nature: they are surplus items prepared with exactly the same material, design and craftsmanship as the products sold as original in high-end boutiques. Even the logo is the 'original' one passed by the mother house to stitch on the final product. These are not cheap imitations but rather 'a sort of true fake'.[29] All that they miss is the authorization by the designer to sell the product under the fashion house's name. The Camorra usurps this authority and its subjects rejoice: a product perfectly identical to the one designed for the upper-class market becomes now accessible to the wider public. Franchetti was right: perverted or not, organized crime has always been a form of 'democratization'.

Although certainly not for the sake of democracy, the Camorra has set up shop everywhere: Hamburg, Dortmund, Frankfurt, Berlin, Barcelona, Madrid, Brussels, Vienna, Oporto, Boavista, London, Dublin, Amsterdam, Denmark, Sarajevo, Belgrade, New York, Miami Beach, New Jersey, Chicago ... Through the business of selling 'true fakes', certainly supplemented by drug money, the Camorra clans have 'acquired stores and shopping centers where genuine articles were increasingly mixed in with the fakes, thus erasing any distinction'.[30] So what is legitimate, and what is illegitimate? Which stamped article of clothing is original, and which one is a fake?

It may be surprising that Italy's major fashion houses have never put an end to this system that makes their original products compete with the identical fake ones. On the other hand, denouncing the situation 'would have meant forgoing once and for all their cheap labor sources' in Secondigliano.[31] The magic of globalization, the logic of low-cost speedy production, has its marginal costs as well. This is one page Saviano adds to the many already written on the economics of globalization. On this page, in capital letters, stands the word 'Camorra'.

But let's turn back our page for a moment and return to this whole business of fakes and originals, and to the issue, once more, of Mafia cinema. As we saw in the last chapter, after John Gotti reality was becoming increasingly confused with fiction. With the Camorra, it is now the fake and the original that have become impossible to tell apart. The situation seems almost allegorical of the Camorra itself – of a criminal organization that always appeared as an avatar, as a copy of the real Mafia.

There was always a profound injustice in all this which Neapolitan criminals must have always lamented. Take, for instance, the scarred face of the mafioso par excellence, the globally renowned Al Capone:

> Most of the criminal archetypes, the acme of Mafia charisma, were from a few square miles of Campania. Even Al Capone was originally from here; his family came from Castellammare di Stabia. Capone was the first boss to measure himself against the movies. His nickname, Scarface, from a scar on his cheek, was used by Brian De Palma for his 1983 film about Tony Montana, but Howard Hawks had used it previously for his 1932 movie about Capone.[32]

Even for *The Godfather*, 'Mario Puzo's inspiration was not a Sicilian but Alfonso Tieri, boss of Pignasecca in downtown Naples.'[33] Yet all these genuine artefacts of the Neapolitan heartland had become the archetype of the *Mafia*! The Mafia, not the Camorra, was always the selling brand.

So if, for Gotti and Gravano, movies had been a way to claim their lineage back to an old, mythical tradition of the Mafia, the situation for the men of the Camorra was altogether different. By the beginning of the new millennium they were the uncontested kings of organized crime, with interests that extended from Naples to the whole of Europe, to China, America, Australia and even Africa (where the Camorra is in the business of radioactive dumping). Yet they were kings without a tradition; with a brand name, Camorra, which signified little in the globalized world.

This lack of tradition, which had, perhaps, helped them in making their nimble moves soon after 1989 when they had capitalized on the fall of the Iron Curtain and the hegemony of neo-liberal globalization, became a branding problem. Turning to the movies and remaking the Scarface villa were, for them, not claims of belonging, but the desire to craft for themselves an image that they lacked. They were not the model for cinema; instead, they needed to model themselves after it, no matter if the resulting image, like the Versace blouses they were selling, was fake:

> Camorristi look to the movies to create for themselves a criminal image they often lack . . . Cinematographic inspiration even conditions technical choices such as the way you handle or shoot a gun: a veteran of the Naples Forensic Division once told me how Camorra killers imitate the movies: 'Ever since Tarantino, these guys don't know the right way to shoot! They don't keep the barrel straight anymore. Now they hold it crooked, like in the movies, which makes for disaster. They hit the guts, groin, or legs, seriously wounding but not killing. And so they have to finish the victim off with a bullet to the nape of the neck. A pool of pointless blood, a barbarism completely superfluous to the goal of execution.' Female bosses have bodyguards who dress like Uma Thurman in Kill Bill: blond hair and phosphorescent yellow outfits. Vincenza Di Domenico, a woman from the Quartieri Spagnoli who collaborated with the authorities for a short while, had the eloquent nickname of Nikita, the heroine killer in Luc Besson's film.[34]

It is not that the Camorra had never captured the cinematic imagination. Luigi Maggi had directed A Glimpse of Neapolitan Camorra in 1911, Marino Girolami filmed Amore e sangue in 1951 and Pasquale Squitieri had completed Camorra in 1972. These, however, were not titles that could compete, in either quantity or quality, with the cornucopia and fame of Mafia movies. At best the Camorra was the topic for the local sceneggiata, a form of lowbrow musical drama typical of Naples. Its star, Mario Merola, did try to bring the Camorra from the sceneggiata to cinema with Sgarro alla Camorra (Affront to the Camorra, 1973), La camorra sfida, la città risponde (The Camorra Challenges the City, 1979) and Il triangolo della camorra (The Camorra Triangle, 1981). Almost as proof of the Camorra's lack of status in the movie industry and in the popular imaginary beyond Naples, the last title was released in the u.s. as The Mafia Triangle. In the end it was always the Mafia!

If, as Saviano says, 'a winning business must have a winning image', then the image the Camorra had to acquire for itself was that of the Mafia.[35] It was the Mafia, and the Mafia alone, that had become 'a brand name for organized crime'.[36] It little mattered if this image represented something other than the Camorra; by putting the celebrated Mafia logo on their deeds, as they had put Armani's on their jeans, *Camorra* clans were not so much 'ruining [their] brand's image, but simply taking advantage of [the Mafia's] advertising and symbolic charisma'.[37] Fake or original, to them, never mattered much.

The Mafia film hero was one avatar whose image the Camorra appropriated. Another was the businessman, emblematic figure of that globalization the Camorra rode in style. Along with the figures of Pasquale, his exploited colleagues and the low-ranking soldiers dressed in made-in-China rags, *Gomorrah* is peopled with elegant mobsters in 'blue jacket and dark blue oxford shirt' and 'Bulgari cuff links'.[38] In an epoch when legal and illegal business are hard to tell apart, when fake and original have become one, the Camorra man too is indistinguishable from the businessman educated at Oxford, Chicago or Milan's business school:

> New generations of bosses don't follow an exclusively criminal path; they don't spend their days on the streets with the local thugs, carry a knife or have scars on their faces. They watch TV, study, go to college, graduate, travel abroad and are, above all, employed in the office of the mechanisms of power.[39]

Fake or original? 'All', says Saviano as if echoing Coppola, 'has obscure origins: such is the law of capitalism.'[40]

Yet another seemingly fake element in *Gomorrah* is the image of the woman mobster. Which Sicilian clan or, for that matter, which Mafia movie could ever conceive of the existence of a woman boss? Not even in Garrone's movie can women have anything more than a 'liminal status'.[41] This is the unwritten rule of the genre. When women do appear in Mafia movies, as for instance in Rosi's *Giuliano* or Marco Tullio Giordana's *One Hundred Steps*, they do so to mourn their dead sons. In *The Godfather*, they are beaten up by husbands, lied to and definitely kept out of the room of command. In *Scarface* (both versions), they are the trophy of the mobster's success. At most they die victims of the Mafia, as Marco Amenta's *La siciliana ribelle* (*The Sicilian Girl*) and Garrone's *Maria*; or are raped, as in Pasquale Scimeca's *Placido Rizzotto*. In Roberta Torre's powerful *Angela*, too, 'they are obliged to be invisible.'[42] As one sociologist remarks, 'female exclusion from the patriarchal order is not simply the consequence of the chauvinistic nature of the organization Cosa Nostra but a projection, albeit distorted, of a set of traditions and a value system, which still survive in southern Italy today.'[43]

Without much of a tradition, in Saviano's *Camorra* women are, instead, always an integral part of the clans' structures of power. While they still, in large part, delegate illegal trafficking and murder to their male counterparts, they hold firmly in their hands the management of the family business, from finances to organization. It would be a mistake to read all this as a sign of emancipation, though. If, in the Camorra, 'women became clan managers, entrepreneurs, and bodyguards', they did so by becoming something other than women – by becoming an image, a spectacle, a representation of a representation:[44]

> I was struck by the fact that both [female bodyguards of boss Anna Mazza] were wearing fluorescent yellow . . . The driver had on yellow sunglasses and the other a bright yellow T-shirt. A yellow that could not have been chosen by chance, a combination that could not have been a mere coincidence. A professional touch. The same yellow as Uma Thurman's motorcycle outfit in *Kill Bill*, the Quentin Tarantino film in which for the first time women are first-rate criminal stars. The same yellow that Uma Thurman wears in the ad for the film, with her bloody samurai sword – a yellow imprinted on your retina and maybe even on your taste buds. A yellow so unreal it becomes a symbol.[45]

A true avatar of both the archetypical female criminal star of cinema and of the Mafia boss, the Camorra woman is so unreal precisely *because* she has morphed into an icon, a declarative emblem – a symbol indeed. And as a symbol her body dematerializes, becoming an image of a filmic image: 'Camorra women of all ranks', writes Saviano, are 'carefully cultivating

The Mafia in suit and tie, *Gomorra*.

their image'.[46] The Camorra female boss, like her male counterpart, is a pure representation of a field of forces that needs to brand itself through a Mafia logo, a dress code, a colour or a filmic image; its body, its sex and gender, are merely incidental in the exercise of power according to an imaginary script. The woman boss, which for the Mafia would have simply been something fake, becomes one original trait of the Camorra. But originality, here, is always fake and copy of a fiction – the myth of the Mafia, of the businessman, of Scarface or Uma Thurman.

It is no wonder, then, that in this context Saviano's *Gomorrah* got caught up in an ongoing diatribe. Was the book fiction or reportage? Was its content real or fake? No doubt Saviano, who at the time of the book's publication was still a journalist working for *L'Espresso* and *La Repubblica*, had researched his topic, at personal risk, as journalism. On the other hand, perhaps in his desire to make his findings accessible to a wider audience, while never succumbing to the temptation of a spectacular Mafia thriller, Saviano had injected a novelistic quality to the dry reporting of facts. As he said in an interview: 'I wanted it to be a "bastard" because I knew that this topic, if it were not treated differently than usual, would have been relegated as either a thriller, or as an essay for experts in the field.'[47] But what to make of a 'bastard' book? Was *Gomorrah* the original, unadulterated truth about the Camorra, or a somewhat fake novelistic allegory of globalization? Quite literally: was Saviano's topic the Camorra, or a biblical parable of Sodom and Gomorrah?

In 2008 one of Italy's most prestigious literary journals, *Allegoria*, organized a debate on this very question. Franco Petroni lamented that, by refusing to make a decision between reportage and fiction, Saviano had ultimately failed to make his book either 'relevant' to debates with real policy consequences or convincingly 'allegorical' in a novelistic fashion.[48] Gilda Policastro, too, saw *Gomorrah* as 'two distinct books' in one, each weakening the other.[49] However, Carla Benedetti and Antonio Tricomi defended Saviano's choice, the former by claiming that any 'great book' invariably 'exceeds these categories', and the latter by insisting that the best thing in *Gomorrah* was that it 'rendered infinitesimally small' the distance between fiction and reality.[50]

In truth, however, while the Camorra is relentlessly at work to erase the difference between fiction and reality, between fake and original, Saviano's book tries to resist precisely that: the distance between fiction and reality in *Gomorrah* does not seem so small. Against a spirit of the time that insists there are neither realities nor facts but only opinions, *Gomorrah*'s intent is precisely to recover facts and realities. Fictions, to put it differently, have, for Saviano, a more complicated relation with reality that neither the culture of the op-ed nor hypocrisy of the reality show can ultimately hide. Take, for instance, the episode of fifteen-year-old Emanuele, killed in a shoot-out with the police in the opening pages of the book. The officers had seen a gun in his hand, but it was only a 'fake pistol . . . a toy wielded as if it were real'.[51] In episodes such as this, the difference between what is real and what is fake is certainly bigger than 'infinitesimally small'. Emanuele dies a real death, as real as Ciro and Marco's in Garrone's movie, that no fiction à la *Scarface* can possibly change.

The problem, however, is that in the world of the Camorra fictions and fakes cannot simply be liquidated as mere unrealities either. Like Emanuele's fake gun, they shape real life and have real consequences, too:

> Young Spartans went to war with the feats of Achilles and Hector in their heads, but around here you go to kill and be killed thinking of *Scarface*, *Goodfellas*, *Donnie Brasco*, and *The Godfather* . . . It's not true that films are a lie, that you can't live as in the movies, that as soon as you stick your head out of the theater, you realize things are not the same.[52]

In the world of the Camorra, on a planet that seems shaped in large part by the goods and logic of the Camorra, one *does* 'live as in the movies'. At the very least, one tries to live as in commercials or advertising. All is transformed into a spectacle, and all is potentially a reality show. As Guy Debord, the thinker that more than anybody else tried to understand the mechanics of what he called 'the society of spectacle', once wrote: 'The Mafia is not an outsider in this world; it is perfectly at home. Indeed, in the integrated spectacle it stands as the model.'[53]

In an epoch when, for organized crime, spectacle has become superior to the old modes of secrecy, Saviano simply tries to uncover the real truth still hidden in the fake spectacle. It is not that all is a fiction. Quite the contrary: all, even fiction, has to turn into reality. What ultimately hides behind the spectacle of obscene amounts of merchandise available for consumption in the feast of neo-liberalism, what lurks under the fiction of globalization's progress for the whole of humankind, is the crude reality of Pasquale's 600 euros, and the incessant traffic of the Camorra between the port of Naples and the rest of the world. While the Camorra hides its real identity behind the icons of Uma Thurman and Tony Montana or behind the logo of a mythical Mafia, the real resurfaces with the force of a scandal on Saviano's page:

> 100 deaths in 1979, 140 in 1980, 110 in 1981, 264 in 1982, 204 in 1983, 155 in 1984, 107 in 1986, 127 in 1987, 168 in 1988, 228 in 1989, 222 in 1990, 223 in 1991, 160 in 1992, 120 in 1993, 115 in 1994, 148 in 1995, 147 in 1996, 130 in 1997, 132 in 1998, 91 in 1999, 118 in 2000, 80 in 2001, 63 in 2002, 83 in 2003, 142 in 2004, 90 in 2005. Since I was born, 3,600 deaths.[54]

Or, as Garrone summed it up in the film's final statement:

> In Europe the Camorra has killed more than any other terrorist or criminal organization. 4,000 deaths in the last 30 years. Once every three days. Scampia is the largest open-air drug trafficking market in the world. Just one clan makes about 500,000 euros a day. If the toxic waste handled by the clans was all lumped together, it would create a mountain that is 14,600 meters tall. Everest is 8,850 meters tall. Cancer rates in poisoned areas have risen twenty per cent. The proceeds from illicit activities are reinvested in numerous legal activities all over the world. The Camorra invested in the reconstruction of the World Trade Center.

All these realities, Saviano insists, are the spectacle's necessary condition – the spectacle's ultimate truth.

By the end of the book, in a chapter devoted to the tourist industry in Aberdeen, Scotland, controlled by the Camorra, Saviano meditates precisely on this truth:

> In a land where truth is considered to be what gets you something and lying what makes you lose, living as if you actually believe truth can exist is incomprehensible. So the people around you feel uncomfortable, undressed by the gaze of one who has renounced the rules of life itself, which they have fully accepted. And accepted without feeling ashamed, because in the end that's just how things are and have always been; you can't change it all on your own, and so it's better to save your energy, stay on track, and live the way you're supposed to live.[55]

In the spectacular ski resorts of Aberdeen, in the comfort and luxury created by Camorra money, violence and exploitation, life goes according to a script – 'the way you're supposed to live', as in Michael Curtiz's *White Christmas*. Like Kay in *The Godfather Part I*, we prefer not to see the truth. Saviano's 'word', patiently, tries to carve it out.

In this whole confusion of fake and original it is difficult to say, after reading Saviano, if the Camorra is, for him, the allegory of neo-liberal globalization or if the reverse is true. For both, the imperative, says Saviano, is the same:

> To be the center of every action, the center of power. To use everything as a means and themselves as the ends. Whoever says that it's amoral, that life can't exist without ethics, that the economy has limits and must obey certain rules, is merely someone who has never been in command, who's been defeated by the market. Ethics are the limit of the loser, the protection of the defeated, the moral justification for those who haven't managed to gamble everything and win it all . . . This is the logic that shapes the economic imperative. It's not the Camorristi who pursue deals, but deals that pursue the Camorristi. The logic of criminal business, of the bosses, coincides with the most aggressive neoliberalism. The rules, dictated or imposed, are those of business, profit, and victory over all the competition. Anything else is worthless. Anything else doesn't exist.[56]

That truth can exist, and that truth could be anything more than 'what gets you something', remains a scandal.

Scandalous too, however, is the way in which spectacle and real life continue to intersect, despite Saviano's and Garrone's most ethical intentions. Bernardino Tracciano, who plays 'Uncle' Bernardino in Garrone's movie, 'was arrested together with six other suspected Camorristi in October of 2008 on suspicion of arms dealing, murder, and extortion'.[57] Saviano received (real) death threats after the publication of *Gomorrah* and remains under police protection. Mondadori, the publishing house owned by the Berlusconi family, still reaps the profits of the book that defied organized crime: the book's author, too, was transformed into an avatar of the author in peril – 'a sort of "Italian Salman Rushdie"'.[58] He, too, became a spectacle.

Mafia 2.0

Immerse yourself in a violent criminal world in an all-consuming
quest to become a man of honour.
– Feral Interactive Ltd, *Mafia II: Director's Cut*

Camorristi acting as mafiosi from the movies; actors playing mobsters in
Garrone's film arrested for mob activities; Neapolitan writers cast in the
role of some 'Italian Salman Rushdie': there is no doubt the time has
come for the final avatar Mafia – what might be called Mafia 2.0.

While cinema seems to have surrendered to the fact that the golden age
of the Mafia film is over and can only be reminisced about – for instance
by an equally old Tony Servillo in Paolo Sorrentino's *The Consequences of
Love* (*Le conseguenze dell'amore*, 2004) – the video gaming industry seems to
enjoy instead a golden age of Mafia games pioneered, perhaps, by Rockstar
Games' *Grand Theft Auto*. Unsurprisingly, given the titles of some games
such as *The Godfather* or *Scarface*, discussions around these games have predictably followed a palimpsest originally conceived to address the alleged
social scandal of gangster cinema. As in the times of Hays's Production
Code, the questions have been whether virtual violence promotes real crime
or not, and if the very mention of the Mafia is not a covert attack on Italian-
American communities.[59]

Besides the cinematic allusion in some titles, video games have abun-
dantly plundered from cinema, most notably, in the case of shooting
games, from cinema's voyeuristic impulse to frame and shoot life as it
unfolds in front of some technical contrivance – a viewfinder, a camera
or a rifle sight. The cinematic revolution begun with Étienne-Jules Marey's
chronophotographic gun (mentioned in chapter Two) continues to give
its fruits, not only in movies such as *The Bourne Identity* but in shooting
games like *Deus Ex: Human Revolution*.

There seems to be something missing, however, from such discussions, and two things in particular seem absolutely relevant to me for a
cultural history of the Mafia. The first is the way in which virtuality *continues*
here a process which we saw beginning with *Cavalleria rusticana*'s confusion between a real Mafia and an ideal or operatic one, intensifying in
John Gotti's blurring of the line between fiction and reality and climaxing
in the Camorra's overlapping of fakes into originals. The second is the
way in which video games *interrupt* a dynamic that I have suggested has
always been central to the Mafia genre – in narrative forms, both literary

and cinematic. The dynamic to which I am referring is one in which, through the devices of the exotic (Verga's Sicily), of the immigrant (Hawks's Italian-American) or of irony (The Sopranos), the figure of the mafioso allows for both identification *and* repulsion on the part of the reader or viewer. What such a dynamic engendered, in turn, was a *distance* between the character and the cultural consumer of his deeds. What happens now to the Mafia in video games when the avatar complicates further the relation between reality and fiction, and when any distance between myself and the character that I guide through the game is finally abolished?

I have been trying to answer this question by playing (with admittedly scarce success) Feral Interactive's *Mafia* II. To begin, in this game the Mafia is certainly not real – but it is not exactly fictional either. It is, in fact, 'virtual' simulation: it contains elements that can be acted upon in ways that fictional content *cannot* be acted upon. I cannot change Verga's story, nor can I change Coppola's. But, within some scripted limits, I can (and in fact, I have to) make my own story out of *Mafia* II. The characters of these video games, in short, are neither real nor fictional:

> they belong to another ontological category than, say Tintin's dog or the pyramid floating over Paris in Hergé's and Bilal's comic books . . . We respond to them differently, they are constructed differently, and the social exchanges they are part of are different from the social uses of fiction.[60]

In other words in *Mafia* II I have neither a real Mafia (something I would rather not experience in real life) nor a purely fictional one that I can read about or watch from the safe distance of the page or screen. Here I *act* the Mafia; I make its story.

In this sense *Mafia* II is a classic third-person game: it involves the player taking the role of an underworld thug. The mobster becomes my avatar in a parallel universe of heroism, violence, triumph and – as happened to me more than it should have – defeat. I drive around the city, eliminating my foes or beating them to a pulp. I grow more powerful, though danger always lurks at every street corner. In a way 'he' is 'me', and no distance between the two can be discerned. My triumphs are his triumphs and so are my defeats. The point is to build, through his, my own Mafia story.

The story begins ('Chapter I' – each discrete mission is divided like a novel into chapters) on a rainy night in the imaginary city of Empire Bay

– the architecture is mostly reminiscent of New York City, with Capone's Chicago appearing here and there. A voice comes in: 'I am Vito Scaletta. I was born in Sicily in 1925.' As I flip through an album of old family photos, Vito retells our story. Born in 'the Old Country' in the poverty of Sicily, Vito moved with the family to the New World, 'to start a new life in America'.

From the outset (Vito's name included) the game is a familiar echo of the *Godfather* saga. As in *The Godfather*, what we are rehearsing here is Mafia film's classic theme of the American Dream. Unlike *Grand Theft Auto*, which declares as its slogan that 'crime does pay' (or 'Ain't the American Dream grand?' in version V), *Mafia II*, like the Mafia film to which it so frequently pays homage, asks more questions than it answers; as Vito Scaletta proffers before launching into the first mission of the game, 'The American Dream was more a nightmare.' Will Vito be the emblem of the American Dream's realization? Or will he be its tragic hero? The classic ambiguity of the American gangster movie returns here. Within the coded programme this ambiguity can only be resolved by the player's ability to accomplish the Dream. Yet, ability notwithstanding, the programme of *Mafia II* – spoiler! – ends with an echo of another Mafia classic. As in *The Sopranos*, at the very end of *Mafia II*'s last mission, in the ending cut-scene, we do not know if Vito Scaletta will kill or be killed. I suppose *Mafia III*, if released, will solve the riddle.

What happens to the player acting through the avatar of the mafioso in a game such as *Mafia II*? What social exchanges are scripted in the play? In a paper delivered at the International Digital Arts and Culture Conference in Melbourne, Australia, in 2003, Mikael Jacobsson and T. L. Taylor famously claimed that gaming produced (or reproduced) a form of sociability not altogether different from a Mafia structure. Not only in their coded purpose of winning at all costs, but in the socialized rituals organized in online chat groups that accompany success with reputation and low benchmarks with marginalization, the gaming world itself resembles some sort of a Mafia community. The player himself, Jacobsson and Taylor concluded, 'saw that instead of having Gandalf as a role model, he would be better off trying to think as Tony Soprano'.[61]

The Australian scholars were looking at the fantasy online game *EverQuest*, which has, in all truth, nothing to do with the Mafia. It is not surprising that their argument applies rather well to a Mafia game. In *Mafia II*, quite literally, the player *ought to* think like Tony Soprano. The goal is to take advantage of the enemy's weaknesses, to accrue money and power, to befriend potentially useful characters and to calculate strategies in view of personal success. In a sense, then, the game truly becomes, as Vito Scaletta's words in its prologue had hinted, a true allegory of an American Dream turning into a nightmare.

To survive the game, we must put aside all ethics in a way starkly reminiscent of Saviano's Camorra. When convenient to score a point, we have to kill whomever the boss wants eliminated. Here, as in *Gomorrah*, 'ethics are the limit of the loser . . . the moral justification for those who haven't managed to gamble everything and win it all.' And here, too, 'the rules are those of business, profit, and victory over all the competition. Anything else is worthless. Anything else doesn't exist.'[62] The ultimate goal, in fact, is not merely to survive, but to accumulate 'money' that we can spend for the purchase of cars, gas ($1.20 a gallon!), guns and leisure. The world coded into *Mafia II* looks more and more like the real world we inhabit. Minus the killings, it may well be our daily life.

Far from estranging the player from society, far from creating a loner not living in the real world, a game like *Mafia II* seems only to replicate the real world and its social mechanics:

> In our neoliberal moment, in which the bottom line becomes self-aggrandizement and financial well-being, it is easy to see how the game becomes an apt metaphor for the way we consumer-citizens wend our way through the world: through the figure of the game, life becomes a veritable sport in which everything is about tactic, calculation, and the means to get ahead and do so before everyone else.[63]

The Mafia becomes once again a metaphor for all-too-real social processes and dynamics. The distance between real and fiction is blurred yet again. So far *Mafia II* has brought us once more in the world of the Mafia as allegory (for good and for bad) of the American Dream. Yet this is no longer the same allegory we had seen, say, in *Scarface* or *The Godfather*. What is missing is precisely the *distance* that, while letting us recognize Tony Camonte's dream as ours, also separates us from him. Lost is that sense of distance that allowed us to identify with Michael Corleone in his search for something other than 'business', while warning us that his way was 'business' too. What remains absent is even that modicum of distance – we had called it 'irony' – that let us live Tony Soprano's life vicariously, while always imagining we *could* be better than him in the end. Without that distance, in *Mafia II* we *are* the Mafia in a radically new way. The virtual identification, in fact, goes beyond the very possibilities of grammar: it is not that 'we R them', as Sandra Gilbert had written apropos *The Sopranos*. Rather 'we' and 'them', 'I' and 'Vito Scaletta', become a homogeneous whole – an avatar. There is nothing other than a unique, virtual 'I': '*I am Vito Scaletta.*'

What has been abolished in *Mafia II* is the *distance* from real life that led the Mafia film director to imagine the Mafia as a fiction of the American Dream while, at the same time, maintaining a critical distance from it. No longer distanced from us as mere fiction, the Mafia of the video game is a dynamic model of personal participation in a predetermined logic. Here lies the difference between fictions and gaming:

> One is made solely of signs, the other of signs and a dynamic model, that will specify its behaviour and respond to our input. It is this model behaviour that makes it different from a fiction since we can get to know the simulation much more intimately than we come to know the fiction. A fiction is rarely, if ever, personal, while a simulation can become so through experience. Simulations allow us to test their limits, comprehend causalities, establish strategies, and effect changes, in ways clearly denied us by fictions, but quite like in reality. We can't have our way with fictions, but with games, we may.[64]

And here, too, lies the profound depression I have felt when playing *Mafia II* after having read and watched so many Mafia books and movies. If from its beginning with Verga the Mafia had been a fiction and a 'perspective' through which the real world could be questioned, re-imagined, or even fantasized about in a faraway mythical 'Sicily' of Don Tommasinos, here the Mafia has become 'quite like in reality', undistinguishable from reality. The ultimate distance – that between fiction and reality – has ultimately been abolished. The world is as it is. It is not that we have identified with that logic; rather, we have no other possible role than becoming its avatars.

In a sense, then, *Mafia II* is the same world inhabited by Tony Soprano: there is 'nowhere to go' and nothing to do but repeat the same mission over and over again to improve our score. To get higher up. To succeed. There is, however, a major difference. Here it is we, not a fictional Tony, who inhabit that world; we experience it and, to an extent, make it turn, realize it in our play – always according to a script, a code, that no longer allows any fictional elsewhere. If melancholia for something lost was the feeling David Chase had for his Sopranos, resignation is the one I felt playing *Mafia* II. While I, Vito Scaletta, may have had the presentiment in the first cut-scene that 'the American Dream was more a nightmare', I have no alternative to inhabiting the nightmare and playing by the rules of the game. No other world is possible.

We may have complained about the fact that the sort of Mafia coming out of novels, short stories and movies risked 'romanticizing' the real thing, making it appear as a myth of courageous Robin Hoods. And yet how much worse the Mafia seems now when it is not even a romantic fiction, a myth, but a routine of scoring points for success! Can the Mafia no longer work as the fiction representing a society's fears and desires? Have fears and desires disappeared with the fictional Mafia in the new world's games? Are we doomed to repeat, time and again, the same play of tactics and calculations? As I ask myself these questions, I restart the game. The only hope is a better score: 'I am Vito Scaletta. I was born in Sicily in 1925 . . .'

References

Unless otherwise specified, translations are by the author.

Preface

1 Sam Roberts, 'Mario Cuomo, Vocal Foe of Italian Stereotyping, Finally Sees *The Godfather'*, *New York Times* (21 October 2013), p. 12.
2 Tracy Wilkinson, 'Luck Finally Runs Out for Italy's Boss of Bosses', *Los Angeles Times* (12 April 2006), pp. 7–8.
3 Hannah Arendt, *Eichmann in Jerusalem: A Report on the Banality of Evil* (New York, 2006), p. 250.

ONE Of Rustic Knights and Godfathers: The Origin of the Mafia

1 Cited in Fred Baker and Ross Firestone, *Movie People* (New York, 1972), p. 53.
2 Francis Ford Coppola, *Francis Ford Coppola: Interviews*, ed. Gene D. Phillips and Rodney Hill (Jackson, 2004), p. 169.
3 Jon Lewis, 'If History Has Taught Us Anything . . . Francis Coppola, Paramount Studios, and *The Godfather Parts I, II, and III'*, in *Francis Ford Coppola's* The Godfather Trilogy, ed. Nick Browne (Cambridge, 2000), p. 47.
4 Phoebe Poon, 'The Corleone Chronicles: Revisiting *The Godfather* Films as Trilogy', *Journal of Popular Film and Television* (2006), p. 193.
5 Bob Mondello, '*Godfather III*: A Staggering Saga', *All Things Considered* (24 December 1990).
6 Naomi Greene, 'Family Ceremonies: or, Opera in *The Godfather* Trilogy', in *Francis Ford Coppola's* The Godfather Trilogy, ed. Browne, p. 133; Marcia J. Citron, 'Operatic Style and Structure in Coppola's *Godfather* Trilogy', *Musical Quarterly*, LXXXVII/3 (2004), p. 452; George De Stefano, *An Offer We Can't Refuse: The Mafia in the Mind of America* (New York, 2006), p. 129.
7 André Bazin, *What is Cinema?*, trans. Hugh Gray (Berkeley, CA, 2004), I, p. 25.
8 Sergei Eisenstein, *Film Form: Essays in Film Theory*, trans. Jay Leyda (New York, 1949), p. 49.
9 Jonathan J. Cavallero, *Hollywood's Italian American Filmmakers: Capra, Scorsese, Savoca, Coppola, and Tarantino* (Urbana, IL, 2011), p. 120.
10 Citron, 'Operatic Style', p. 452; Greene, 'Family Ceremonies', p. 135.
11 John Paul Russo, 'Redemption in Francis Ford Coppola *The Godfather: Part III'*, in *Mafia Movies: A Reader*, ed. Dana Renga (Toronto, 2011), pp. 153–4.

12 Citron, 'Operatic Style', p. 438.

13 Greene, 'Family Ceremonies', p. 140.

14 Cited in Lars Franke, 'The Godfather Part III: Film, Opera, and the Generation of Meaning', in Changing Tunes: The Use of Pre-existing Music in Film, ed. Phil Powrie and Robynn Jeananne (Aldershot, 2006), p. 31.

15 Vera Dika, 'The Representation of Ethnicity in The Godfather', in Francis Ford Coppola's The Godfather Trilogy, ed. Browne, pp. 82–92.

16 Michele Colombo, Il romanzo dell'Ottocento (Bologna, 2011), p. 102.

17 Benedetto Croce, La letteratura della nuova Italia (Bari, 1964), IV, p. 332.

18 Giovanni Verga, Luigi Capuana and Gino Raya, Lettere a Luigi Capuana (Florence, 1975), p. 31.

19 Ibid., p. 49.

20 Giovanni Verga, Tutte le novelle, ed. Carla Riccardi (Milan, 1979), p. 202.

21 Gino Tellini, Il romanzo italiano dell'Ottocento e Novecento (Milan, 1998), p. 180.

22 Cited in Giacomo Debenedetti, Verga e il naturalismo (Milan, 1993), p. 318.

23 Verga, Capuana and Raya, Lettere a Luigi Capuana, p. 114.

24 Ibid., p. 114.

25 Cited in Claudia Petraccone, Le due civiltá. Settentrionali e meridionali nella storia d'Italia dal 1860 al 1914 (Bari, 2000), p. 166.

26 Verga, Novelle, p. 130.

27 Piero Bevilacqua, Breve storia dell'Italia meridionale dall'Ottocento a oggi (Bari, 1993), p. 34.

28 Salvatore Scarpino, La guerra cafona. Il brigantaggio meridionale contro lo Stato unitario (Milan, 2005), p. 10.

29 Christopher Duggan, A Concise History of Italy (Cambridge, 1984), p. 140.

30 Salvatore Lupo, History of the Mafia, trans. Anthony Shugaar (New York, 2009), pp. 31–2.

31 Petraccone, Le due civiltà, p. 57.

32 Daniel Pick, Faces of Degeneration: A European Disorder, c. 1848–c. 1918 (Cambridge, 1989), pp. 109–54.

33 Salvatore Cafiero, Questione meridionale e unità nazionale 1861–1995 (Rome, 1996), pp. 32–5.

34 Pasquale Villari, Le lettere meridionali ed altri scritti sulla questione sociale in Italia (Florence, 1878), p. 308.

35 Cited in Rosario Romeo, L'Italia liberale. Sviluppo e contraddizioni (Milan, 1987), p. 99.

36 Villari, Lettere meridionali, p. 11.

37 Ibid., p. 27.

38 Ibid., p. 3.

39 Leonardo Sciascia, Opere, ed. Claude Ambroise (Milan, 1987), II, p. 1107.

40 Napoleone Colajanni, Nel regno della mafia (Rome, 2008), p. 25.

41 Massimo Onofri, Tutti a cena da don Mariano. Letteratura e mafia nella Sicilia della nuova Italia (Milan, 1996), p. 40; Remo Ceserani, Mario Domenichelli and Pino Fasano, 'Mafia', in Dizionario dei temi letterari, (Turin, 2007), I, p. 349.

42 Antonino Traina, Nuovo vocabolario siciliano-italiano (Palermo, 1868), p. 550; Giuseppe Giarrizzo, 'Mafia', in Enciclopedia italiana (Rome, 1993), pp. 277–8; Mario Alinei, 'Origini pastorali e italiche della camorra, della mafia e della 'ndrangheta: un esperimento di Archeologia Etimologica', Quaderni di semantica, XXVIII/2 (2007), pp. 270–74.

43 James Mannion, *101 Things You Didn't Know about the Mafia: The Lowdown on Dons, Wiseguys, Squealers, and Backstabbers* (Avon, MA, 2005); pp. 3–4; Lupo, *History of the Mafia*, p. 137.

44 Villari, *Lettere meridionali*, p. 63.

45 Ibid., p. 70.

46 Lupo, *History of the Mafia*, p. 115.

47 Villari, *Lettere meridionali*, p. 28.

48 Ibid., p. 36.

49 Lupo, *History of the Mafia*, p. 84.

50 Villari, *Lettere meridionali*, p. 32.

51 Ibid., p. iii.

52 Cited in Lupo, *History of the Mafia*, p. 58.

53 Cited ibid., pp. 61–2.

54 Cited in John Dickie, *Cosa Nostra: A History of the Sicilian Mafia* (New York, 2004), p. 73.

55 Ibid., p. 51.

56 Leopoldo Franchetti, *La Sicilia nel 1876* (Florence, 1877), p. 64.

57 Cited in Onofri, *Tutti a cena da don Mariano*, p. 29.

58 James Fentress, *Rebels and Mafiosi: Death in a Sicilian Landscape* (Ithaca, NY, 2000), pp. 153–4.

59 Franchetti, *La Sicilia nel 1876*, p. 162.

60 Ibid., p. 172.

61 Ibid., pp. 196, 240, 37, 158, 180.

62 Ibid., p. 159.

63 Lupo, *History of the Mafia*, p. 33.

64 Dickie, *Cosa Nostra*, p. 58.

65 Lupo, *History of the Mafia*, p. 43.

66 Dickie, *Cosa Nostra*, p. 48.

67 Ibid., p. 48.

68 Giuseppe Marchesano, *Processo contro Raffaele Palizzolo e c.i. . . . resoconto stenografico* (Palermo, 1902), p. 332.

69 Fentress, *Rebels and Mafiosi*, p. 238.

70 Lupo, *History of the Mafia*, p. 149.

71 Cited in Paolo Pezzino, 'Stato violenza società. Nascita e sviluppo del paradigma mafioso', in *Le regioni dall'unità d'Italia ad oggi. La Sicilia*, ed. Maurice Aymard and Giuseppe Giarrizzo (Turin, 1987), p. 922.

72 Giuseppe Pitrè, *Biblioteca delle tradizioni popolari siciliane* (Palermo, 1889), V, pp. 289–90.

73 Dickie, *Cosa Nostra*, p. 105.

74 Lynn H. Nicholas, *Cruel World: The Children of Europe in the Nazi Web* (New York, 2005), pp. 77–8.

75 Verga, Capuana and Raya, *Lettere a Luigi Capuana*, pp. 37, 43.

76 Francesco De Sanctis, *La scienza e la vita: discorso inaugurale letto nella Università di Napoli il 16 novembre 1872* (Naples, 1872), p. 88.

77 Verga, Capuana and Raya, *Lettere a Luigi Capuana*, p. 208.

78 Antonio Di Grado, *L'isola di carta: incanti e inganni di un mito*, 2nd edn (Syracuse, 1984), p. 29.

79 Pitrè, *Biblioteca*, p. 294.

80 Ibid., p. 306.

81 Walter Benjamin, *The Origin of German Tragic Drama*, trans. John Osborne (London, 1977), p. 44.
82 Raimondo Catanzaro, 'Enforcers, Entrepreneurs, and Survivors: How the Mafia Has Adapted to Change', *British Journal of Sociology*, XXXVI/1 (March, 1985), p. 36.
83 Ibid., pp. 36–7.
84 Michael Herzfeld, 'The European Self: Rethinking an Attitude', in *The Idea of Europe: From Antiquity to the European Union*, ed. Anthony Pagden (Washington, DC, 2002), p. 167.
85 Giovanni Verga, *Cavalleria Rusticana and Other Stories*, trans. D. H. Lawrence (New York, 1928), pp. 40–41.
86 Onofri, *Tutti a cena da don Mariano*, p. 90.
87 Verga, *Cavalleria*, p. 37.
88 Ibid., p. 42.
89 Ibid., p. 45.
90 Ibid., p. 47.
91 Pitrè, *Biblioteca*, p. 309.
92 Letizia Paoli, *Mafia Brotherhoods: Organized Crime, Italian Style* (Oxford, 2003), p. 34.
93 Onofri, *Tutti a cena da don Mariano*, p. 85.
94 D. H. Lawrence, *Collected Letters* (New York, 1962), p. 88.
95 D. H. Lawrence, 'Translator's Preface', in Giovanni Verga, *Cavalleria Rusticana and Other Stories* (New York, 1928), p. 24.
96 Max Weber, *The Protestant Ethic and the Spirit of Capitalism*, trans. Peter Baehr and Gordon C. Wells (London, 2002), p. 93.
97 Lawrence, 'Preface', pp. 17–18.
98 Ibid., p. 21.
99 Greene, 'Family Ceremonies', p. 154; Dika, 'The Representation of Ethnicity', p. 92.
100 Franco Sciannameo, *Nino Rota's The Godfather Trilogy: A Film Score Guide* (Lanham, MD, 2010), p. 56.
101 Dika, 'The Representation of Ethnicity', p. 98.
102 Vittorio Albano, *La mafia nel cinema siciliano. Da 'In nome della legge' a 'Placido Rizzotto'* (Manduria, 2003), p. 78.
103 Coppola, *Interviews*, p. 36.
104 Leo Buscaglia, *Loving Each Other: The Challenge of Human Relationships* (New York, 1986), p. 12.
105 Cavallero, *Hollywood's Italian American Filmmakers*, p. 109.
106 Tom Santopietro, *The Godfather Effect: Changing Hollywood, America, and Me* (New York, 2012), p. 254.
107 Gene D. Phillips, *Godfather: The Intimate Francis Ford Coppola* (Lexington, KY, 2004), p. 135.
108 Giovanni Verga, *Lettere al suo traduttore [Édouard Rod]*, ed. Fredi Chiappelli (Florence, 1954), p. 244.
109 Giorgio Bertellini, *Italy in Early American Cinema: Race, Landscape, and the Picturesque* (Bloomington, IN, 2010), p. 83.
110 Luigi Capuana, *La Sicilia e il brigantaggio* (Rome, 1892), p. 57.
111 Ibid., p. 7.
112 Ibid., pp. 7–8.
113 Ibid., pp. 9–10.
114 Dickie, *Cosa Nostra*, p. 112.

115 Ermanno Sangiorgi, *Il tenebroso sodalizio. Il primo rapporto di polizia sulla mafia siciliana*, ed. Salvatore Lupo (Rome, 2011), pp. 131–3.

116 Paolo Valera, *L'assassinio Notarbartolo, o, Le gesta della mafia*, ed. Michela Sacco Messineo (Lecce, 2006), p. 55.

117 Cited in Dickie, *Cosa Nostra*, p. 117.

118 Giuseppe Carlo Marino, *L'opposizione mafiosa. Mafia, politica, stato liberale* (Palermo, 1986), pp. 70–76.

119 Cited in Umberto Santino, *Storia del movimento antimafia. Dalla lotta di classe all'impegno civile* (Rome, 2000), p. 70.

120 Dickie, *Cosa Nostra*, p. 127.

121 Onofri, *Tutti a cena da don Mariano*, p. 95; Matteo Di Gesù, 'Verga e la mafia', *Allegoria*, 59 (2009), p. 57.

TWO From Corleone to Hollywood

1 Mark A. Vieira, *Sin in Soft Focus: Pre-code Hollywood* (New York, 1999), p. 69.

2 Cited in Tino Balio, *The American Film Industry* (Madison, WI, 1985), p. 308.

3 Cited in Steven Mintz and Randy W. Roberts, *Hollywood's America: Twentieth-century America Through Film* (London, 2010), p. 118.

4 Luigi Pirandello, *Tutti i romanzi*, ed. Giovanni Macchia and Mario Costanzo (Milan, 1973), II, p. 73.

5 Karla Oeler, *A Grammar of Murder: Violent Scenes And Film Form*, www.myilibrary.com (Chicago, 2009).

6 Sergei Eisenstein, *Selected Works*, ed. Richard Taylor (Bloomington, IN, 1988), II, p. 16.

7 Ibid., II, p. 41.

8 Cited in Vieira, *Sin in Soft Focus*, p. 30.

9 Cited ibid., p. 69.

10 Cited in Gregory D. Black, *Hollywood Censored: Morality Codes, Catholics, and the Movies* (Cambridge, 1996), p. 124.

11 Cited ibid., p. 124.

12 Thomas A. Reppetto, *American Mafia: A History of its Rise to Power* (New York, 2005), p. 28.

13 John Dickie, *Cosa Nostra: A History of the Sicilian Mafia* (New York, 2004), p. 169.

14 Giuseppe Carlo Marino, *Storia della mafia* (Rome, 1997), p. 100.

15 Robert T. Anderson, 'From Mafia to Cosa Nostra', *American Journal of Sociology*, LXXI/3 (1965), p. 302.

16 Eric J. Hobsbawm, *Primitive Rebels: Studies in Archaic Forms of Social Movement in the 19th and 20th Centuries* (New York, 1965), pp. 30–56.

17 Anderson, 'From Mafia to Cosa Nostra', p. 309.

18 Cited in Tommaso Astarita, *Between Salt Water and Holy Water: A History of Southern Italy* (New York, 2005), p. 281.

19 Cited in Nelson Moe, *The View from Vesuvius: Italian Culture and the Southern Question* (Berkeley, CA, 2002), p. 145.

20 Giuseppe Sergi, *Origine e diffusione della stirpe mediterranea* (Rome, 1895).

21 Cesare Lombroso, *Delitto, genio, follia. Scritti scelti*, ed. Delia Frigessi, Ferruccio Giacanelli and Luisa Mangoni (Turin, 1995), p. 514.

22 Petraccone, *Le due civiltà. Settentrionali e meridionali nella storia d'Italia dal 1860 al 1914* (Bari, 2000), p. 164.

23 John E Coxe, 'The New Orleans Mafia Incident', *Louisiana Historical Quarterly*, 20 (1937), p. 1067.

24 Cited in Dickie, *Cosa Nostra*, p. 162.

25 Cited ibid., p. 171.

26 Ibid., p. 169.

27 William Paul Dillingham, *Reports of the Immigration Commission: Dictionary of Races of Peoples* (Washington, DC, 1911), p. 83.

28 Anton Blok, 'Mafia and Blood Symbolism', in *Risky Transactions: Trust, Kinship, and Ethnicity*, ed. Frank K. Salter (New York, 2002), p. 109.

29 Hamilton Cravens, *The Triumph of Evolution: The Heredity-environment Controversy, 1900–1941* (Baltimore, MD, 1978), p. 179.

30 Giorgio Bertellini, 'Black Hands and White Hearts: Italian Immigrants as Urban Racial Types in Early American Film Culture', *Urban History*, XXXI/3 (2004), pp. 392–3.

31 Dickie, *Cosa Nostra*, p. 172.

32 Lupo, *History of the Mafia*, p. 145.

33 Kevin Brownlow, *Behind the Mask of Innocence* (New York, 1990), pp. 71–80.

34 Norma Bouchard, 'Ethnicity and Classical Gangster Film: Mervin Le Roy's *Little Caesar* and Howard Hawks' *Scarface*', in *Mafia Movies: A Reader*, ed. Dana Renga (Toronto, 2011), p. 69.

35 Jeanne Ruvoli, '"Most Thrilling Subjects": D. W. Griffith and the Biograph Revenge Films', in *Mafia Movies: A Reader*, ed. Dana Renga (Toronto, 2011), p. 59.

36 Dickie, *Cosa Nostra*, p. 175.

37 Peter E. Bondanella, *Hollywood Italians: Dagos, Palookas, Romeos, Wise Guys, and Sopranos* (New York, 2005), pp. 176–83.

38 Francis Edwards Faragoh, *Little Caesar* (Madison, WI, 1981), p. 9.

39 Laura Beshears, 'Honorable Style in Dishonorable Times: American Gangsters of the 1920s and 1930s', *Journal of American Culture*, XXXIII/3 (2010), p. 197.

40 J. E. Smyth, 'Revisioning Modern American history in the Age of Scarface (1932)', *Historical Journal of Film, Radio and Television*, XXIV/4 (2004), p. 538.

41 William McAdams, *Ben Hecht: The Man Behind the Legend* (New York, 1990), p. 128.

42 Bertellini, 'Black Hands', p. 399.

43 Beshears, 'Honorable Style', p. 197.

44 Robert Warshow, 'The Gangster as Tragic Hero', in *The Immediate Experience: Movies, Comics, Theatre, and Other Aspects of Popular Culture* (Cambridge, MA, 2002), pp. 130–31.

45 Taeko Kitahara, 'Why Are They So Disturbing?: A Study of Classic American Gangster Movies', *Journal of American and Canadian Studies*, 30 (2012), p. 35.

46 Warshow, 'The Gangster as Tragic Hero', pp. 130–33.

47 Jeff Hill, *Defining Moments: Prohibition* (Detroit, IL, 2004), p. 69.

48 David E. Ruth, *Inventing the Public Enemy: The Gangster in American Culture, 1918–1934* (Chicago, IL, 1996), p. 63.

49 Beshears, 'Honorable Style', p. 197.

50 Bertellini, 'Black Hands', p. 388.

51 Bondanella, *Hollywood Italians*, p. 183.

52 Bouchard, 'Ethnicity and Classical Gangster Film', p. 71.

53 Faragoh, *Little Caesar*, p. 11; J. David Slocum, *Violence and American Cinema* (London, 2001), p. 141.

54 Warshow, 'The Gangster as Tragic Hero', p. 133.

55 F. Scott Fitzgerald, *The Great Gatsby* [1925] (New York, 1953), pp. 93–4.
56 Marshall McLuhan, *Understanding Media: The Extensions of Man* (New York, 1964),
    p. 290; Fitzgerald, *The Great Gatsby*, p. 160.
57 Marilyn Roberts, 'Scarface, The Great Gatsby, and the American Dream',
    Literature-film Quarterly, XXXIV/1 (2006), p. 77.
58 Ibid., p. 77.
59 Cited in Todd McCarthy, *Howard Hawks: The Grey Fox of Hollywood*
    (New York, 2000), p. 144.
60 Donald L. Bartlett and James B. Steel, *Howard Hughes: His Life and Madness*
    (London, 2003), p. 73.
61 Cited ibid., p. 74.

THREE The Far West is Here

1 Joseph McBride and Michael Wilmington, *John Ford* (New York, 1975), p. 95.
2 Mark Slobin, 'The Steiner Superculture', in *Global Soundtracks: Worlds of Film Music*
   (Middletown, CT, 2008), pp. 19–21.
3 Don Stancavish, *The Pass* (New York, 2004), p. 119.
4 Mary Lea Bandy and Kevin L. Stoehr, *Ride, Boldly Ride: The Evolution of the American
   Western* (Berkeley, CA, 2012), p. 90; Marcia Landy, '"Which Way Is America?":
   Americanism and the Italian Western', *boundary 2*, XXIII/1 (1996), p. 49.
5 Danielle Hipkins, 'Which Law Is the Father's? Gender and Generic Oscillation
   in Pietro Germi's *In the Name of the Law*', in *Mafia Movies: A Reader*, ed. Dana
   Renga (Toronto, 2011), p. 203.
6 Giuseppe De Santis, 'Per un paesaggio italiano', in *Rosso fuoco. Il cinema di
   Giuseppe De Santis*, ed. Sergio Toffetti (Turin, 1996), p. 270.
7 Giuseppe De Santis and Mario Alicata, 'Verità e poesia. Verga e il cinema
   italiano', in *Rosso fuoco*, ed. Toffetti, p. 276.
8 Gian Piero Brunetta, *Cent'anni di cinema italiano* (Bari, 2003), II, p. 11.
9 Cited in David W. Ellwood, 'The Propaganda of the Marshall Plan in Italy in a
   Cold War Context', in *The Cultural Cold War in Western Europe, 1945–60*, ed. Giles
   Scott-Smith and Hans Krabbendam (Independence, KY, 2004), p. 225.
10 David Forgacs, 'Americanisation: The Italian Case, 1938–1954', *Borderlines:
    Studies in American Culture*, 1/2 (1993), pp. 157–69.
11 Brunetta, *Cent'anni*, pp. 400–401.
12 Giuseppe Carlo Marino, *Storia della mafia* (Rome, 1997), p. 112.
13 Cited in Salvatore Lupo, *History of the Mafia*, trans. Anthony Shugaar
    (New York, 2009), p. 156.
14 Umberto Santino, *Storia del movimento antimafia. Dalla lotta di classe all'impegno
    civile* (Rome, 2000), pp. 109–11.
15 Giuseppe Carlo Marino, *L'opposizione mafiosa. Mafia, politica, stato liberale*
    (Palermo, 1986), p. 121.
16 Ibid., p. 124.
17 Steven Ricci, *Cinema and Fascism: Italian Film and Society, 1922–1943*
    (Berkeley, CA, 2008), p. 145.
18 Cited in John Dickie, *Cosa Nostra: A History of the Sicilian Mafia* (New York, 2004),
    p. 145.
19 Ibid., p. 146.
20 Ibid., p. 147.

21 Jack E. Reece, 'Fascism, the Mafia, and the Emergence of Sicilian Separatism (1919–43)', *Journal of Modern History*, XLV/2 (1973), p. 265.

22 Ibid., p. 268.

23 Mikel J. Koven, *La dolce morte: Vernacular Cinema and the Italian Giallo Film* (Lanham, MD, 2006), p. 3.

24 Timothy Newark, *The Mafia at War: Allied Collusion with the Mob* (London, 2007); Ezio Costanzo, *The Mafia and the Allies: Sicily 1943 and the Return of the Mafia* (New York, 2007).

25 Peter Khiss, 'Secret Report Cites', *New York Times* (9 October 1977).

26 Costanzo, *The Mafia and the Allies*, p. 128.

27 Norman Lewis, *The Honoured Society: The Mafia Conspiracy Observed* (Harmondsworth, 1967), p. 58.

28 Dickie, *Cosa Nostra*, p. 191.

29 Ibid., p. 194.

30 Marino, *Storia*, pp. 145–6.

31 Dickie, *Cosa Nostra*, p. 197.

32 Lupo, *History of the Mafia*, p. xiii.

33 Cited in Mario Sesti, *Tutto il cinema di Pietro Germi* (Milan, 1997), p. 163.

34 Giuseppe Pitrè, *Biblioteca delle tradizioni popolari siciliane*, 25 vols (Palermo, 1889), pp. 289–90.

35 Eric J. Hobsbawm, *Primitive Rebels: Studies in Archaic Forms of Social Movement in the 19th and 20th Centuries* (New York, 1965), pp. 19–22.

36 Ibid., p. 24.

37 Vittorio Albano, *La mafia nel cinema siciliano. Da 'In nome della legge' a 'Placido Rizzotto'* (Manduria, 2003), p. 13.

38 Ermanno Sangiorgi, *Il tenebroso sodalizio. Il primo rapporto di polizia sulla mafia siciliana*, ed. Salvatore Lupo (Rome, 2011), pp. 7–8.

39 Leonardo Sciascia, *Opere*, ed. Claude Ambroise (Milan, 1987), I, pp. 1214–15.

40 Monte S. Finkelstein, *Separatism, the Allies, and the Mafia: The Struggle for Sicilian Independence, 1943–1948* (Bethlehem, PA, 1998), p. 178.

41 Dickie, *Cosa Nostra*, p. 211.

42 Lupo, *History of the Mafia*, p. 193.

43 Hobsbawm, *Primitive Rebels*, p. 19.

44 Austin Fisher, *Radical Frontiers in the Spaghetti Western: Politics, Violence and Popular Italian Cinema* (London, 2011), p. 62.

45 Laura Wittman, 'The Visible, Unexposed: Francesco Rosi's Salvatore Giuliano' in *Mafia Movies: A Reader*, ed. Dana Renga (Toronto, 2011), p. 211.

46 Sciascia, *Opere*, I, pp. 1220–21.

47 Ibid.

48 Angelo Restivo, *The Cinema of Economic Miracles: Visuality and Modernization in the Italian Art Film* (Durham, NC, 2002), p. 51.

49 Francesco Bolzoni, *I film di Francesco Rosi* (Rome, 1986), p. 68.

50 Cited in Newark, *The Mafia at War*, p. 239.

51 Cited in Costanzo, *The Mafia and the Allies*, p. 149.

52 Cited in Santino, *Storia*, p. 135.

53 Hobsbawm, *Primitive Rebels*, p. 13.

54 Dickie, *Cosa Nostra*, pp. 203–4.

55 Lupo, *History of the Mafia*, p. 198.

56 Peter Robb, *Midnight in Sicily* (New York, 1999), Kindle edition.

57 A.G.D. Maran, *Mafia: Inside the Dark Heart* (New York, 2011), Kindle edition.
58 Marino, *Storia*, p. 201.
59 Michael Newton, *The Mafia at Apalachin, 1957* (Jefferson, NC, 2012).
60 Francesco Barbagallo, *La modernità squilibrata del Mezzogiorno d'Italia* (Turin, 1994), pp. 48–59.
61 Dickie, *Cosa Nostra*, p. 222.
62 Wittman, 'The Visible, Unexposed', p. 215.
63 Ibid., p. 216.
64 Marcia Landy, *Italian Film* (Cambridge, 2000), p. xiv.
65 Albano, *La mafia nel cinema italiano*, p. 27.
66 Cited in Miriam Mafai, *Il sorpasso. Gli straordinari anni del miracolo economico (1958–1963)* (Milan, 1997), p. 3.
67 Valerio Castronuovo, 'La storia economica', in *Storia d'Italia*, ed. Ruggiero Romano and Corrado Vivanti (Turin, 1975), p. 400; Guido Crainz, *Storia del miracolo italiano. Culture, identità, trasformazioni fra anni Cinquanta e Sessanta* (Bari, 1996), p. 83.
68 Giuseppe Goffredo, *Cadmos cerca Europa. Il Sud fra il Mediterraneo e l'Europa* (Milan, 2000), p. 58.
69 Nelson Moe, 'Modernity, Mafia Style: Alberto Lattuada's Il mafioso', in *Mafia Movies: A Reader*, ed. Dana Renga (Toronto, 2011), p. 219.
70 Marino, *Storia*, pp. 259–60.
71 Dickie, *Cosa Nostra*, p. 243.

FOUR The Godfather

1   Estes Kefauver, U.S. *Senate Committee to Investigate Organized Crime in Interstate Commerce* (Washington, DC, 17 April 1951), Kindle edition.
2   Selwyn Raab, *Five Families: The Rise, Decline, and Resurgence of America's Most Powerful Mafia Empires* (New York, 2005), pp. 97–8.
3   Ibid., p. 98.
4   Peter Maas, *The Valachi Papers* (New York, 1968).
5   John McClellan, *Select Committee on Improper Activities in the Labor or Management Field* (1958), 16512.
6   Francis Ford Coppola, *Francis Ford Coppola: Interviews*, ed. Gene D. Phillips and Rodney Hill (Jackson, MS, 2004), p. 30.
7   Jon Lewis, 'If History Has Taught Us Anything . . . Francis Coppola, Paramount Studios, and *The Godfather Parts I, II, and III*', in *Francis Ford Coppola's The Godfather Trilogy*, ed. Nick Browne (Cambridge, 2000), p. 27.
8   Coppola, *Interviews*, p. 19.
9   Anthony Julian Tamburri, 'Michael Corleone's Tie: Francis Ford Coppola's *The Godfather*', in *Mafia Movies: A Reader*, ed. Dana Renga (Toronto, 2011), p. 94.
10 Vittorio Albano, *La mafia nel cinema siciliano. 'Da In nome della legge' a 'Placido Rizzotto'* (Manduria, 2003), p. 43.
11 Coppola, *Interviews*, p. 28.
12 Giuseppe Pitrè, *Biblioteca delle tradizioni popolari siciliane* (Palermo, 1889), V, p. 290.
13 Alessandro Camon, 'The Godfather and the Mythology of Mafia', in *Francis Ford Coppola's The Godfather Trilogy*, ed. Browne, pp. 65–6.
14 Coppola, *Interviews*, p. 28.

15 Balázs Szigeti, 'The Dialects of Sin in Shakespeare's *Macbeth* and Francis Ford Coppola's *The Godfather*', *The AnaChronisT*, 14 (2009), pp. 24–46.

16 Sergio di Giorgi, cited in Albano, *La mafia nel cinema siciliano*, p. 64.

17 Fredric Jameson, *Signatures of the Visible* (New York, 2013), p. 32.

18 Gene D. Phillips, *Godfather: The Intimate Francis Ford Coppola* (Lexington, KY, 2004), p. 171.

19 Coppola, *Interviews*, p. 35.

20 Alessandra Dino, *La mafia devota. Chiesa, religione, Cosa nostra* (Rome, 2008), p. 13.

21 Émile Durkheim, *Professional Ethics and Civic Morals* (Glencoe, IL, 1958), p. 115.

22 Alessandra Dino, 'For Christ's Sake: Organized Crime and Religion', in *Organised Crime and the Challenge to Democracy*, ed. Felia Allum and Renata Siebert (New York, 2003), p. 164.

23 Carlo Rotella, 'Praying for Stones Like This: *The Godfather* Trilogy', in *Catholics in the Movies*, ed. Colleen McDannell (Cary, NC, 2007), p. 228.

24 Ibid., p. 229.

25 Phoebe Poon, 'The Corleone Chronicles: Revisiting *The Godfather* Films as Trilogy', *Journal of Popular Film and Television* (2006), p. 190; 'Blood in the Marketplace: The Business of Family in *The Godfather* Narratives', in *Ethnic Passages: Literary Immigrants in Twentieth-Century America* (Chicago, IL, 1993).

26 Poon, 'Corleone Chronicles', p. 190.

27 Michael William Doyle, 'Staging the Revolution: Guerrilla Theater as a Countercultural Practice, 1965–68', in *Imagine Nation: The American Counterculture of the 1960s and '70s*, ed. Peter Braunstein and Michael William Doyle (London, 2002), pp. 80–81.

28 Tamburri, 'Michael Corleone's Tie', p. 97.

29 Glenn Man, 'Ideology and Genre in the *Godfather* Films', in *Francis Ford Coppola's The Godfather Trilogy*, ed. Browne, p. 115.

30 Robert Warshow, 'The Gangster as Tragic Hero', in *The Immediate Experience: Movies, Comics, Theatre, and Other Aspects of Popular Culture* (Cambridge, MA, 2002), pp. 130–33.

31 Marshall McLuhan, *Understanding Media: The Extensions of Man* (New York, 1964), p. xxi.

32 Robert Warshow, 'The Gangster as Tragic Hero', in *The Immediate Experience: Movies, Comics, Theatre, and Other Aspects of Popular Culture* (Cambridge, MA, 2002), p. 133.

33 Camon, 'The Mythology of Mafia', p. 70.

34 Phillips, *The Intimate Francis Ford Coppola*, p. 27.

35 Coppola, *Interviews*, pp. 26–7.

36 Raab, *Five Families*, p. 94.

37 Mark Seal, 'The Godfather Wars', *Vanity Fair* (March 2009), p. 270.

38 Cited in Stanley Karnow, *Vietnam: A History*, 2nd edn (Harmondsworth, 1997), p. 339.

39 Coppola, *Interviews*, pp. 128–9.

40 Ibid., p. 127.

41 Ibid., p. 129.

42 Ibid., p. 29.

43 Ibid., pp. 128–9.

44 Phillips, *The Intimate Francis Ford Coppola*, p. 27.

45 Coppola, *Interviews*, p. 33.

FIVE Prime Time

1 Cited in Claire Sterling, *Octopus: The Long Reach of the International Sicilian Mafia* (New York, 1990), p. 353.
2 Alexander Stille, *Excellent Cadavers: The Mafia and the Death of the First Italian Republic* (New York, 1995), p. 65.
3 Salvatore Pappalardo, *Da questa nostra isola* (Milan, 1986), p. 52.
4 Cited in Francesco Barbagallo, *La modernità squilibrata del Mezzogiorno d'Italia* (Turin, 1994), p. 84.
5 Rocco Chinnici, 'Testo integrale del diario personale del Dr Rocco Chinnici', www.ecorav.it/arci/documenti, accessed 7 November 2013.
6 Cited in Stille, *Excellent Cadavers*, p. 100.
7 Cited ibid., p. 134.
8 Cited ibid., p. 148.
9 Marino, *Storia della mafia* (Rome, 1997), pp. 401–39.
10 Ibid., p. 338.
11 Peter Robb, *Midnight in Sicily* (New York, 1999), Kindle edition.
12 The list of twelve requests went as follows:
  1 Reversal of the sentences of the Maxi trial
  2 Annulment of the law 41bis [requiring a regime of total isolation for Mafia associates]
  3 Revision of the law Rognoni-La Torre [Mafia association]
  4 Reform of the law on *pentiti*
  5 Benefits for those convicted of Mafia-association
  6 House arrests for those aged 70 years old or older
  7 Closing the maximum-security prisons
  8 Incarceration closer to the residence of family members
  9 No censorship on family members' letters
  10 Increased visitations
  11 Arrests only for in flagrante crimes
  12 Tax exemption for petrol sold in Sicily
13 Nando dalla Chiesa, *Contro la mafia. I testi classici* (Turin, 2010), p. xi.
14 Andrea Bisicchia, *Teatro e mafia, 1861–2011* (Milan, 2011), p. 121.
15 Leonardo Sciascia, *Opere*, ed. Claude Ambroise (Milan, 1987), III, pp. 862–9.
16 Alfio Leotta, 'Do Not Underestimate the Consequences of Love: The Representation of the New Mafia in Contemporary Italian Cinema', *Italica*, LXXXVIII/2 (2011), p. 289; Gian Piero Brunetta, *Cent'anni di cinema italiano* (Bari, 2003), II, p. 249.
17 Aldo Grasso, 'Storia della televisione italiana', in *Storia della televisione italiana* (Milan, 2000), p. 134.
18 Brunetta, *Cent'anni*, II, p. 249.
19 Stefano Tani, *The Doomed Detective: The Contribution of the Detective Novel to Postmodern American and Italian Fiction* (Carbondale, IL, 1984).
20 Umberto Santino, *Storia del movimento antimafia. Dalla lotta di classe all'impegno civile* (Rome, 2000), pp. 328–9; Nicola Tranfaglia, *Più di cento anni ma la mafia c'è sempre. Crisi della Repubblica e ascesa delle mafie, 1861–2011* (Alessandria, 2011), p. 199.
21 Vittorio Albano, *La mafia nel cinema siciliano. Da 'In nome della legge' a 'Placido Rizzotto'* (Manduria, 2003), p. 69.

22 Tobias Jones, *The Dark Heart of Italy: Travels Through Space and Time across Italy* (London, 2004).

23 Millicent Marcus, 'In Memoriam: The Neorealist Legacy in the Contemporary Sicilian Anti-Mafia Film', in *Italian Neorealism and Global Cinema*, ed. Laura E. Ruberto and Kristi Wilson (Detroit, IL, 2007), p. 290.

24 Cited in Albano, *La mafia nel cinema siciliano*, p. 71.

25 John Dickie, *Cosa Nostra: A History of the Sicilian Mafia* (New York, 2004), pp. 333–4.

26 Jones, *The Dark Heart of Italy*, p. 107.

27 Giuseppe D'Avanzo, 'Arriva la decima piovra, ma la mafia non è un serial TV', *La Repubblica* (10 January 2001), p. 4.

28 Selwyn Raab, *Five Families: The Rise, Decline, and Resurgence of America's Most Powerful Mafia Empires* (New York, 2005), p. 196.

29 Cited ibid., p. 338.

30 Karen Gravano and Lisa Pulitzer, *Mob Daughter: The Mafia, Sammy 'the Bull' Gravano and Me* (New York, 2012), p. 223.

31 Ibid., p. 79.

32 Raab, *Five Families*, p. 375.

33 James Poniewozik, 'The Mafia Gave the Movie Material: The Movies Gave John Gotti a Script', *Time*, CLIX/25 (24 June 2002), p. 64.

34 'What John Gotti Had Over Al Capone', Editorial, *Media Industry Newsletter* (17 June 2002), p. 1.

35 Cited in Raab, *Five Families*, p. 462.

36 Poniewozik, 'The Mafia Gave the Movie Material', p. 64.

37 Steve Fishman, 'We're Going to Take Over F—-ing Hollywood', *New York Magazine* (24 September 2012), p. 29.

38 Edwin Diamond, 'Media: Romancing the Don?', *New York* [magazine] (19 February 1999), p. 20.

39 Frederick T. Martens and Michele Cunningham-Niederer, 'Media Magic, Mafia Mania', *Federal Probation*, 49 (1985), p. 60.

40 George S. Larke, 'Organized Crime: Mafia Myths in Film and Television', in *Criminal Visions: Media Representations of Crime and Justice*, ed. Paul Mason (New York, 2012), p. 125.

41 Imani Perry, *Prophets of the Hood: Politics and Poetics in Hip Hop* (Durham, NC, 2004), p. 129.

42 Raab, *Five Families*, p. 689.

43 Robert F. Worth, 'Fond Tales of Gotti, and a Lot of "No Comment"', *New York Times* (11 June 2002), section B, p. 4.

44 Peter E. Bondanella, *Hollywood Italians: Dagos, Palookas, Romeos, Wise Guys, and Sopranos* (New York, 2005), p. 297.

45 Sigmund Freud, *An Outline of Psychoanalysis*, ed. James Strachey (New York, 1989), p. 32.

46 Bondanella, *Hollywood Italians*, p. 313.

47 Albert Auster, 'The Sopranos: The Gangster Redux', *Television Quarterly*, XXI/4 (2001), p. 38.

48 Cited in Gary R. Edgerton, *The Sopranos* (Detroit, MI, 2013), p. 53.

49 Cynthia Burkhead, 'Fishes and Football Coaches: The Narrative Necessity of Dreams in *The Sopranos*', in *The Essential Sopranos Reader*, ed. David Lavery (Lexington, KY, 2011), p. 162.

50 Elizabeth Wurtzel, *Prozac Nation: Young and Depressed in America*
    (Boston, MA, 1994).
51 Auster, 'Gangster Redux', p. 38.
52 Stephen J. Sills, 'Social Mobility', in *Encyclopedia of Social Problems*, ed. Vincent
    N. Parrillo (New York, 2008), p. 880.
53 Edgerton, *The Sopranos*, p. 69.
54 Ibid., p. 54.
55 Ibid., p. 68.
56 Maurice Yacowar, 'The Sopranos and the American Dream', *Queen's Quarterly*,
    CXII/3 (2005), p. 392.
57 Martha P. Nochimson, 'Waddaya Lookin'At?: Re-reading the Gangster Genre
    Through *The Sopranos*', *Film Quarterly*, LVI/2 (2003), p. 7.
58 Dana Polan, *The Sopranos* (Durham, NC, 2009), p. 85.
59 Ava Collins, 'Intellectuals, Power and Quality Television', *Cultural Studies*, VII/I
    (1993), pp. 28–45.
60 Sandra M. Gilbert, 'Life with (God)father', in *A Sitdown with the Sopranos:
    Watching Italian American Culture on TV's Most Talked-about Series*, ed. Regina Barreca
    (New York, 2002), pp. 11–15.
61 Polan, *The Sopranos*, p. 149.
62 Larke, 'Mafia Myths in Film and Television', p. 122.
63 Polan, *The Sopranos*, p. 65.
64 John Barth, 'The Literature of Exhaustion', in *Friday Book: Essays and Other
    Non-Fiction* (Baltimore, MD, 1984), p. 63.
65 Ibid., p. 74.
66 Ellen Willis, 'Our Mobsters, Ourselves: Why *The Sopranos* is Therapeutic TV',
    The Nation (2 April 2001), p. 27.
67 For a very partial list of way too many allusions, see Edgerton, *The Sopranos*,
    pp. 39–49.
68 Polan, *The Sopranos*, p. 66.
69 Ibid., p. 59.
70 Cited in Edgerton, *The Sopranos*, pp. 58–9.

SIX Avatars

1 Cited in John Hooper, 'Mafiosi Given "Soft Jail Time" by Berlusconi',
   The Guardian (24 July 2004), p. 3.
2 Ministero degli Interni, 'Rapporto sulla criminalità in Italia' (2012),
   www.interno.gov.it.
3 John Dickie, *Cosa Nostra: A History of the Sicilian Mafia* (New York, 2004), p. 337.
4 Ibid., p. 311.
5 Cited in Nicola Tranfaglia, *Più di cento anni ma la mafia c'è sempre. Crisi della
   Repubblica e ascesa delle mafie, 1861–2011* (Alessandria, 2011), p. 242.
6 Luciano Violante, *Non è la piovra. Dodici tesi sulle mafie italiane* (Turin, 1994).
7 Albert Auster, 'The Sopranos: The Gangster Redux', *Television Quarterly*, XXI/4
   (2001), p. 38.
8 Don Liddick, 'Organized Crime 2006: A Global Overview of Current Events,
   Recent Trends, and Emerging Patterns', in *Organized Crime: From Trafficking to
   Terrorism*, ed. Frank Shanty and Patit Paban Mishra (Santa Barbara, CA, 2008),
   pp. xiv–xxv.

9 Jean-François Bayart, 'The Paradoxical Invention of Economic Modernity', in *Globalization*, ed. Arjun Appadurai (Durham, NC, 2001), p. 332; Jennifer L. Hesterman, *The Terrorist-criminal Nexus: An Alliance of International Drug Cartels, Organized Crime, and Terror Groups* (Boca Raton, FL, 2013), p. 17.

10 Carla Benedetti et al., 'Roberto Saviano, Gomorra', *Allegoria: per uno studio materialistico della letteratura*, 57 (2008), p. 183; Luca Pocci, '"Io so": A Reading of Roberto Saviano's *Gomorra*', *Modern Language Notes*, CXXVI/1 (2011), p. 229.

11 Ray Conlogue, 'A Grim and Compelling Hit', *Globe and Mail* (12 April 2002), p. 4; Neil Norman, 'The Mafia in His Sights', *Evening Standard* (8 March 2001), p. 31.

12 Benedetti et al., 'Roberto Saviano, Gomorra', p. 192.

13 Cited in Pierpaolo Antonello, 'Dispatches from Hell: Matteo Garrone's *Gomorrah*', in *Mafia Movies: A Reader*, ed. Dana Renga (Toronto, 2011), p. 181.

14 Stuart Klawans, 'Waste Management', *The Nation* (23 February 2009), p. 24.

15 Antonello, 'Dispatches From Hell', p. 383.

16 Dana Renga, *Unfinished Business: Screening the Italian Mafia in the New Millennium* (Toronto, 2013), p. 147.

17 Cited in Aurelio Benevento, 'Saviano's *Gomorra di Saviano*', *Critica letteraria*, XXXVI/3 (2008), p. 602.

18 Giovanni Verga, Luigi Capuana and Gino Raya, *Lettere a Luigi Capuana* (Florence, 1975), p. 114.

19 Roberto Saviano, *Gomorrah: A Personal Journey into the Violent International Empire of Naples' Organized Crime System*, trans. Virginia Jewiss (New York, 2007), p. 212.

20 Ibid., p. 236.

21 Ibid., pp. 35–6.

22 Ibid., p. 15.

23 Ibid., p. 41.

24 Ibid., p. 6.

25 Ibid., p. 34.

26 Ibid., pp. 34–5.

27 Ibid., pp. 25–6.

28 Ibid., p. 19.

29 Ibid., p. 39.

30 Ibid., p. 43.

31 Ibid., p. 42.

32 Ibid., pp. 250–51.

33 Ibid., p. 250.

34 Ibid., p. 251.

35 Ibid., p. 145.

36 William A. Darity, 'Mafia', in *International Encyclopedia of the Social Sciences* (Detroit, MI, 2008), p. 550.

37 Saviano, *Gomorrah*, p. 42.

38 Ibid., p. 218.

39 Ibid., p. 218, 250.

40 Ibid., p. 29.

41 Renga, *Unfinished Business*, p. 134.

42 Ibid., p. 53.

43 Alison Jamieson, 'Mafiosi and Terrorists: Italian Women in Violent Organizations', *SAIS Review*, XX/2 (2000), p. 52.

44 Ibid., p. 144.

45 Ibid., p. 145.
46 Ibid.
47 Daniela Borgi and Paola Cioni, 'Quando c'è l'inondazione la prima cosa che manca è l'acqua potabile: Intervista a Roberto Saviano', *Inostrannaya Literatur*, 10 (2008), p. 195.
48 Benedetti et al., 'Roberto Saviano, Gomorra', p. 181.
49 Ibid., p. 187.
50 Ibid., pp. 174, 193.
51 Saviano, *Gomorrah*, p. 20.
52 Ibid., pp. 255–6.
53 Guy Debord, *Comments on the Society of the Spectacle*, trans. Malcolm Imrie (London, 1990), p. 67.
54 Saviano, *Gomorrah*, pp. 119–20.
55 Ibid., pp. 279–80.
56 Ibid., pp. 112–13.
57 Renga, *Unfinished Business*, p. 146.
58 Pierpaolo Antonello, 'Dispatches from Hell: Matteo Garrone's *Gomorrah*', in *Mafia Movies: A Reader*, ed. Dana Renga (Toronto, 2011), p. 377.
59 *Violence in Video Games: Hearing before the Subcommittee on Telecommunications and Finance of the Committee on Energy and Commerce, House of Representatives*, One Hundred Third Congress, 2nd Session (Washington, DC, 1994); Anon., 'Italian Americans Protest Mafia II Game', *Italian America*, XV/4 (2010), p. 53.
60 Espen Aarseth, 'Doors and Perception: Fiction vs Simulation in Games', *Intermédialités: Histoire et théorie des arts, des lettres et des techniques*, 9 (2007), p. 36.
61 Mikael Jacobsson and T. L. Taylor, 'The Sopranos Meets EverQuest: Social Networking in Massively Multiplayer Online Games', in *International Digital Arts and Culture Conference* (Melbourne, 2003), p. 81.
62 Saviano, *Gomorrah*, pp. 112–13.
63 Dana Polan, *The Sopranos* (Durham, NC, 2009), p. 82.
64 Aarseth, 'Doors and Perception', p. 37.

Bibliography

Aarseth, Espen, 'Doors and Perception: Fiction vs Simulation in Games', *Intermédialités: Histoire et théorie des arts, des lettres et des techniques*, 9 (2007), pp. 35–44

Albano, Vittorio, *La mafia nel cinema siciliano. Da 'In nome della legge' a 'Placido Rizzotto'* (Manduria, 2003)

Alinei, Mario, 'Origini pastorali e italiche della camorra, della mafia e della 'ndràngheta: un esperimento di Archeologia Etimologica', *Quaderni di semantica*, XXVIII/2 (2007), pp. 247–86

Anderson, Robert T., 'From Mafia to Cosa Nostra', *American Journal of Sociology*, LXXI/3 (1965), pp. 302–10

Anon., 'Italian Americans Protest Mafia II Game', *Italian America*, XV/4 (2010), p. 3

Antonello, Pierpaolo, 'Dispatches from Hell: Matteo Garrone's *Gomorrah*', in *Mafia Movies: A Reader*, ed. Dana Renga (Toronto, 2011), pp. 377–84

Arendt, Hannah, *Eichmann in Jerusalem: A Report on the Banality of Evil* [1963] New York, 2006)

Astarita, Tommaso, *Between Salt Water and Holy Water: A History of Southern Italy* (New York, 2005)

Auster, Albert, 'The Sopranos: The Gangster Redux', *Television Quarterly*, XXI/4 (2001), pp. 34–8

Baker, Fred, and Ross Firestone, *Movie People* (New York, 1972)

Balio, Tino, *The American Film Industry* (Madison, WI, 1985)

Bandy, Mary Lea, and Kevin L. Stoehr, *Ride, Boldly Ride: The Evolution of the American Western* (Berkeley, CA, 2012)

Barbagallo, Francesco, *La modernità squilibrata del Mezzogiorno d'Italia* (Turin, 1994)

Barth, John, 'The Literature of Exhaustion', in *Friday Book: Essays and Other Non-Fiction* (Baltimore, MD, 1984), pp. 62–76

Bartlett, Donald L., and James B. Steel, *Howard Hughes: His Life and Madness* (London, 2003)

Bayart, Jean-François, 'The Paradoxical Invention of Economic Modernity', in *Globalization*, ed. Arjun Appadurai (Durham, NC, 2001), pp. 307–34

Bazin, André, *What is Cinema?*, trans. Hugh Gray (Berkeley, CA, 2004)

Benedetti, Carla, Franco Petroni, Gilda Policastro and Antonio Tricomi, 'Roberto Saviano, Gomorra', *Allegoria: per uno studio materialistico della letteratura*, 57 (2008), pp. 173–95

Benevento, Aurelio, 'Gomorra di Saviano', *Critica letteraria*, XXXVI/3 (2008), pp. 602–6

Benjamin, Walter, *The Origin of German Tragic Drama*, trans. John Osborne (London, 1977)

Bertellini, Giorgio, 'Black Hands and White Hearts: Italian Immigrants as Urban Racial Types in Early American Film Culture', *Urban History*, XXXI/3 (2004), pp. 375–99
——, *Italy in Early American Cinema: Race, Landscape, and the Picturesque* (Bloomington, IN, 2010)
Beshears, Laura, 'Honorable Style in Dishonorable Times: American Gangsters of the 1920s and 1930s', *Journal of American Culture*, XXXIII/3 (2010), pp. 197–206
Bevilacqua, Piero, *Breve storia dell'Italia meridionale dall'Ottocento a oggi* (Bari, 1993)
Bisicchia, Andrea, *Teatro e mafia, 1861–2011* (Milan, 2011)
Black, Gregory D., *Hollywood Censored: Morality Codes, Catholics, and the Movies* (Cambridge, 1996)
Blok, Anton, 'Mafia and Blood Symbolism', in *Risky Transactions: Trust, Kinship, and Ethnicity*, ed. Frank K. Salter (New York, 2002), pp. 109–28
Bolzoni, Francesco, *I film di Francesco Rosi* (Rome, 1986)
Bondanella, Peter E., *Hollywood Italians: Dagos, Palookas, Romeos, Wise Guys, and Sopranos* (New York, 2005)
Borgi, Daniela, and Paola Cioni, 'Quando c'è l'inondazione la prima cosa che manca è l'acqua potabile: Intervista a Roberto Saviano', *Inostrannaya Literatur*, 10 (2008), pp. 195–201
Bouchard, Norma, 'Ethnicity and Classical Gangster Film: Mervin Le Roy's *Little Caesar* and Howard Hawks' *Scarface*', in *Mafia Movies: A Reader*, ed. Dana Renga (Toronto, 2011), pp. 68–75
Brownlow, Kevin, *Behind the Mask of Innocence* (New York, 1990)
Brunetta, Gian Piero, *Cent'anni di cinema italiano* (Bari, 2003)
Burkhead, Cynthia, 'Fishes and Football Coaches: The Narrative Necessity of Dreams in *The Sopranos*', in *The Essential Sopranos Reader*, ed. D. Lavery (Lexington, KY, 2011)
Buscaglia, Leo, *Loving Each Other: The Challenge of Human Relationships* (New York, 1986)
Cafiero, Salvatore, *Questione meridionale e unità nazionale 1861–1995* (Rome, 1996)
Camon, Alessandro, 'The Godfather and the Mythology of Mafia', in *Francis Ford Coppola's The Godfather Trilogy*, ed. Nick Browne (Cambridge, 2000), pp. 149–56
Capuana, Luigi, *La Sicilia e il brigantaggio* (Rome, 1892)
Castronuovo, Valerio, 'La storia economica', in *Storia d'Italia*, ed. Ruggiero Romano and Corrado Vivanti (Turin, 1975)
Catanzaro, Raimondo, 'Enforcers, Entrepreneurs, and Survivors: How the Mafia Has Adapted to Change', *British Journal of Sociology*, XXXVI/1 (March, 1985), pp. 34–57
Cavallero, Jonathan J., *Hollywood's Italian American Filmmakers: Capra, Scorsese, Savoca, Coppola, and Tarantino* (Urbana, IL, 2011)
Ceserani, Remo, Mario Domenichelli and Pino Fasano, 'Mafia', in *Dizionario dei temi letterari*, 3 vols (Turin, 2007)
Chinnici, Rocco, 'Testo integrale del diario personale del Dr Rocco Chinnici', www.ecorav.it/arci/documenti, accessed 7 November 2013
Citron, Marcia J., 'Operatic Style and Structure in Coppola's Godfather Trilogy', *The Musical Quarterly*, LXXXVII/3 (2004), p. 423
Colajanni, Napoleone, *Nel regno della mafia* (Rome, 2008)
Collins, Ava, 'Intellectuals, Power and Quality Television', *Cultural Studies*, VII/1 (1993), pp. 28–45
Colombo, Michele, *Il romanzo dell'Ottocento* (Bologna, 2011)
Conlogue, Ray, 'A Grim and Compelling Hit', *Globe and Mail* (12 April 2002)
Coppola, Francis Ford, *Francis Ford Coppola: Interviews*, ed. Gene D. Phillips and Rodney Hill (Jackson, MS, 2004)

Costanzo, Ezio, *The Mafia and the Allies: Sicily 1943 and the Return of the Mafia*
  (New York, 2007)
Coxe, John E., 'The New Orleans Mafia Incident', *Louisiana Historical Quarterly*, 20
  (1937), pp. 1067–110
Crainz, Guido, *Storia del miracolo italiano. Culture, identità, trasformazioni fra anni Cinquanta
  e Sessanta* (Bari, 1996)
Cravens, Hamilton, *The Triumph of Evolution: The Heredity-Environment Controversy*,
  1900–1941 (Baltimore, MD, 1978)
Croce, Benedetto, *La letteratura della nuova Italia* (Bari, 1964)
Dalla Chiesa, Nando, *Contro la mafia. I testi classici* (Turin, 2010)
Darity, William A., 'Mafia', in *International Encyclopedia of the Social Sciences*
  (Detroit, MI, 2008)
D'Avanzo, Giuseppe, 'Arriva la decima piovra, ma la mafia non è un serial TV', *la
  Repubblica* (10 January 2001)
De Sanctis, Francesco, *La scienza e la vita: discorso inaugurale letto nella Università di Napoli
  il 16 novembre 1872* (Naples, 1872)
De Santis, Giuseppe, 'Per un paesaggio italiano', in *Rosso fuoco. Il cinema di Giuseppe De
  Santis*, ed. Sergio Toffetti (Turin, 1996), pp. 269–72
——, and Mario Alicata, 'Verità e poesia. Verga e il cinema italiano', in *Rosso fuoco.
  Il cinema di Giuseppe De Santis*, ed. Sergio Toffetti (Turin, 1996), pp. 273–6
De Stefano, George, *An Offer We Can't Refuse: The Mafia in the Mind of America*
  (New York, 2006)
Debenedetti, Giacomo, *Verga e il naturalismo* (Milan, 1993)
Debord, Guy, *Comments on the Society of the Spectacle*, trans. Malcolm Imrie (London, 1990)
Di Gesù, Matteo, 'Verga e la mafia', *Allegoria*, 59 (2009), pp. 56–70
Di Grado, Antonio, *L'isola di carta: incanti e inganni di un mito*, 2nd edn (Syracuse, 1984)
Diamond, Edwin, 'Media: Romancing the Don?', *New York* [magazine]
  (19 February 1999)
Dickie, John, *Cosa Nostra: A History of the Sicilian Mafia* (New York, 2004)
Dika, Vera, 'The Representation of Ethnicity in *The Godfather*', in *Francis Ford Coppola's
  The Godfather Trilogy*, ed. Nick Browne (Cambridge, 2000), pp. 76–108
Dillingham, William Paul, *Reports of the Immigration Commission: Dictionary of Races of
  Peoples* (Washington, DC, 1911)
Dino, Alessandra, 'For Christ's Sake: Organized Crime and Religion', in *Organised Crime
  and the Challenge to Democracy*, ed. Felia Allum and Renata Siebert (New York, 2003)
——, *La mafia devota. Chiesa, religione, Cosa nostra* (Rome, 2008)
Doyle, Michael William, 'Staging the Revolution: Guerrilla Theater as a Countercultural
  Practice, 1965–68', in *Imagine Nation: The American Counterculture of the 1960s and '70s*,
  ed. Peter Braunstein and Michael William Doyle (London, 2002), pp. 71–98
Duggan, Christopher, *A Concise History of Italy* (Cambridge, 1984)
Durkheim, Émile, *Professional Ethics and Civic Morals*, trans. Cornelia Brookfield
  (Glencoe, IL, 1958)
Edgerton, Gary R., *The Sopranos* (Detroit, MI, 2013)
Eisenstein, Sergei, *Film Form: Essays in Film Theory*, trans. Jay Leyda (New York, 1949)
——, *Selected Works*, ed. Richard Taylor, 3 vols (Bloomington, IN, 1988)
Ellwood, David W., 'The Propaganda of the Marshall Plan in Italy in a Cold War
  Context', in *The Cultural Cold War in Western Europe, 1945–60*, ed. Giles Scott-Smith
  and Hans Krabbendam (Independence, KY, 2004), pp. 225–36
Faragoh, Francis Edwards, *Little Caesar* (Madison, WI, 1981)

Fentress, James, *Rebels and Mafiosi: Death in a Sicilian Landscape* (Ithaca, NY, 2000)

Ferraro, Thomas, 'Blood in the Marketplace: The Business of Family in *The Godfather* Narratives', in *Ethnic Passages: Literary Immigrants in Twentieth-century America* (Chicago, IL, 1993), pp. 19–52

Finkelstein, Monte S., *Separatism, the Allies, and the Mafia: The Struggle for Sicilian Independence, 1943–1948* (Bethlehem, PA, 1998)

Fisher, Austin, *Radical Frontiers in the Spaghetti Western: Politics, Violence and Popular Italian Cinema* (London, 2011)

Fishman, Steve, 'We're Going to Take Over F——ing Hollywood', *New York Magazine* (24 September 2012)

Fitzgerald, F. Scott, *The Great Gatsby* [1925] (New York, 1953)

Forgacs, David, 'Americanisation: The Italian Case, 1938–1954', *Borderlines: Studies in American Culture*, I/2 (1993), pp. 157–69

Franchetti, Leopoldo, *La Sicilia nel 1876*, 2 vols (Florence, 1877)

Franke, Lars, 'The Godfather Part III: Film, Opera, and the Generation of Meaning', in *Changing Tunes: The Use of Pre-existing Music in Film*, ed. Phil Powrie and Robynn Jeananne (Aldershot, 2006), pp. 31–45

Freud, Sigmund, *An Outline of Psychoanalysis*, ed. James Strachey (New York, 1989)

Giarrizzo, Giuseppe, 'Mafia', in *Enciclopedia italiana* (Rome, 1993)

Gilbert, Sandra M., 'Life with (God)father', in *A Sitdown with the Sopranos: Watching Italian American Culture on TV's Most Talked-about Series*, ed. Regina Barreca (New York, 2002), pp. 11–25

Goffredo, Giuseppe, *Cadmos cerca Europa. Il Sud fra il Mediterraneo e l'Europa* (Milan, 2000)

Grasso, Aldo, *Storia della televisione italiana* (Milan, 2000)

Gravano, Karen, and Lisa Pulitzer, *Mob Daughter: The Mafia, Sammy 'the Bull' Gravano and Me* (New York, 2012)

Greene, Naomi, 'Family Ceremonies: or, Opera in *The Godfather* Trilogy', in *Francis Ford Coppola's The Godfather Trilogy*, ed. Nick Browne (Cambridge, 2000), pp. 133–55

Herzfeld, Michael, 'The European Self: Rethinking an Attitude', in *The Idea of Europe: From Antiquity to the European Union*, ed. Anthony Pagden (Washington, DC, 2002), pp. 139–70

Hesterman, Jennifer L., *The Terrorist-criminal Nexus: An Alliance of International Drug Cartels, Organized Crime, and Terror Groups* (Boca Raton, FL, 2013)

Hill, Jeff, *Defining Moments: Prohibition* (Detroit, IL, 2004)

Hipkins, Danielle, 'Which Law Is the Father's? Gender and Generic Oscillation in Pietro Germi's *In the Name of the Law*', in *Mafia Movies: A Reader*, ed. Dana Renga (Toronto, 2011), pp. 203–10

Hobsbawm, Eric J., *Primitive Rebels: Studies in Archaic Forms of Social Movement in the 19th and 20th Centuries* (New York, 1965)

Hooper, John, 'Mafiosi Given "Soft Jail Time" by Berlusconi', *The Guardian* (24 July 2004)

Jacobsson, Mikael, and T. L. Taylor, 'The Sopranos Meets EverQuest: Social Networking in Massively Multiplayer Online Games', in *International Digital Arts and Culture Conference* (Melbourne, 2003), pp. 81–90

Jameson, Fredric, *Signatures of the Visible* (New York, 2013)

Jamieson, Alison, 'Mafiosi and Terrorists: Italian Women in Violent Organizations', *SAIS Review*, XX/2 (2000), pp. 51–64

Jones, Tobias, *The Dark Heart of Italy: Travels Through Space and Time across Italy* (London, 2004)

Karnow, Stanley, *Vietnam: A History*, 2nd edn (Harmondsworth, 1997)

Kefauver, Estes, U.S. *Senate Committee to Investigate Organised Crime in Interstate Commerce* (Washington, DC, 17 April 1951), Kindle edition

Khiss, Peter, 'Secret Report Cites', *New York Times* (9 October 1977)

Kitahara, Taeko, 'Why Are They So Disturbing?: A Study of Classic American Gangster Movies', *Journal of American and Canadian Studies*, 30 (2012), pp. 31–53

Klawans, Stuart, 'Waste Management', *The Nation* (23 February 2009)

Koven, Mikel J., *La dolce morte: Vernacular Cinema and the Italian Giallo Film* (Lanham, MD, 2006)

Landy, Marcia, '"Which Way Is America?": Americanism and the Italian Western', *boundary 2*, XXIII/1 (1996), pp. 35–59

——, *Italian Film* (Cambridge, 2000)

Larke, George S., 'Organized Crime: Mafia Myths in Film and Television', in *Criminal Visions: Media Representations of Crime and Justice*, ed. Paul Mason (New York, 2012), pp. 116–32

Lawrence, D. H., *Collected Letters* (New York, 1962)

——, *Cavalleria Rusticana and Other Stories* (New York, 1928)

Leotta, Alfio, 'Do Not Underestimate the Consequences of Love: the Representation of the New Mafia in Contemporary Italian Cinema', *Italica*, LXXXVIII/2 (2011), pp. 286–96

Lewis, Jon, 'If History Has Taught Us Anything . . . Francis Coppola, Paramount Studios, and The *Godfather Parts I, II*, and *III*', in *Francis Ford Coppola's* The Godfather Trilogy, ed. Nick Browne (Cambridge, 2000), pp. 23–56

Lewis, Norman, *The Honoured Society: The Mafia Conspiracy Observed* (Harmondsworth, 1967)

Liddick, Don, 'Organized Crime 2006: A Global Overview of Current Events, Recent Trends, and Emerging Patterns', in *Organized Crime: From Trafficking to Terrorism*, ed. Frank Shanty and Patit Paban Mishra (Santa Barbara, CA, 2008), pp. xiii–xix

Lombroso, Cesare, *Delitto, genio, follia. Scritti scelti*, ed. Delia Frigessi, Ferruccio Giacanelli and Luisa Mangoni (Turin, 1995)

Lupo, Salvatore, *History of the Mafia*, trans. Anthony Shugaar (New York, 2009)

Maas, Peter, *The Valachi Papers* (New York, 1968)

McAdams, William, *Ben Hecht: The Man Behind the Legend* (New York, 1990)

McBride, Joseph, and Michael Wilmington, *John Ford* (New York, 1975)

McCarthy, Todd, *Howard Hawks: The Grey Fox of Hollywood* (New York, 2000)

McClellan, John, *Select Committee on Improper Activities in the Labor or Management Field* (1958)

McLuhan, Marshall, *Understanding Media: The Extensions of Man* (New York, 1964)

Mafai, Miriam, *Il sorpasso. Gli straordinari anni del miracolo economico (1958–1963)* (Milan, 1997)

Man, Glenn, 'Ideology and Genre in the *Godfather* Films', in *Francis Ford Coppola's* The Godfather Trilogy, ed. Nick Browne (Cambridge, 2000), pp. 109–32

Mannion, James, *101 Things You Didn't Know about the Mafia: The Lowdown on Dons, Wiseguys, Squealers, and Backstabbers* (Avon, MA, 2005)

Maran, A.G.D., *Mafia: Inside the Dark Heart* (New York, 2011)

Marchesano, Giuseppe, *Processo contro Raffaele Palizzolo e c.i. . . . resoconto stenografico* (Palermo, 1902)

Marcus, Millicent, 'In Memoriam: The Neorealist Legacy in the Contemporary Sicilian Anti-Mafia Film', in *Italian Neorealism and Global Cinema*, ed. Laura E. Ruberto and Kristi Wilson (Detroit, IL, 2007), pp. 290–305

Marino, Giuseppe Carlo, *L'opposizione mafiosa. Mafia, politica, stato liberale* (Palermo, 1986)
——, *Storia della mafia* (Rome, 1997)
Martens, Frederick T., and Michele Cunningham-Niederer, 'Media Magic, Mafia Mania', *Federal Probation*, 49 (1985), pp. 60–68
Ministero degli Interni, 'Rapporto sulla criminalità in Italia' (2012), www.interno.gov.it
Mintz, Steven, and Randy W. Roberts, *Hollywood's America: Twentieth-century America through Film* (London, 2010)
Moe, Nelson, 'Modernity, Mafia Style: Alberto Lattuada's *Il mafioso*', in *Mafia Movies: A Reader*, ed. Dana Renga (Toronto, 2011), pp. 219–25
——, *The View from Vesuvius: Italian Culture and the Southern Question* (Berkeley, CA, 2002)
Mondello, Bob. '*Godfather* III: A Staggering Saga', *All Things Considered* (24 December 1990)
Newark, Timothy, *The Mafia at War: Allied Collusion with the Mob* (London, 2007)
Newton, Michael, *The Mafia at Apalachin, 1957* (Jefferson, NC, 2012)
Nicholas, Lynn H., *Cruel World: The Children of Europe in the Nazi Web* (New York, 2005)
Nochimson, Martha P., 'Waddaya Lookin'At?: Re-reading the Gangster Genre Through *The Sopranos*', *Film Quarterly*, LVI/2 (2003), pp. 2–13
Norman, Neil, 'The Mafia in His Sights', *Evening Standard* (8 March 2001)
Oeler, Karla, *A Grammar of Murder: Violent Scenes And Film Form* (Chicago, 2009)
Onofri, Massimo, *Tutti a cena da don Mariano. Letteratura e mafia nella Sicilia della nuova Italia* (Milan, 1996)
Paoli, Letizia, *Mafia Brotherhoods: Organized Crime, Italian Style* (Oxford, 2003)
Pappalardo, Salvatore, *Da questa nostra isola* (Milan, 1986)
Perry, Imani, *Prophets of the Hood: Politics and Poetics in Hip Hop* (Durham, NC, 2004)
Petraccone, Claudia, *Le due civiltá. Settentrionali e meridionali nella storia d'Italia dal 1860 al 1914* (Bari, 2000)
Pezzino, Paolo, 'Stato violenza società. Nascita e sviluppo del paradigma mafioso', in *Le regioni dall'unità d'Italia ad oggi. La Sicilia*, ed. Maurice Aymard and Giuseppe Giarrizzo (Turin, 1987), pp. 903–82
Phillips, Gene D., *Godfather: The Intimate Francis Ford Coppola* (Lexington, KY, 2004)
Pick, Daniel, *Faces of Degeneration: a European Disorder, c. 1848–c. 1918* (Cambridge, 1989)
Pirandello, Luigi, *Tutti i romanzi*, ed. Giovanni Macchia and Mario Costanzo, 2 vols (Milan, 1973)
Pitrè, Giuseppe, *Biblioteca delle tradizioni popolari siciliane*, 25 vols (Palermo, 1889)
Pocci, Luca, '"Io so": A Reading of Roberto Saviano's *Gomorra*', *Modern Language Notes*, CXXVI/1 (2011), pp. 224–44
Polan, Dana, *The Sopranos* (Durham, NC, 2009)
Poniewozik, James, 'The Mafia Gave the Movie Material: The Movies Gave John Gotti a Script', *Time*, CLIX/25 (24 June 2002), p. 64
Poon, Phoebe, 'The Corleone Chronicles: Revisiting *The Godfather* Films as Trilogy', *Journal of Popular Film and Television* (2006), pp. 187–95
Raab, Selwyn, *Five Families: The Rise, Decline, and Resurgence of America's Most Powerful Mafia Empires* (New York, 2005)
Reece, Jack E., 'Fascism, the Mafia, and the Emergence of Sicilian Separatism (1919–43)', *Journal of Modern History*, XLV/2 (1973), pp. 261–76
Renga, Dana, *Unfinished Business: Screening the Italian Mafia in the New Millennium* (Toronto, 2013)

Reppetto, Thomas A., *American Mafia: A History of its Rise to Power* (New York, 2005)

Restivo, Angelo, *The Cinema of Economic Miracles: Visuality and Modernization in the Italian Art Film* (Durham, NC, 2002)

Ricci, Steven, *Cinema and Fascism: Italian Film and Society, 1922–1943* (Berkeley, CA, 2008)

Robb, Peter, *Midnight in Sicily* (New York, 1999)

Roberts, Marilyn, 'Scarface, The Great Gatsby, and the American Dream', *Literature-Film Quarterly*, XXXIV/1 (2006), pp. 71–8

Roberts, Sam, 'Mario Cuomo, Vocal Foe of Italian Stereotyping, Finally Sees The Godfather', *New York Times* (21 October 2013)

Romeo, Rosario, *L'Italia liberale. Sviluppo e contraddizioni* (Milan, 1987)

Rotella, Carlo, 'Praying for Stones Like This: The Godfather Trilogy', in *Catholics in the Movies*, ed. Colleen McDannell (Cary, NC, 2007), pp. 227–52

Russo, John Paul, 'Redemption in Francis Ford Coppola The Godfather: Part III', in *Mafia Movies: A Reader*, ed. Dana Renga (Toronto, 2011), pp. 149–56

Ruth, David E., *Inventing the Public Enemy: The Gangster in American Culture, 1918–1934* (Chicago, IL, 1996)

Ruvoli, Jeanne, '"Most Thrilling Subjects": D. W. Griffith and the Biograph Revenge Films', in *Mafia Movies: A Reader*, ed. Dana Renga (Toronto, 2011), pp. 59–67

Sangiorgi, Ermanno, *Il tenebroso sodalizio. Il primo rapporto di polizia sulla mafia siciliana*, ed. Salvatore Lupo (Rome, 2011)

Santino, Umberto, *Storia del movimento antimafia. Dalla lotta di classe all'impegno civile* (Rome, 2000)

Santopietro, Tom, *The Godfather Effect: Changing Hollywood, America, and Me* (New York, 2012)

Saviano, Roberto, *Gomorrah: A Personal Journey into the Violent International Empire of Naples' Organized Crime System*, trans. Virginia Jewiss (New York, 2007)

Scarpino, Salvatore, *La guerra cafona. Il brigantaggio meridionale contro lo Stato unitario* (Milan, 2005)

Sciannameo, Franco, *Nino Rota's The Godfather Trilogy: A Film Score Guide* (Lanham, MD, 2010)

Sciascia, Leonardo, *Opere*, ed. Claude Ambroise, 3 vols (Milan, 1987)

Seal, Mark, 'The Godfather Wars', *Vanity Fair* (March 2009), p. 270

Sergi, Giuseppe, *Origine e diffusione della stirpe mediterranea* (Rome, 1895)

Sesti, Mario, *Tutto il cinema di Pietro Germi* (Milan, 1997)

Sills, Stephen J., 'Social Mobility', in *Encyclopedia of Social Problems*, ed. Vincent N. Parrillo (New York, 2008)

Slobin, Mark, 'The Steiner Superculture', in *Global Soundtracks: Worlds of Film Music* (Middletown, CT, 2008), pp. 3–35

Slocum, J. David, *Violence and American Cinema* (London, 2001)

Smyth, J. E., 'Revisioning Modern American History in the Age of Scarface (1932)', *Historical Journal of Film, Radio and Television*, XXIV/4 (2004), pp. 535–63

Stancavish, Don, *The Pass* (New York, 2004)

Sterling, Claire, *Octopus: The Long Reach of the International Sicilian Mafia* (New York, 1990)

Stille, Alexander, *Excellent Cadavers: The Mafia and the Death of the First Italian Republic* (New York, 1995)

Szigeti, Balázs, 'The Dialects of Sin in Shakespeare's Macbeth and Francis Ford Coppola's The Godfather', *The AnaChronisT*, 14 (2009), pp. 24–46

Tamburri, Anthony Julian, 'Michael Corleone's Tie: Francis Ford Coppola's The Godfather' in *Mafia Movies: A Reader*, ed. Dana Renga (Toronto, 2011), pp. 64–101

Tani, Stefano, *The Doomed Detective: The Contribution of the Detective Novel to Postmodern American and Italian Fiction* (Carbondale, IL, 1984)

Tellini, Gino, *Il romanzo italiano dell'Ottocento e Novecento* (Milan, 1998)

Traina, Antonino, *Nuovo vocabolario siciliano-italiano* (Palermo, 1868)

Tranfaglia, Nicola, *Più di cento anni ma la mafia c'è sempre. Crisi della Repubblica e ascesa delle mafie, 1861–2011* (Alessandria, 2011)

Valera, Paolo, *L'assassinio Notarbartolo, o, Le gesta della mafia*, ed. Michela Sacco Messineo (Lecce, 2006)

Verga, Giovanni, *Cavalleria Rusticana and Other Stories*, trans. D. H. Lawrence (New York, 1928)

——, *Lettere al suo traduttore* [Édouard Rod], ed. Fredi Chiappelli (Florence, 1954)

——, *Tutte le novelle*, ed. Carla Riccardi (Milan, 1979)

——, Luigi Capuana and Gino Raya, *Lettere a Luigi Capuana* (Florence, 1975)

Vieira, Mark A., *Sin in Soft Focus: Pre-code Hollywood* (New York, 1999)

Villari, Pasquale, *Le lettere meridionali ed altri scritti sulla questione sociale in Italia* (Florence, 1878)

Violante, Luciano, *Non è la piovra. Dodici tesi sulle mafie italiane* (Turin, 1994)

Violence in Video Games: Hearing before the Subcommittee on Telecommunications and Finance of the Committee on Energy and Commerce, House of Representatives, One Hundred Third Congress, 2nd Session (Washington, DC, 1994)

Warshow, Robert, 'The Gangster as Tragic Hero', in *The Immediate Experience: Movies, Comics, Theatre, and Other Aspects of Popular Culture* (Cambridge, MA, 2002), pp. 127–33

Weber, Max, *The Protestant Ethic and the Spirit of Capitalism*, trans. Peter Baehr and Gordon C. Wells (London, 2002)

'What John Gotti Had Over Al Capone', Editorial, *Media Industry Newsletter* (17 June 2002)

Wilkinson, Tracy, 'Luck Finally Runs Out for Italy's Boss of Bosses', *Los Angeles Times* (12 April 2006)

Willis, Ellen, 'Our Mobsters, Ourselves: Why *The Sopranos* is Therapeutic TV', *The Nation* (2 April 2001)

Wittman, Laura, 'The Visible, Unexposed: Francesco Rosi's *Salvatore Giuliano*', in *Mafia Movies: A Reader*, ed. Dana Renga (Toronto, 2011), pp. 211–18

Worth, Robert F., 'Fond Tales of Gotti, and a Lot of "No Comment"', *New York Times* (11 June 2002)

Wurtzel, Elizabeth, *Prozac Nation: Young and Depressed in America* (Boston, MA, 1994)

Yacowar, Maurice, 'The Sopranos and the American Dream', *Queen's Quarterly*, CXII/3 (2005), pp. 383–92

Acknowledgements

This book began as a series of conversations with my students in a 'Mafia at the Movies' class at Duke University. Their voices – too many to acknowledge properly – can still be heard in these pages. I thank Martin Eisner for having suggested that I taught that class in the first place; Claudia Milian for her always useful suggestions; Michael Newcity for our chats on the Russian mafia; Anthony Fragola for our conversations on the *Beautiful Memories* elicited by his aptly titled documentary on Peppino Impastato; and Antonio Nicaso for sharing his coffee pot with me while discussing the intricacies of organized crime during a tropical summer in Vermont.

A special thank you goes to Elizabeth Tremmel, the most scrupulous and attentive reader I have ever enjoyed. Last but not least, I am very grateful to Ben Hayes and Robert Williams at Reaktion Books for their encouragement and support.

Photo Acknowledgements

The author and publishers wish to express their thanks to the below sources for illustrative material and/or permission to reproduce it.

Library of Congress Prints and Photographs Division, Washington, DC: pp. 27, 63, 70, 72, 93, 97, 115, 122, 133.

Index

Page numbers in *italics* refer to illustrations